Dories and Dorymen
by Otto P. Kelland

Two dorymen retrieve their gear on an offshore bank — (Courtesy Wilfred Eisnor, Knickle Studios, Lunenburg).

Dories and Dorymen

by Otto P. Kelland

Newfoundland Writer, Balladeer and author of the song "Let Me Fish off Cape St. Mary's"

A rare sight and an unusual photo, the becalmed Newfoundland salt banker 'Robert Max' in command of Captain Frank Thornhill, being towed out of St. John's harbour by her dories in the summer of 1936 —(Courtesy Ern Maunder).

The publisher acknowledges the financial contribution of the *Department of Tourism and Culture, Government of Newfoundland and Labrador,* which has helped make this publication possible.

Appreciation is expressed to *The Canada Council* for publication assistance.

Cover Photo: K. Bruce Lane

∝ Printed on acid-free paper

Published by
RB Books
Robinson-Blackmore Printing & Publishing
P.O. Box 8660, St. John's, Newfoundland A1B 3T7

First Printing, May 1984
Second Printing, October 1985
Third Printing, June 1986
Fourth Printing, February 1996
Fifth Printing, February 1997

Printed in Canada by:
ROBINSON-BLACKMORE PRINTING & PUBLISHING

ISBN 0-920884-12-1

Contents

Badly iced-up with her chilled crewmen huddled for'ard, the Gloucester schooner 'Killarney' is shown returning from the Grand Bank in January of 1924 — (Courtesy Peabody Museum, Salem, Massachusetts).

Acknowledgements

To begin with I wish to express my thanks to Canada Council for awarding me a grant which enabled me to conduct research in areas where without that assistance the completion of this project would have been impossible.

I am grateful also, to former Newfoundland Banks fishing captains: Jacob Thornhill, Alexander (Sandy) Thornhill, Thomas Farrell, Chesley Rose, George Follett, Hugh Grandy, Thomas Grandy, Gordon Harris, the late Captain Clarence Williams, and the late Captain Archibald Thornhill.

I am indebted to dory builders: Messrs. Ralph and John Lowell of Amesbury, Massachusetts, U.S.A.; Mr. William Cox of Shelburne, Nova Scotia, Captain Lawrence Allen, Mr. Robert Cram and Mr. Freeman Rhuland of Lunenburg, Nova Scotia, Mr. Roy Grandy and Mr. Leonard Grandy of Grand Bank, Newfoundland; Mr. John Monk Jr. of Monkstown, Placentia Bay, Newfoundland; Mr. Randell Roberts of Epworth, Placentia Bay; and Monsieur Elie Jugan of Saint Pierre et Miquelon.

In addition, I should like to thank: Mayor Fred Tessier, Mr. Harry Walsh, Mr. Leonard Matthews Sr., Grand Bank; Mr. Michael Harrington, Mrs. Bobbi Robertson, Mrs. Bride Daly, Mr. Edwin Dicks, Mr. Amos March, Mr. William Murley, St. John's; Mr. Patrick Rossiter, Fermeuse; Mr. John P. Malloy and Mr. John Myrick, St. Shotts; Mr. Archibald Williams and Mr. William May, Pool's Cove; Ex-Sergeants of the Newfoundland Constabulary, Lawrence V. Dutton and Maxwell Rose, and R.C.M.P. Staff-Sergeant Richard Jarvis.

Special thanks to: Mrs. Lillian Walsh of Mount Pearl for graciously consenting to tell me the story of the terrible tragedy which took her husband and three sons; Gordon W. Thomas of Gloucester and Ipswich, Massachusetts, a friend of long standing who unstintingly supplied me with a considerable amount of material which went into the making of this book; Mrs. Francois Bowring and Mr. Hubert Plante who acted as interpreters; Senator Fredrick W. Rowe and Dr. C.R. Barrett, President of the College of Fisheries.

My very special thanks and love to my wife Hilda, my son Jerry and my daughter Jocelyn for their support and help.

Introduction

DORIES AND DORYMEN
by Otto P. Kelland
(Copyrighted 1976)

A slight built boat is the dory,
But she lives a tough career,
Woven through the fisherman's story
At all seasons of the year.

She tops each wave like a battle tank,
With a buoyancy that's grand,
And has weathered gales when schooners sank
On the Banks of Newfoundland.

Our fancy made her a pirate ship,
In the pond by the harbour bend,
And we went on many a raiding trip,
Conveyed by our dory friend.

Her mast would be a garden post,
The sail an old brin bag,
When as pirates bold we harried the coast
And returned with imaginary swag.

She carries the fisherman down to the seas,
Where she helps him to earn his bread,
And has brought him safe through many a breeze
When, he's been given up for dead.

She was there to take you near and far,
To church or to make the hay,
And was prized as much as your family car
By the people of yesterday.

Down through the years a page she wrote,
A brave and romantic story,
Lauded by seamen as the finest small boat,
Little Queen of the Seas: THE DORY.

Nearly twenty years have passed by since I wrote these verses. I guess I was inspired to write them by the profound admiration and respect which I've always had for the dory.

While growing up at Lamaline, on Newfoundland's Burin Peninsula, on more than one occasion I've witnessed that little boat bringing men safely ashore over mountainous, gail-ripped seas where no other type of small craft could possibly have survived. On one such occasion my father and elder brother were the potential victims of a drowning accident. But thanks to the seaworthy qualities of their dory, they made it to land.

Our section of the Burin Peninsula was a very dangerous strip of coast to attempt to land on when high seas were running, owing to its shoal water propensity and the underwater rocks which scattered off its shoreline. Very often when men went out fishing the water would be smooth, the wind moderate. Then while they were in the act of hauling a codtrap or a trawl, huge combers would suddenly commence to roll in, the big seas having been created by some severe windstorm that had occurred far off in the Atlantic. As a result, in a few minutes the giant waves would be breaking furiously on rocks and shoals, turning the water, for a considerable distance offshore, feather white and very lethal.

Fishermen caught on the grounds tending fishing gear under such conditions became cut off from shore. In some instances they managed to land after experiencing great difficulty. But I can recall that on a couple of occasions some of the fishermen could not get ashore in our area at all. They were forced to row to the deep water harbour of Lawn, twenty miles to the east, in order to make a safe landing.

In the stories of Banks dorymen presented herein the reader may well marvel at the tremendous amount of punishment those men could take and yet survive, then live to attain great age. These accounts of their courage as well as their powers of endurance go beyond the pale of simple amazement and credability.

The reader will observe that throughout the book, whenever I refer to our land based fisheries, I use the term 'shore fishery' instead of 'inshore fishery', for the reason that prior to our entering union with Canada the former term was used by all Newfoundlanders. A few years after we joined the great Dominion, however, our people slowly but surely started to use the Canadian term, 'inshore fishery'. In that respect, I do not hesitate to say that I refuse to become a copycat, for I will keep using the words 'shore fishery'. I guess it is not too important today which term is used, but as far as I am concerned I am very reluctant to dispense with that tiny bit of folklore nostalgia of old Newfoundland.

In the meantime, the terms as they were used by Canadians and Newfoundlanders in days gone by presented two different meanings. When Newfoundlanders referred to the shore fishery they meant that the men who were engaged at the industry were fishing from shore-based premises, not from a schooner; whereas when Canadians used the term inshore fishery it meant that the undertaking was being carried out by men who fished on grounds near the shore, not on the farflung Banks.

When one speaks of dorymen today most people are under the impression that reference is being made to men who are engaged at prosecuting the Banks fishery. However, such is far from being the case. For from Bay Bulls to Port aux Basques on Newfoundland's South Coast, then around Cape Ray and north along the coast of the Great Northern Peninsula, men fished the shore in dories since the early 1880s. So they too have every right to be classed as dorymen. Although the dangers they encountered may have varied several degrees from those which were experienced by Banks fishermen, they were very real and ever present.

Before the marine motor was introduced shore fishermen were compelled to row, or if the wind was fair, sail distances of from five to eight miles. They had to put up with dense fogs, high seas, sudden storms and racing tides: the same conditions that their counterparts faced on the Banks.

In some areas, shore fishing dorymen had to contend with another grave danger, that from the off-shore rocks and shoals I mentioned earlier, which lay a short distance below the surface. When getting off course during heavy fog or in a snow squall while engaged at late fall fishing, with a mean swell in the water, it could spell disaster for the unfortunate dorymen who ran over one of these just as a big sea broke. For the dory despite her sprightliness and buoyancy cannot rise on a broken sea; no boat can. Instead, while her bottom is floating on firmer water, this foam, comprised of bubbles, will encircle her, then boil over her bow, gunnels and stern, swamping her. In ninety-nine cases out of a hundred the dory will capsize to drown her crew in the surrounding maelstrom.

After such a fatal accident, if the wind is blowing towards the land, the dory will heave ashore, very often in a badly damaged condition, caused when she collided with rocks enroute.

> The capsized, broken dory,
> Cast upon some wave-lashed shore,
> Tells the mute, sad story
> Of brave men, who will fish no more.

Sometimes the bodies of drowned fishermen will wash ashore also, with their pitiable remains lying half covered by sand and rolled up in seaweed.

There was scarcely a Banks fisherman who did not cut his eye teeth in a shore fishing dory. In the barrisways, coves, harbours and ponds near their homes, small boys who lived on a dory coast sometimes ventured out in those craft with their fathers, elder brothers, neighbours and even their mothers, who taught them how to row. At first they would have sufficient strength to handle only one oar, while their larger, stronger dorymate held the other. Then as the youngsters developed in size and strength they would take an oar in each hand to gradually master the art of rowing, so that by the time they reached the age of eighteen years they had become expert dorymen. Later you will read of the time when my cousin Jack and I set out on a voyage in a dory, which might have ended differently if my nine-year-old relative had been a little older, a bit stronger and more experienced in dory handling. Former fishing skippers, Banks dorymen and shore fishing dorymen can tell you that once a man learns how to handle a dory properly, she is the safest small rowboat that ever went upon the face of the waters.

That phrase, "Once a man learns how to handle a dory properly", speaks volumes from a safety point of view. For not only does he need to learn how to row a boat of that type, he must also make himself familiar with the correct method of loading and placing heavy anchors, logs, salt, coal, etc. in a proper position. He must learn how deeply she should be loaded and the safest way to come alongside a vessel, particularly in a choppy sea. More especially should he learn how to set out and haul up anchors, grapnels or killicks from a dory.

The shore-fishing doryman had several advantages which the Banks-fishing doryman were not in a position to enjoy. For example, when the shore fisherman reached home after a hard row bucking against adverse winds, his wife and children who had anxiously been waiting his return would be on hand to give him a joyous welcome. Then there would be a hot meal ready for him. He would enjoy the luxury of sleeping in a comfortable bed, which came as a tremendous relief from the bobbing around he had endured all day in his wave-tossed dory.

His Banks-fishing brother, on the other hand, went from a bouncing dory to a pitching, rolling schooner where his hard, narrow bunk in a crowded fo'csle could not in any way compare with the nightly comfort of a shore fisherman.

This book is by no means all about Newfoundland and Newfoundlanders, for embodied herein are the exploits of Nova Scotian, American, French and Portuguese dorymen and dory builders. The verses which you have read and others that you will encounter, with the exception of three, are my own compositions. The three which I refer are: one rather bawdy verse concerning the advertures of a sea-going lady while she was gallivanting around in dories and flats. The second verse was composed by an old fisherman-rymster, to aid a French policeman in finding a lost purse. The third one praises the skill of a dory builder, named Jim Tuff.

Since I commenced to write this book in 1976 the following persons who rendered me very valuable assistance and to whom I will always feel deeply indebted, have regretably passed away:

Captain Clarence Williams
Captain Archibald Thornhill
Captain George Follett
Mr. Gordon W. Thomas
Mr. Patrick Rossiter
Mrs. Lillian Walsh
Mr. Leonard Matthews Sr.
Sergeant L.V. Dutton

I wish to extend special thanks to photographer Ben Hansen, who reproduced many of the pictures in this book.

Otto P. Kelland

CHAPTER ONE

The Birthplace of the Dory

Many people have assumed that the true origin of the fishing row dory would never be discovered. For a considerable period of time I was under the impression that this boat was either a French or a Portuguese invention.

The reason for my entertaining this belief was the fact that I was born, and lived until I was sixteen years of age, in the shore-fishing town of Lamaline, situated on Newfoundland's Burin Peninsula and fourteen miles from the French Islands of Saint Pierre et Miquelon, which lie to the westward.

Prior to the outbreak of World War One and for some time following its progression the fishermen of our harbour purchased all their dories in the town of Saint Pierre or from the French or Portuguese vessels which frequently harboured there. Consequently, for several years the only dory types known to us were the French and Portuguese. Thinking, therefore, as I did, that these were the only dories in existence, I can be pardoned for labouring under the impression that the dory was invented in France or Portugal. The dories procured from French and Portuguese fishing schooners were usually those which had been damaged when heavy seas whacked them up against bulwarks or fiferails, while on the Banks.

Those large bankers always carried four or five spare dories to take care of the problem when smash-ups occurred. Unless the damages were of a minor nature they rarely repaired broken dories while at sea. On their first trip to Saint Pierre, however, they obtained replacements from one of the two dory factories which were in full-time operation there. Meanwhile, the damaged craft were put ashore and sold to Newfoundland fishermen at bargain prices.

Many of the dories cast ashore were brand new and had suffered what our fishermen considered to be minor damages. For example, on one side a stove in top board, a broken gunnel, a cracked timber, with the opposite side, stempost and stern remaining intact. The broken side boards, gunnels and timbers were quickly and expertly replaced. In the majority of cases our fishermen buyers effected the necessary repairs themselves, as nearly all

1

Ralph Lowell, direct descendant of Simeon Lowell, inventor of the dory. Ralph is the seventh generation of dory-builders in Amesbury, Massachusetts — (Courtesy Gordon Thomas).

outport men, through absolute necessity, had become adapted to using carpenter's tools. Most of the dories used by our fishermen were of the secondhand variety and were purchased from French shore fishermen who had acquired new ones.

I have always been interested in attempting to discover the birthplace of the dory. In recent years, after conducting an intensive research in connection with the origin of that spry little boat, I have been compelled to revise my ideas concerning her having been invented by the French or the Portuguese. Regardless of the number of trails I followed, they eventually merged with a single path that led to a little town in Massachusetts, U.S.A. For unless and until there are other claimants, who hitherto have not put in an appearance, the credit for the invention of the dory must go to the late Simeon Lowell of Salisbury Point, which since his time has been absorbed into the town of Amesbury in that New England state.

I had the pleasure of visiting the Lowell Marine Works in Amesbury during the month of June, 1973, where I talked with the present managing-owner, Ralph Lowell, and his son John. They are the seventh and eighth generations of ship, small keel-boat and dory builders and are the direct descendents of Simeon Lowell, who turned out his first dory in the summer of 1793.

Simeon Lowell graduated from youth to manhood as a seaman. At an early age he rose to command ships. After going through his share of storms, hardships and narrow escapes from drowning, he apparently decided to take up an avocation on land. Being handy with carpenter's tools and having an overdose of salt in his blood, it was quite natural for him to settle on boat building as a suitable trade.

The first Lowells came to America from England during the 1630s. They settled in Newbury, a few miles from Amesbury. After a time a segment of the family branched off and moved to Boston, where it acquired considerable affluence, eventually producing judges, bankers, mill owners, a Harvard president and two poets. Ralph Lowell says of his branch of the family: "They didn't write poems, just built ships, keel boats and dories." Neither Ralph, nor the existing Lowell or town documents can explain how or why Simeon Lowell came to invent the dory or why he so named it.

Some marine reference books mention 'dory' not as a boat, but as a fish that inhabits the English Channel, and in Nova Scotia they call the redfish a 'John Dory' fish. One writer suggested that our dory had her origin in Nicaragua, Central America, because they have a boat there that they call a 'duri'. As that boat is hollowed out of a tree trunk, not built with an affixed stempost, stern and timber frames, and is not constructed of individual boards, it can only be classed as a dugout canoe. Accrediting the Nicaraguans with the invention of the dory would be as senseless as giving some overheated

3

African tribe the credit for inventing the Eskimo parka. Regardless of the many opinions that have been brought forward down through the years respecting the inventor of that reliable little lady of the North Atlantic and concerning her birthplace as well, one fact stands out very clearly: The Lowells of Amesbury were building dories long before there is any record of others doing so.

The Yankees were first in many nautical endeavors. In 1885 Captain Frank Foster, a native of Gloucester, Massachusetts, chartered the steamer *William Floyd* and outfitted her for mackerel seining. She was the first vessel of her type to become engaged at the fishery.

In 1898 the famous schooner designer, Captain Thomas McManus of Boston, produced from his board the first round-bowed fishing schooner *Mattakeesett*. Then in 1901 he came up with *Helen B. Thomas,* the first knockabout (no bowsprit) type banker. Incidentally, I built and equipped a six-foot model of this vessel which is now on display in the Newfoundland College of Fisheries, St. John's.

Rob Roy, another Banks fishing schooner, was the first spoon-bowed craft. This vessel was the brainchild of Benjamin Crownenshield, a noted Boston yacht designer.

The birthplace of the dory in Amesbury, Massachusetts —(Courtesy Gordon Thomas).

4

The biggest ship built by the Lowells was the *Alliance*, one of the first frigates authorized by Continental Congress at the time that America was striving to free herself from British rule to become an independent nation.

The *Alliance*, in command of a renegade Frenchman, sailed in company with the *Bon Homme Richard*, flagship of the famous American admiral, John Paul Jones. When they met the English warship, *Serapis*, the Frenchman must have got his wires crossed, for he fired broadside into Jones' flagship instead of at the Britisher.

From Simeon, the Lowells descended as follows, with the sons entering the business, then learning the boat building trade from their fathers: Benjamin, Hiram, Frederick E., Frederick A., Walter, Ralph, and John.

Although they were extremely busy at getting a rush order of half a dozen fibreglass boats out when I visited them, the Lowells were very genial and co-operative and took time out to answer my questions. Ralph explained that out of a whole harbour filled with dories from different builders, he can spot one of their's every time.

"Maybe it's because of the way she sits in the water," he said. "Or it could be the stock we use. The side boards and skillets (bottoms) are of seasoned white pine; stempost, stern, timber frames, gunnels and gunnel caps are of oak. Some dory builders," he said, "use applewood for timbers, while spruce makes up the remainder of the parts. Then a few don't wait for the wood to season. But," he continued, "even when our design is copied exactly a marked difference is apparent to me."

Ralph recalled that a few years ago the Coast Guard people came to him when they were in the market for dories and said that they told builders to copy a Lowell dory. But the Coast Guard didn't have plans or specifications, so Ralph drew up a set of plans for them, only to discover later that the Coast Guard had put it out for competative bidding and another builder got the contract. He was kicking himself, he said, for giving away their plans, but after the boats were delivered the Government condemned them and the Lowell firm ended up by building the dories anyway.

John Lowell took me down to the paint shop on the wharf, underneath the boat factory, where the floor is covered with what appears to be six inches of plastic, but which is actually a build-up of paint drippings of one hundred and eighty years. On the chimney is layer upon layer of paint where dory painters have been cleaning their brushes for the same period of time. John explained that when a strong summer sun shines on the floor, it softens the paint and you get the feeling that you are walking on foam rubber.

Ralph Lowell went to work for his grandfather, Fred W. Lowell, when he was thirteen. He is a well set-up man in his late fifties. He selects all the stock and watches carefully every board and plank that goes into his dories, skiffs

5

This old chimney in the birthplace of the dory (Amesbury, Massachusetts) shows where dory and boat painters cleaned their brushes for 183 years! —(Jerry Kelland Photo).

and outboards.

The men who went to fish from dories, particularly on the Banks during the winter season, developed into a hardy race. But not only on the fishing Banks were hardihood and stamina required, for the dory builders had to be pretty rugged also. Their daily task entailed the endless shaping of the different parts that went into the construction of the dory: the continuous driving and clinching of chisel-pointed nails that strengthened her sides. Some men employed by the Lowells and others in the dory factory in Shelburne, Nova Scotia, spent more than half a century building dories. It was a tedious business and there were times when they must have been bored to the point of desparation.

Ralph Lowell recalls that on bitter winter mornings it was his job to light a fire in the factory wood stove at 6:30 a.m., after which he would lug buckets of water from his grandfather's place across the street. One bucket always stood a dozen feet from the stove and on an especially cold day the water in it would freeze over.

"I can tell you," he added, "working in that brand of cold wasn't exactly fun. But," he added, "we've been modern for several years now, being equipped with a furnace and electricity."

Fred E. Lowell, Ralph's grandfather, who taught him the boat-building business, witnessed both the peak and decline of dory building, which occurred between 1870 and 1920.

In the olden days a Lowell dory cost a dollar an overall foot. A little extra was paid the builder if he delivered them. Thus, a fifteen foot dory would cost $15. The same dory today costs $600. When I asked Ralph how they could employ a gang of men (they numbered twenty-five during the peak years) even in that far-off day of cheap materials and low salaries, so that they could sell dories so cheaply, he laughed and replied: "Well, you see, white pine lumber could be purchased for $10 a thousand, dory paint cost $0.75 a gallon and our foreman, yes our foreman, mind you, was paid $18 a week.

"Sometimes Grandfather Lowell made extra money by delivering dories himself. When the wind and tide were in his favour he would set out in a row-dory towing a half dozen of his masterpieces six miles down the Merrimack River, then seventeen miles across Ipswich Bay to Cape Ann and Gloucester." Ralph said: "My Grandfather often told me that he didn't think my generation was nearly as rugged as his.

"My Grandfather wasn't a big man," Ralph stated, "but he certainly possessed great physical strength. I witnessed him putting out that power on several occasions and the muscular feats which he performed were truly amazing."

In 1941 the old man suffered a stroke which damaged him so much that one of his arms became useless and he was unable to move about as his legs were also affected. When he was able to walk once more he would come to the shop with a wheelbarrow, then load it up with firewood. He'd hold one handle with his good hand and the other handle was held by a rope sling which he had fashioned to loop around his neck.

Great physical strength was not the only quality possessed by Fred E. Lowell. His brain must have been in tune with his muscles, for he developed the skill of mass production in dory building to an amazing degree. He had perfected a system whereby he could get the most out his twenty-five skilled workers in the shortest possible time without killing them physically or mentally or impairing their efficiency.

Even after dory factories had been activated in France and Portugal as well as in Saint Pierre et Miquelon, the supply which their factories put out could not always keep up with the demand, as more vessels were added to the fishing fleets of both nations year after year. Consequently, quite frequently orders for dories would be received from them by the Lowell factory in Amesbury.

A terrific example, resulting from Fred Lowell's mass production system, is revealed by the Lowell records of 1911. Late in the winter of that year his factory received a rush order from the Portuguese for two hundred dories. The order carried a deadline shipping date and Fred Lowell started right in to meet it. He began by setting twenty-three of his men to work manufacturing all the separate parts that go into building the dories, while he kept the two remaining men busy sharpening tools and cleaning up after the chip and shaving makers. He had each man assigned to shaping particular sections, arranging the employment so that one man's work would not overlap that of another. When each and every part was ready for the two hundred dories, the actual building of them commenced. Then with twenty men divided into building crews, the remaining five were given the job of painting the finished dories as they came off the horses or cradles. It was a round-the-clock job with hurried meals and little time for sleep. A tough assignment, but from the time the first nail was driven, until the final brushful of paint had been applied, a period of only eighteen days had elapsed. Fred Lowell and his boys had beaten the deadline with two days to spare.

The day following the completion of the dories they were nested on flat cars and shipped off to Boston, where a big Portuguese steamer took delivery of them. Two hundred dories built in the space of eighteen days. It was indeed a very remarkable feat that portrayed man's ingenuity, skill and endurance at its finest.

Of course, speed coupled with efficiency was always the American way. Yankees earned the enviable reputation of being amongst the finest schooner builders in the world, for not only were the vast majority of their vessels fast under sail, they were excellent sea boats. The workmanship and materials that went into their construction enabled those that were not lost during violent storms or from crashing on reefs to endure and remain seaworthy far beyond the lifespan normally expected of them.

A fine example of this is the schooner *Effie M. Morrissey* which for many years was commanded by the famous Newfoundlander, Captain Bob Bartlett, as an Arctic exploratory vessel. The *Morrissey* was built by Willard Burnham in Essex, Massachussets during the winter of 1893-94. She sailed on her maiden voyage in command of Captain William Morrissey, whose daughter she was named after. From that date until 1914 this great vessel was used in every branch of the fisheries, including making trips many times to Newfoundland to pick up herring cargoes.

In 1914 she was sold to Harold Bartlett of Brigus. Captain Bob Bartlett purchased her from Harold in 1917.

After Captain Bob's death in New York in 1946 the vessel was sold to parties who engaged her in the Cape Verde Packet Trade. She was renamed *Ernestina* and sailed under the Portuguese flag. My old friend Gordon Thomas of Ipswich, Massachusetts, informed me that as far as he can determine the old schooner was still afloat at Fogo, Cape Verde Islands in 1972. Afloat after seventy-eight years of battling her way through Atlantic storms and butting Arctic ice. What greater testimony can one offer to the consciousness efficiency of her builders than that?

Hiram Lowell, grandson of Simeon Lowell, took over the boat-building business shortly after the American Revolution. He hung out his shingle which read:

HIRAM LOWELL and SONS
Boat Builders, Lumber, Paint,
Marine Supplies.
est. 1793

Down to the present day the wording of that sign has never been changed.

CHAPTER TWO

The Dory and Me

I guess I was three years old when I first noticed dories. I can easily recall that I was standing on a chair looking out through our kitchen window at Lamaline when I observed my father and his codtrap fishing crew bring two dories up from the nearby barrisway and set them down, bottoms up, between our house and the store.

I should explain that the name 'store' in this instance did not mean a shop, but a building set apart from the dwelling house. It was usually equipped with a long work bench, which in turn was outfitted with all varieties of carpenter's tools necessary for men who were engaged in the fisheries, who wee compelled to make by hand nearly all the units pertaining to their occupation. Just about every householder in Newfoundland outports owned such a store. From the work benches of those stores there were manufactured cod splitting tables, hand tubs, trawls tubs, fish barrows, wheelbarrows, dory scoops or water bailers, dory thwarts, dory bulkheads, cod jiggers, squid jiggers and handline reels, tholepins, etc. The store also housed putty, white lead, paints, screws, nails, bolts, and odds and ends of lumber.

To come back to my father's dories, I observed that they were pretty shabby looking, for they had been in service throughout the winter where they had been used for hunting salt water ducks and in ferrying freight ashore from the coastal steamer. In many places their sideboards had been chafed bare of paint where they had come in contact with ice. The rough usage had also knocked oakum out of the bottom board seams, which caused them to become leaky.

As it was the month of May, the time had arrived to prepare for the approaching cod fishery. Consequently, lines and twines had to be completely overhauled, trapskiffs and dories repaired and painted. After which they would be outfitted with new painters and stern straps. I watched with considerable interest as the men with a roll of tarry oakum around one arm deftly filled the seams in the dories' bottoms with the reliable material, using caulking irons driven by wooden mallets, the rolls of oakum becoming smaller by the minute as they uncoiled from the men's arms with the filling of each seam.

The caulking iron is a chisel-like instrument about six inches long with the blade measuring one and a half to two inches wide. Although it is rather thin at the blade edge, it is not sharp like a chisel.

When the caulking was finished the men went along the seams with another iron, very similar to the caulking iron, but very blunt at the edge of the blade. Its purpose is to flatten out the oakum in the seams and to set it down firmly. This tool is called a making iron. The crew then fashioned a fireplace from stones, placing kindling and billets of wood inside, they started a fire. When the flames were burning brightly, they placed an iron pot over the fire. This pot contained a substance known as pitch, which was purchased locally in solid form, but heat from the fire quickly melted it into liquid form. When it was sufficiently melted, the men using mops, smeared it into the caulked seams.

Of course the names of impliments and materials used during the repair job were unknown to me at the time and a considerable space of time had to go by before I became familiar with all of them. I learned later, also, that the idea of applying pitch to caulked seams was in order for it to form a hard surface over the oakum, to bind it and prevent it from dropping out, for when applied in the open air it quickly cooled and became hard at once. When this condition was finalized, iron scrappers were used to remove all excess pitch from the bottom boards and to level it over the seams.

After the scrapping had been finished, the dories were painted, first on the outside, then they were turned right side up and painted on the inside. The paint was golden yellow, later when I became old enough to learn to read I noticed stamped or stencilled on the cans the words, 'Dory Yellow', on others 'Dory Buff'. Those name brands of course meant that the paint came from different manufacturers. Dory paints which were imported from the United States differed from those of Nova Scotia and that which was manufactured in St. John's differed from both.

Finally the gunnels of the dories were painted a pretty shade of green. I might insert here that neither the shades of 'Dory Buff', 'Dory Yello', nor the gunnel green used in those days can be found in any paint shop today. I build dory models and I have to mix my own shades and colours in order that my little boats will resemble as closely as possible those which were painted by the old dory builders and painters of years gone by.

Then again, all dories in those days weren't painted buff or yellow, many of our fishermen used grey, red, blue and green. The fresh coat of paint transformed our dories completely. Gazing at them with the eyes of a three-year-old youngster, I thought that they looked very beautiful. I am a long distance from being a three-year-old today, but I still think that a well-built, newly and neatly painted dory is the finest looking small row boat.

Two months after I'd watched so interestedly while my father's dories were being repaired and painted, I came within an ace of losing my life by falling overboard from one of them.

The day was warm and fine, I was playing around near our back door, which was only about thirty feet from the barrisway previously mentioned. A breastwork of stout logs placed tightly together and driven ends down deep into the beach surrounded this section of the waterway, for when the wind blew strongly from the northwest quite a wind lop would be kicked up; so, without the protection of the breastwork, the road which ran around the barrisway would be washed away.

Like I said, I was playing near the back door when I noticed that one of our dories was tied broadside to the breastwork. The tide was top high and the water very calm. Suddenly, I got the idea that I would like to be onboard the dory. So I went down and clambered over the breastwork, landing in the dory near the bow. I recall very vividly that I slowly made my way aft, seized the rope stern-strap which was dangling down on the inside and with its aid I walked up the raking stern. What I had in mind was to go high enough so as I could peer over the boat's counter and see what was going on down in the water; but unfortunately for me I went too far with my climbing act for suddenly I overbalanced and, losing my grip on the stern strap, plunged headlong overboard.

The water was about four feet deep at that point. I came to the surface gasping and struggling; then I went down again. As I broke water the second time I remember reaching up to try and grasp the dory's gunnel which appeared to be awfully high and far away. By this time I could only see things dimly. I fancied that I could hear someone yelling; then I started to sink for the traditional third time. As I was about to disappear I felt a terrible pain in the top of my head and I felt myself being lifted clear out of the water by my top-knot. It was my mother who saved my life. She had seen me fall overboard from her kitchen window. With her hampering long skirts and all she managed to board that dory just in the nick of time.

My mother lived to be one hundred years, two months old and up to three weeks before she died she was in full possession of all her faculties. When we were celebrating her ninety-eight birthday, I pointed to my bald head and said:

"Mother, but for you I would have a nice head of fuzzy hair today, because when you pulled me out of the water by my curls when I was a tiny boy, you must have loosened up my hair roots. No wonder it is nearly all gone." Very quickly came her reply, "My son, if I had not yanked you into the dory by your head mop, you wouldn't be around today to worry about falling hair."

My second venturing onboard a dory nearly ended in disaster also. It happened when I was six years old and my cousin Jack Pittman was nine. Jack fancied himself to be quite a man and he really acted the part. One day he and I were catching tomcods from our stagehead, which overlooked the western end of Lamaline harbour. His father was a member of our trap crew and he had gone out with my father and the other crew members to haul the codtrap; in fact every ablebodied man in the place was absent, being engaged in similar occupations. It was about three o'clock in the afternoon. Jack's father's dory was tied to our stagehead. Suddenly Jack turned to me and said in an authoritive voice, "Come on, b'y, we're goin' for a row." At the time the wind was blowing off our shore, straight towards the mouth of the harbour a mile away. As young as I was I noticed that it appeared to be blowing pretty hard. So in reply to Jack I returned rather timidly: "It's kinda windy out there."

"Aw! Come on," said Jack. "Don't be such a bloody baby. You got nuttin' to worry about with me rowing. So get aboard, set down in the stern and keep quiet." So aboard I got, sitting down in the stern Jack untied the dory, jumped aboard, shipped his oars and we were on our way.

Under the lee of the land Jack didn't fare too badly and he managed the heavy oars very well. I might say that Uncle Bob's dory was the fifteen foot size, known both in the Banks and shore fisheries as the double or two-man type. When we arrived out to where the wind was blowing stronger, Jack apparently realized that he was too far off shore and managing the heavy dory was fast becoming a problem that he could not handle. Then he made a valiant attempt to turn around and head back to safety. Unfortunatley, an exceptionally heavy squall descended upon the dory at the same time he made that decision, with the result, in spite of Jack's efforts, she turned completely broadside. Any empty, improperly managed dory when so assailed will do that every time and it takes a strong man to handle such a boat to keep her on course before the wind or to bring her head into it. A nine-year-old boy simply didn't have a chance. When the dory turned broadside the strong wind blowing on her win'ard sice caused her to tilt precariously. It also caused her to bear down heavily on the leeward oar which made it twist violently in the oarlock. Jack could not hold it and lost his grip, with the result that the lum or handle of the oar shot forward, striking my cousin full on the chest, knocking him off the thwart, down upon the bottom of the dory. Whilst he was falling he lost his grip on the win'ard oar. When he managed to get back on the thwart again both oars had slipped out of the oarlocks and were now some distance astern, where I could spot them bobbing along in our wake.

Now the wind started to increase in volume with heavy squalls becoming more frequent. Driving hard on the side of our dory, they pushed the craft towards the harbour mouth with gathering speed. As the wind became stronger the lops rose higher, causing the dory to rock so violently I thought for sure that we would be tossed overboard. Today, when ever I reflect on our wild boat ride I think of that grand old hymn, 'Rocked in the Cradle of the Deep'. The man who wrote that beautiful number was away better off than Jack and I, for according to his verses he could lay himself down in peace to sleep. No such luxury was in store for us. Speaking for myself, I was too terrified even to think of slumber and I suspect that my cousin was experiencing similar feelings. As we sped along I became aware that the dory's stern strap was within my reach, whereupon I promptly seized it with both hands. All through the remainder of our unpleasant voyage I stuck to that strap like goo to a diaper. In fact my fear was so great that it caused me to clutch the rope so firmly that one of our rescurers experienced considerable difficulty in prying my fingers loose from it.

The stern straps were fashioned from stout manila rope, the two ends being pushed through holes in the top section of the dory's stern and secured on the outside by the forming of knots, leaving a loop or becket approximately sixteen inches long hanging down on the inside. On Banks fishing vessels they were used to hoist dories outboard and inboard. On shore-fishing dories they served as an attachment for a stern line anchor rope to prevent the boats from drifting ashore to chafe on the rocks.

I shifted my gaze from the tumbling creamy tipped waters to peer at Jack. To my dismay I noticed that he was lying on his side on the bottom of the dory vomiting all over the place. I could see one side of his face, his ruddy complexion had disappeared. It had been replaced by a ghosly blue tint that was shaded with a greenish hue not unlike one sees on a hunk of fresh water ice.

The redoutable Jack had become violently seasick, although at the time I didn't know exactly what ailed him. I remembered hearing people talking of seasickness but I had never before witnessed a person being afflicted with it. At least in one respect I was the more fortunate one for I did not get seasick and later during my more than five years at sea on various ships I am thankful to be able to say I was never visited by that obnoxious malady.

I have seen many of my fellow crewmen so ill that you would imagine they were on the verge of death. Big strong men, some of them, but once they became seasick they'd lie on their bunks listless and helpless as newborn infants. I have known shore fishermen who went to sea from boyhood to elderly manhood who suffered from seasickness every day they were afloat, yet they bravely carried on. Why? Because they had families to feed and very few land-based jobs were available in times past.

As our dory shot out through the harbour mouth I thought of our fathers who were fishing three or four miles to the west'ard. We cartainly could not expect any aid from them. I thought also of our mothers and sisters, all of them unaware of our terrible plight. I guessed that they would never see us again. Frightened as I was I managed to raise myself by the stern strap until I could peer over the dory's counter to take one last look at that beloved strip of land on which our homes stood.

As I gazed disconsolately shoreward a movement in that direction caught my eye. I stared harder, then I could discern a yellow painted dory being rowed by two people coming rapidly before the wind in our direction. I kept gazing for another few minutes because I wanted to be certain that I was actually seeing what I thought I saw. Shortly afterward all doubt was removed from my mind; that yellow dory was no mirage, those blades flashed up and down in quick succession were very real. Overjoyed, I turned to my cousin.

"Jack," I yelled excitedly, "Someone is comin', we're gettin' saved!"

With both stomach and ego considerably deflated by this time, poor Jack moaned, "It don't matter, I'm dying."

The yellow dory caught up with us several yards outside the harbour mouth. When the craft came alongside ours, I discovered that the people rowing her were two women. I recognized them easily for they were both neighbours of ours, namely, Mrs. Martha Haley and Mrs. Eva Longeau. Neither of them had children of their own and though they were only in their thirties, they and their husbands had been given the honourary titles of Uncle and Aunt, as it was often the customary practise in many Newfoundland outports to grant childless couples such titles. Everyone in the community addressed these fine women as Aunt Eva and Aunt Martha. Both of them were tall, well built and in top physical condition, as they had been used to hard work from early girlhood. Furthermore, very luckily for us, they were expert at rowing dories.

The barrisway referred to earlier was an excellent area on whose waters young people both male and female could learn to row as well as sail boats. It is a miniature inland sea, completely landlocked with the exception of a narrow gut that connects it with the waters of the harbour and through which its tides rise and fall.

Many dories that had been more or less condemned as fishing boats because of age were harboured in the barrisway. It was in those craft that we learned how to handle dories, both in rowing and sailing them. Consequently, girls as well as boys, by the time they reached the age of eighteen years, could handle a dory as well as a man.

"Now, Martha!" yelled Aunt Eva, as her strong hands gripped our gunnel, "I'll hold on here while you take the boys onboard our dory."

Acting quickly, Aunt Martha, apparently realizing Jack's sorry condition, rescued him first and laid him down in the bow of their boat.

"I'm dyin', Aunt Eva," groaned the miserable Jack.

"Oh, you'll get over it," replied Eva tartly. "The only way you're goin' to die, me b'y, is if your father kills you for takin' his dory out on a windy day like this with that youngster aboard."

While this exchange was going on I too had been rescued by the efficient Aunt Martha, who by superhuman strength had managed to pry my fingers loose from that blessed stern strap.

"Eva, what are we goin' to do about Bob's dory?" queried Aunt Martha.

"To hell with Bob's dory," snapped Aunt Eva. "You know very well that we can't tow her back against this wind, we'll be lucky if we manage to row our own dory back. Let her go adrift."

Our timely rescue by those two sturdy women was no mean feat, as the high wind and heavy lop caused the two dories to bob up and down like bucking broncos, and as they tossed they banged together so hard you would imagine that they would be smashed to pieces. The women had a hard row back to the beach, a distance of over a mile, but they certainly were equal to the task. Like I said, they were expert dory rowers even against a strong head wind.

It seemed as though our plight had been noticed by an old, retired fisherman who was so crippled by rheumatism that he was unable to help us. However, he notified Aunt Eva and Aunt Martha who quickly commandeered the first dory they came across and set out after us.

After we were safely back on land Jack, who had soon recovered from the effects of seasickness, became extremely worried over the loss of his father's dory. But as it turned out, Uncle Bob's dory was not lost after all, for later in the evening word was received from the settlement of Point au Gaul, three miles to the east'ard, that the boat had come ashore on the soft sand of Point au Gaul Point and was undamaged. We were more than delighted to learn that our dory, too, had made a happy landing.

When our fathers returned from fishing and learned of our escapade they only administered a mild scolding to us. Very mild, indeed, for that day and age. But I suspect that deep down they were so delighted we had not been drowned or driven off to sea that they held back the heavy artillery.

The third incident wherein a dory was involved and which terminated in nearly sending me to Davey Jones' locker occurred when I was thirteen years old. It happened in July, 1918. One day my father purchased a brand new Shelburne dory from the firm of Samuel Harris and Company, whose premises were located on the south side of Lamaline harbour.

The codtrap fishing season was at its peak and large catches were being brought in every day. Although fish out in the Bights were devil deep, as the old fishermen used to say, there was one vitally needed commodity which was fast becoming scarce. That was salt. In 1918, fresh fish processing plants were a long distance beyond the horizon as far as Newfoundland was concerned. As a result, the fishermen's only hope for continuing the fishery was to get salt, and plenty of it, for there was no other means available whereby they could perserve their catches.

The salt shortage was accounted for by the fact that World War One was raging. German submarines and surface raiders were sending our salt-carrying vessels to the bottom of the sea at such a rate that the salt coming from Cadiz had been slowly reduced to a mere trickle. At the time of which I am writing, supplies had dwindled to such an extent that the firms were rationing it out, allowing one dory load, approximately a ton, to each codtrap operator and a lesser amount to dory trawl men.

At three o'clock a.m. on the day following the one on which my father had bought his new dory, our crew was getting ready to go out and haul the codtrap. I had intended to go along with them but the skipper had other ideas. He told me:

"While we are gone to the trap, you take the new dory, go over to Harris' and bring back a load of salt. Because if we get a big tuck of fish we'll need more salt to stow it away."

I was disappointed at not being able to go out to the trap, but those were the days when one's father's instructions were obeyed without question.

The day broke fine and clear, no breeze stirred, the waters of the harbour were flat calm as I set out on my errand. Actually, I was quite pleased that my father had entrusted me with what I then considered to be a very important mission. Meanwhile, I felt proud of the new dory, having the same feelings concerning her as my grandsons have today about a new sports model car. The dory was light to row and easy to manoeuvre. The fog which usually plagued our coast during that season of the year was absent and the sun was shining brightly, while the water glistened like a huge mirror.

As I rowed past the rocky bar which forms the western end of our harbour, I noted that the coastal boat S.S. Argyle was anchored in the road, discharging cargo. I mention the steamer for the very good reason that she was the indirect cause of the accident which nearly made me meet my waterloo, with special emphasis on the water part of the word. The road is a body of water lying to the west of Lamaline harbour. It is encompassed by Allen's Island and the harbour bar to the east, Morgan's Island to the south, Green Island to the west and the mainland to the north. It can be entered or departed from by two routes, namely, the opening between Allen's Island and Morgan's Island to the south, or the passageway between Green's Island and the mainland to the west. When strong winds were blowing from a southerly or a westerly direction it could and did become a very rough place, but as the entrance to Lamaline harbour was considered by coastal steamer captains to be too shallow or navigate safely, they always anchored in the road, winter and summer, whether it was rough or smooth. The freight was landed from the steamers by trap skiffs and dories.

When I reached Harris' wharf I observed that the tern or three-masted schooner *General Currie* was tied up there. The *Currie*, which had been built in Grand Bank by Eli Harris during the winter of 1917-18, was launched in the spring of the latter year. The vessel was one of the great white fleet of foreign-going craft owned by the Samuel Harris firm, all of them bearing the names of Allied generals, like: *General Trenchard, General Smutts, General Horne, General Allenby,* etc.

The *General Currie* had arrived with cargo a few days previously, she had been unloaded and was awaiting orders. The vessel had been slacked off from the pier for the distance of twenty feet. This was done in order to permit fishermen bringing in fish catches or making purchases from the firm free access to the wharf and its facilities. I estimate the time of my arrival to be six thirty a.m. I found the premises entirely deserted, as work did not commence there until seven a.m.

I tied my dory to a gump on the pier head and went to search for Mr. Ambrose Saint, the wharf manager, who usually took the orders for salt. After considerable hunting around, I finally located him in the firm's general store which despite the early hour was open for business. I placed my order for salt with Mr. Saint and we strolled back to the wharf. The manager remarked as we neared it that he would get a couple of men to load my dory. Ambrose Saint was a man of middle age. He was a very likeable, genial and efficient person who was well qualified to handle the position he held.

As we reached the edge of the wharf, we noticed a large, heavily laden trapskiff aproaching at a fast clip from a westerly direction. She was heading straight for the passageway between the big schooner and the pier. I glanced down towards my dory and noticed to my dismay that a light breeze which had arisen during my absence had pushed the little boat around so that her stern was jammed against the fore channel irons or chain plates of the 'General Currie' and her stemhead was wedged solidly underneath a wharf stringer or cross beam. In short she had formed a complete barrier right across the waterway with the big, motor driven skiff being pointed exactly at her.

Neddy Walsh, the lone occupant of the skiff, was a very short man and his boat was piled up so high over his head with the boxes and bales which he had just taken off the steamer *Argyle* that his for'ard visibility was completely obscured, but Neddy apparently reasoned that he did not need to see ahead,

18

he was steering by the shoreline and had navigated in that manner so many times that he could probably make that passageway with his eyes shut. I guess that the phrase, 'unknown factor' had not been coined at that time, even if it was on the books, evidently Neddy Walsh was unaware of its existance for he kept right on coming without bothering to stretch up and take a peek over his piled up freight.

Although Neddy was unable to see straight ahead, he could easily see us standing on the pier, at right angles to his starboard side. In vain did Mr. Saint and I wave our arms and yell to him to go out around the bow of the schooner. But Neddy only grinned and waved back with his free hand. He told us later that the noise from his exhaust was making such a hellish racket that he could not distinguish our words, he added that he thought we were waving a friendly greeting to him. The wharf manager's reply to that statement is unprintable even in this modern age when people like a little spice added to their reading matter. Then with the heavy trapskiff scant yards away I did a very foolhardy thing, I slid down over the wharf and stood on the bow of the dory in an attempt to save her, by holding the wharf piling with both hands and pressing down hard with my feet I tried to free her nose with a view to swinging her out of the path of the uncoming skiff. But I discovered that neither my weight nor my strength were equal to the task.

I heard Mr. Saint scream, "You damn fool!"

Then the sturdy, hardwood stempost of the big boat struck the dory right amidships slicing her in two halves as quickly as you would sever a hunk of ham with an electric carving knife. When I felt the dory's bow being jerked out from under my feet, with more luck than I probably deserved, I managed to get a grip on her painter with both hands as it was still fastened securely to the gump on the pier head, but before I could tighten my grip, I slid down into the water up to my waist where the bow wave that had been kicked up by the skiff swung me back and forth like a pendulum of a grandfather clock. Seconds later, Mr. Saint and another man reached down, seized my wrists and pulled me up to safety. At this juncture, a crewmember of the *General Currie* who had evidently been rudely awakened from slumber by our yelling and the noise of the collision appeared on deck, sporting a hard hat and clad in a suit of long underwear which obviously had not been visited by water since the last time he fell overboard. This trouserless individual stared gloomily at the severed dory and the bow of the trapskiff which was festooned with a long section of the little boat's sideboard and gunnel. Then a moment later he added another useless question to the archives of useless questions when he shouted, "What in the name of merry hell have been goin' on around here?"

We ignored him and walked toward John Hyde, the general manager who had now put in an appearance, and Mr. Saint briefed him as to what had occurred. My Hyde instructed the wharf manager to load one of the company's dories with salt, "As his father will probably be waiting for it." Then turning to me he said, "Son, tell your father when he gets his fish stowed away to come over and see me so as we can arrange some sort of deal over his busted dory."

I, of course, did not know what kind of deal they made, but when my father returned that afternoon he was towing another new Shelburne after his trapskiff. As for myself, one fact was certainly becoming very apparent. As an aspiring doryman I was really coming up the hard way.

CHAPTER THREE

The Dory Builders

Dory builders may be placed in three categories. Firstly, there were fishermen around the coasts of New England, Nova Scotia and along the south and west coasts of Newfoundland, who were very handy with carpenter's tools and who did an excellent job of building their own dories. Very often too, those men would build dories for relatives and friends who did not happen to be too well versed in the use of boat building implements. Those builders did not build dories commercially per se, but were acting more in the role of an obliging person who was proud of his handiwork and who would charge a small fee when the job was completed, with the people for whom he performed the work paying for the cost of materials used.

Secondly, there were the part-time builders. Those were the men who fished all through the summer months and built dories during the winter. Their operation was usually conducted on a small scale and they would turn out from three to six dories each winter. Very often those men worked alone, though sometimes a brother or son would volunteer their services as a helper. Of course, the output from two men would be greater than that of a man who worked alone.

Prospects regarding the sale of his dories had to be taken into consideration also, by the part-time builder. But, if he was the type of man who built a strong, neat, good looking dory, he normally had no difficulty in selling his product. As a rule, the past-time builder did not cater to the Banks fishing trade, but if a banker entered a port with one of her dories smashed beyond repaid and there happened to be a dory available that had been built by a part-time craftsman and if the boat was of a size where she would fit snugly or nest into the dories he already had onboard, the captain would buy her as a replacement.

The matter of dories nesting properly on a vessel's deck was in itself important. Banks fishermen have told me that when dories were purchased for the outfitting of a banker, it was essential that they should all come from the same builder, who had turned them out by using the same mould or pattern. For it had been discovered that dories which had been manufactured by one builder, rarely, if ever nested or fitted into those produced by another builder. This was caused by differences in side flare and in bow and stern rake. For example, the Shelburne dory was a misfit when slipped into one of the French type. Although their bottom sizes in length were the same, the French dory having a heavier rake at the stern and stem was much longer on the top sides. The Shelburne, on the other hand, carried a wider bottom which gave her a broader flare on both sides. Consequently, when the latter type was joisted into the French dory, her additional width prevented her from settling down properly. Then, when the positions were reversed, the French dory was prevented from nesting into the Shelburne snugly as she would be held up by her longer overhang fore and aft. So, not only would ill fitting dories rock back and forth when the parent ship was wallowing in a side roll or plunging in a head pitch, such nesting had the effect of pyramiding the stacked dories too high where they could be clobbered and wrecked by the flailing, heavy boom of the foresail, when a schooner luffed up to come about on another tack.

When the part time dory builders in Newfoundland could not find buyers for their boats in settlements along the coasts where they lived, they often brought them into St. John's on the decks of the coasting schooners skippered by friends who were voyaging to the capital to deliver or take on cargo. On several occasions I have viewed such dories being landed from schooners and put up for sale on wharves along the city's waterfront where they were often disposed of in a few days, having been bought by the skippers of coasting vessels or by shore fishermen working out of St. John's or nearby settlements.

In the third category of dory builders, a man or a company established a regular factory wherein the employment was persued on a full time basis. The factory owners engaged the services of skilled workers, who may have been diverted from time and time from dory building to construct craft of other types for which orders had been placed. However, most of their time was dedicated to the building of dories. The first dory factory was activated, as I have already stated, in Salisbury Point, Massachusetts, during 1793 by Simeon Lowell, the inventor of the dory. That enterprising man may be truly classed as the great, great grandfather of the dory builders.

As time marched on, dory factories were set up in Shelburne and Lunenburg in Nova Scotia; Bay of Islands, St. John's, Grand Bank, Monkstown and Lamaline in Newfoundland. There were many others, of course, as far as part-time builders went along our south, southwest and west coasts, as well as on the French islands of Saint Pierre et Miquelon.

As far as I am able to determine, the first dory factory to appear in Canada was established in the town of Shelburne, by Isaac Cowell, about one hundred and twenty years ago. Later dory factories were activated there by Harvey Hipson, John C. Morrison, J.B. Williams and Son, and John Ethrington, Limited.

I remember when the first dories arrived in our harbour from Shelburne, reading the names, J.B. Williams and Son and John Ethrington which were stencilled on the inside of the boats' sterns.

To present day, landlubber eyes, all dories look exactly alike. But they definitely are not. I will now set forth the reason why. As dory building

Models of six types of rowdories and a motor dory built by the author for the New-foundland College of Fisheries —(Dianne Lackie Photo).

developed in countries apart from America, builders with possible attempts at improvement departed somewhat from the original Lowell design, with regard to bow and stern rake, side flare and sheer as well as other features. But basically, nobody changed the overall style of the first dory in appearance. Indeed it has remained unchanged after nearly two centuries of use, for the craft built today still carries a 'V' shaped stern, outward flaring sides and with stem-post and stern strongly raked. Whereas distinctive features employed by different builders may be invisible to inexperienced eyes, they make each dory type easily identifiable when brought before the gaze of an experienced doryman. Apart from that, dories which had been built in separate factories possessed different handling characteristics. That fact can be confirmed by men who have used all types while they were engaged in both the Banks and shore fisheries.

There were seven distinct types of row dories which gained recognition as such, in the various settlements of Newfoundland's south and west coasts. There were the Lowell Americans, which first made their appearance in Newfoundland nested on the decks of American bankers during the 1870s. This craft also became known as the Gloucester dory and the Cape Ann dory, despite the fact that they were neither built on Cape Ann nor in Gloucester, but were turned out in Salisbury Point exclusively. Then there was the Shelburne, French, Lunenburger, Monk, Portuguese and the Grandy.

The differences respecting certain methods pertaining to the construction of each type which made one identifiable from the other went as follows. The French dory had a high steamhead, was very crooked in the sheer (upper lengthwise profile of the boat), she carried a very strong rake at the ends, and her rubbers (protective strips nailed along the outer edge of the gunnels) were rounded. She was fitted with an iron breasthook which was fastened on the inside of the stempost and gunnels. In addition, she was built with six bed of timber frames, while all other fifteen footers were built with five. Then her paint scheme, particularly in the early days, comprised three, four or even five colours, depending, of course, on the number of side boards that went into her construction.

On a sunny morning, years ago, when we were on a trip to Saint Pierre and were approaching a fleet of French dories fishing on the grounds between

The only French type rowdory the author could locate on the island of St. Pierre —(Jerry Kelland Photo).

Lamaline and the French islands, one would imagine that a whole circus had gone to sea, for the dories presented a riot of colour which flashed in the sun as they rose and fell with the motion of each lop.

Each set of timbers in the French dory was made up of four pieces which were pinned together at the limbo holes (water channels) by galvanized metal locks or clips. The Shelburne dory was straighter in the sheer than the French type and did not have so much rake at the ends, particularly in the stempost. She was fitted with flat square edge rubbers and the tip of her stemhead was sawn off which gave her a flat-nosed appearance. But like the French dory she was built with locked timber frames. The Shelburne, more frequently than other types, was constructed with three boards to a side. She was painted, invariably a shade of lemon yellow with green gunnels.

The Lunenburg dory is built with frames of grown timber where in the natural curvature of the wood is maintained, similar to the blade of a hockey stick. This type of timber framing was always considered by both builders and fishermen to be far stronger than the locked or slipped style. The Lunenburger received high praise from many of the Newfoundland fishing skippers I talked with concerning the capabilities of various dory types which they had used on the Banks. They claimed that she was an excellent carrier and a wonderful rough water boat.

This dory could be easily identified from the French and the Shelburne as she had (and still has, as she is being built today) a short stemhead, was not equipped with rubbers and she carried a raised gunnel cap at the for'ard end. I have been informed by Mr. Robert Cram, present owner of the dory factory in Lunenburg, that placing an extra cap or raised gunnel on the bow of his dories has been discontinued. The timber frames, gunnels, gunnel caps, stemposts and sterns of the Lunenburg dory are fashioned from native oak, while her bottom and side boards are of pine. In the fifteen foot Lunenburg Banks dory, I have never seen one with more or less than four boards to a side, although the smaller sizes were often built with three to a side. This reliable craft was usually painted a medium shade of buff with green gunnels.

The Lunenburger also possesses another feature which I have never found on other makes. That is at the bow where the holes for the painter are bored through the top side board, she is fitted with a hardwood block or breasthood that was fastened to the inside of the stempost and reached fully across from side board to side board. Then the nose strap ends, instead of coming through the side boards and crossing the stempost, will pass through holes bored in the block which are in line with those bored in the side boards. Then, either Matthew Walker or Crown Knots are tied in the nose strap ends to prevent them being drawn back through the holes when strain is centered upon the strap. I think the idea of fitting a dory to take a nose strap in this manner is

25

Lunenburg-type dories used in the races at the Nova Scotia Fisheries Exhibition held annually in Lunenburg —(Jerry Kelland Photo).

excellent, as all stress and strain is placed directly on the sturdy hardwood stempost instead of it being placed, partly on the much frailer pine side boards. Where Banks fishing dories were not equipped with the Lunenburg type painter or nose strap breasthook, both ends of the strap had to be spliced together, for if they were knotted the entire strain, when the dory was being hoisted or towed, would be placed on the two sideboards, which was not advisable.

Painters of shore fishing dories were usually fastened by passing one end of the rope through both bow holes, then it was brought around and spliced into the standing part. Nose straps were rarely used in shore fishing dories but were essential to Banks dories to accommodate the jigs or hooks fastened to the tackle by which they were hoisted inboard and outboard. The Lunenburg dory was also, erroneously, called the Dutch dory by many Newfoundlanders. They mispronounced the word Deutschland for Dutchland and thus the Lunenburg dory got the wrong name.

The American dory is similar to the Shelburne in outward appearances. It is quite apparent that the Shelburne was patterned after the American, a style which she held down to the end of her days. But anyone who is familiar with both types can detect some differences between the two. For example, the American has a broader flare at the sides and her sheer is deeper or more crooked. Her rubbers are flat and square edged as are those of the Shelburne, but they are shaped differently where they were fastened outside the stempost. She is also built with locked timber frames. In classing the American I am referring to the Lowell dory of Amesbury. The present managing owner of the factory there informed me that in the early days the timber frames of their dories were fashioned from the roots of the native oak trees, but after these became impossible to obtain, they were compelled to build with locked timbers.

For neatness and perfection in workmanship, the handsome little American dory is mighty hard to beat. She was usually painted with a golden yellow hull and green gunnels.

The Newfoundland dory of the Grandy type was designed by the late Stephen Grandy of Grand Bank. Although this craft resembles both the American and Shelburne dories, possibly because of her flat nose, a close-up view, however, easily identifies her from the other two, owing to the fact that she possesses four distinct features. Firstly, her rubbers do not extend fully to the bow and stern, but are fastened about two feet back from those extremities. Secondly, the rubbers are bevelled on the lower side. Thirdly, she is built with kneed or naturally grown timbers. Fourthly, she has a raised gunnel for'ard, which extends from the stemhead back to approximately five inches abaft the fore timbers. The Grandy was always recognized as a good carrier

27

and an excellent seaboat.

This fine dory was usually painted buff with green gunnels. I have heard nothing but high compliments paid to the Grandy, by men who are familiar with her while pursuing the Banks and shore fisheries, as well as those who have served on vessels engaged in the coastal trade.

The Monk Newfoundland built dory was designed and perfected by the brothers, John and Henry Monk of Monkstown, Placentia Bay. This craft has

The Monk-type Newfoundland dory —(Courtesy John Monk Jr.).

often been mistaken for the Lunenburg dory as she bears a strong resemblance to her, although she is not equipped with rubbers and her timber frames are shaped from the roots of trees. I have never seen one of the Monk dories with locked timbers. She does not have raised gunnel caps for'ard as does the Lunenburg dory and I have seen her displaying five and occasionally six boards to a side. Although the stempost of the Monk appears to be more upright than the Nova Scotian dory, her stern has a much stronger rake. In addition, she carries a broader side flare which gives her a wider beam. The Monk dory also has her side boards set into notches cut in the timber which leaves no spaces between boards and frames, a condition which is quite apparent in other builds.

The Monk dory was a great favorite with fishing skippers and dorymen who conducted operations from small, usually tan-sailed schooners known as western boats, that followed their avocations on the stormy seas off Cape St.

Mary's, the Virgin Rocks and even out on the far flung Grand Banks. This sturdy dory was in great demand also, by trawl and codtrap shore fishermen as she could bear up a very heavy load and was a fine stiff boat from which to set out and haul up heavy trap anchors.

The Portuguese Banks fishermen showed a preference for the cross-handed or single man dory. Although during the days of dory hand-lining many American vessels were equipped with single man dories which were used for certain types of fishing, the Portuguese carried those little dories without variation. Their huge vessels which ranged in size from three hundred to seven hundred tons, nested from forty to seventy-five single man dories.

Whereas the Portuguese purchased many of their dories from factories in America and Nova Scotia, the boats which came from their own builders can be identified from the others. For these have a much heavier rake at both ends, more even than the French type and they were always constructed with four boards to a side. Other identifying marks are, they carry iron breasthooks on the inside of the bow, with iron clamps on the inside of the stern, these are fastened to both sides of the counters and to the sections of the gunnels. In addition, these dories are equipped with galvanized iron oarlocks, which are inserted into the gunnels via a single hole, all other types are fitted out with wooden tholepins. In painting their dories, the Portuguese seemed to

Two boxes of nails, two shavings and a gunnel clamp rest on and near the abandoned dory building cradle in the closed-down Shelbourne dory factory —(Jerry Kelland Photo).

29

favour the two-toned style. I have seen them painted yellow with black trim, white with orange trim, red with white trim, white with red trim, white with green trim and sun tan with white trim. Occasionally I have noticed dories on some Portuguese vessels painted with a single colour.

Before a banking voyage commenced both dories and dorymen were assigned to port or starboard sides. The practise of having the port and starboard dories painted with different colours proved to be a great time saver, when necessity compelled a captain to retrieve his small craft in a hurry.

Although the Shelburne dory was widely used on Newfoundland Banks fishing schooners which sailed from ports of Burin, Grand Bank, Fortune and points further west, her type was not too well known in the shore fishing settlements of Lamaline and other nearby places until the summer of 1918. For as I stated earlier, our fishermen had nearly always used French dories which they purchased second hand in Saint Pierre et Miquelon. These were perfectly sound boats and they came much cheaper than a new Shelburne, which at that time cost $40.00. But by 1918, war conditions had slowed up dory building materials coming into Saint Pierre to such an extent that French fishermen were no longer selling used dories to Newfoundland fishermen, because they could not get the new ones to replace them. When the Lamaline branch of the firm of Samuel Harris and Company imported a couple of dozen dories from Shelburne early in the summer of 1918, it was the second time that many of our fishermen had ever seen that type. On making an inspection of the new dories, they weren't very impressed. Comments voiced concerning them were unfavorable to say the least. They condemned her flat nose, straight sheer and rake. They also condemned her lemon yellow paint scheme, used all their lives to seeing the smarter appearing French dory with her deeply curved sheer, high stemhead, heavily raked ends and rainbow coloured hulls, to them it was like comparing a sleek, thoroughbred racer with a ragged haired work horse.

But they had no choice, it was either use the Shelburne, or stay ashore. With dried salt codfish selling at the fabulous price of $20.00 per quintel and raw codliver oil bringing them in $65.00 per cask, to remain on the beach was out of the question. Naturally the Shelburnes were quickly bought up. My father acquired one of them. By the way, this was the same dory which was unceremoniously sliced in two halves by Neddy Walsh's motor boat.

Shortly after the Shelburne dories had been put into service, a coal laden schooner arrived in our harbour to sell her cargo. A man went onboard to purchase a quantity of the fuel, towing after his trapskiff his new Shelburne dory and an older French dory. Now although she could bear up more, a ton of coal was always considered to be a safe and comfortable dory load, so his two dories were loaded accordingly. But, when he took his departure from the vessel, he immediately returned. Jumping back upon the schooner's deck, he accused the mate who was checking out the coal of short-weighing him.

"Look!" he shouted. "That Shelburne dory is not near so deep in the water as the French dory. You must have held back a tub or two."

Calmly the mate produced his tally sheet.

"There it is," he told the irate man, "in black and white. Your two dories are carrying exactly the same weights, what you don't realize is that the Shelburne with her straighter sheer in the center and broaded flare at the sides is a far better carrier and won't settle so deeply in the water as the French dory with a comparative load." The mate was proven to be right and the accusation made against him was withdrawn, his accusor offering him an apology.

It does not take too much, sometimes, to change the minds of men from condemnation to praise. For as soon as it was discovered that the Shelburne dory could carry a heavier load than the French dory, she became popular overnight. Compliments in her favour commenced to pour in from all sides. "Hellish great carrier," said one. "Damned easy to row and handles well under sail," voiced another. "Not so cranky as the Frenchman," commented a third. As time went by her popularity increased. The Shelburne had come to stay.

While in the town of Shelburne, during June, 1973, I visited the one and only dory factory left standing there today. There were five in 1920. I had hoped to be able to view the dory builders in action, but unfortunately the

William Cox, last owner of the last dory factory in Shelbourne —(Courtesy W. Cox).

factory had been closed down shortly before my arrival. I talked with William Cox, of the ship building firm of Harley Cox and Sons, the last managing owner of the dory factory. I asked Mr. Cox if the lack of orders were the causes for his ceasing operations.

"Not at all," he replied. "We get plenty of orders for dories, our old dory builders simply wore out."

He went on to explain that the men who were employed by him had been building dories for more than half a century. Now being in their late seventies and early eighties, they had come to advise him that they had decided to quit because of their advanced ages. Mr. Cox said that he had prevailed upon them to remain until he could get them to train a group of younger men to take their places. They agreed to stay.

"Three times," continued Mr. Cox, "I brought in three separate groups of young men, putting them under the tutorage of the old masters. But they'd only hang on for a fortnight or so then quit. Their excuses being that they could not get along with the old fellows." Mr. Cox has his own ideas as to why they gave up the job.

"Welfare payments," he said disgustedly, "are probably a lot easier to take."

Mr. Cox then took me out to the paint shop. There, resting on the floor awaiting delivery, were the last three dories which had been built. I could not

The last three dories built in the now defunct dory factory at Shelbourne, Nova Scotia —(Jerry Kelland Photo).

help feeling sad as well as disappointed to discover that this fine little dory which had brought ashore so much of the ocean's wealth and which had been responsible for having saved the lives of countless fishermen on rough waters, was finally bowing out.

As salt banking declined, the dory building firms in Shelburne slowly went out of business, one was destroyed by fire, until only one of the five that were in operation in the 1920s remained active, that of John Ethrington, Limited. That firm shipped dories to points near and far, in Canada, Newfoundland and the United States. When John Ethrington died in 1938, his factory was taken over by Henry Wyman. When the firm was under Mr. Wyman's management a whole fleet of Shelburne dories were shipped to India, in connection with the Columbo Plan. After the death of Mr. Wyman, ten years ago, the present owner, William Cox, continued the operation. I was in a telephone conversation with Mr. Cox in August, 1975 and he informed me that the dory factory was still idle, which in my humble opinion, is very regretable.

Lunenburg, Nova Scotia, was named after the town of Lunenburg, Hanover province, in what is now West Germany. The first settlers to come from there arrived in Nova Scotia during 1753, having answered the call sounded throughout Europe for settlement in the New World, and published in Germany in 1750. Each was given fifty acres of land, tax free for ten years, plus implements to till the soil.

By June, 1754, nineteen houses and ten huts had been erected and one hundred German families settled on their farm lots. As they gazed out over the waters of the Atlantic, it probably never occurred to those deeply rooted farmers that many of them and their descendants would become some of the finest deepsea fishermen in the world.

Governor Lawrence visited Lunenburg during the summer of 1760. He reported that the settlers had been maintaining themselves by farming their good land and wood cutting. They had few vessels to take their produce to Halifax and there was little sign of the farmers transforming into notable fishermen. Fifteen years later, farming was still the only means of support.

At Halifax, fishing was more attractive than agriculture. After more than a generation the Lunenburg settlers began to look seriously toward the sea. It is reasonable to assume that on their trips to Halifax to sell farm produce and viewing fish laden vessels entering that port, the realization came to those thrifty, hard-working Germans that fishing could augment their farming returns. For by 1786, the Germans and Swiss were manning a large number of vessels employed at the cod fishery. As everyone knows today, the descendents of those men turned the port of Lunenburg from a farming community into a great deep sea fishing base.

When I visited the town of Lunenburg in June, 1973, I wasn't altogether too greatly interested in the port's past history, my primary reason for going there was to view the Lunenburg dory being built and if possible, to get her story. This boat was not unfamiliar to me, I had known and admired her for years. I was aware that along with other achievements, the Lunenburgers had come up with a dory which carried her own brand of distinction. There was a time not too far distant when a thousand dories left the harbour of Lunenburg nested on the decks of those big, handsome vessels which had been built by the ship building firm of Smith and Rhuland, amongst them being the mighty fishing-racing schooner, *Bluenose*.

A few years ago I read a short article featuring Nova Scotian-built dories, wherein the writer stated that the Shelburne dory had descended from one developed in Swampscott, Massachusetts, while the Lunenburg dory derives from the original Gloucester dory. I have no idea where the writer got this information, but I can state emphatically that it is not correct. Whereas the Shelburne dory was patterned after an American dory, it certainly did not descend from one developed in Swampscott, as the Swampscott dory possesses a different style of construction altogether from that of the original Banks fishing dory. Actually, the Shelburne was patterned from the Lowell Salisbury Point dory.

Later, I will be describing and showing pictures of the Swampscott dory.

The so-called Gloucester dory was also the Salisbury Point dory. It is true that for a short period a number of dories were built in Gloucester by the firm of Higgins and Griffith, but their main efforts were concentrated on the construction of seine boats. It is quite probable that the reason why the Salisbury Point dory was called the Gloucester dory is because so many of them, several thousand down through the years, were nested on the decks of Gloucester owned ships. In any case, the Lunenburg dory does not even closely resemble either the American or Shelburne dories, in general appearance or in accessories. The only item of relationship to the other two designs is the 'V' shaped stern and even that is finished off differently on the top edge.

Personally, I have always been as much interested in dories as I have been in schooners and that means a lot of interest. I grew up amongst the various types of dories which were used by our own fishermen and those that came into our harbour and the neighbouring harbours of Saint Pierre, Grand Bank and Fortune, nested on the decks of vessels representing four separate nations. Consequently, I had an excellent opportunity to study and have always remembered the features which distinguished one build from another, with the result that I can state with every assurance the dory turned out in Lunenburg is strictly of Lunenburg design, built by Lunenburg craftsmen

Freeman Rhuland and Charles Beck fit the gunnels to a new dory in the Lunenburg factory —(Jerry Kelland Photo).

and is definitely not copied from the lines of any craft that has been produced by other builders.

When I walked into Robert Cram's dory factory, situated on the Lunenburg waterfront, it happened to be at the right moment to see Freeman Rhuland, the factory foreman and his two helpers, Charles Beck and Wallace Schnare, builders of long experience, in the act of completing a fifteen foot (bottom size) Banks type dory. Rhuland and Beck were busy clinching side boards which they had already fastened to the stempost and stern, while Schnare was industriously bevelling the next side boards they would use. I noticed that in the bevelling operation, Schnare first used the old fashioned drawknife, after which he smoothed the bevel and brought it to the correct thickness with a hand operated plane. In the Shelburne dory factory they had used a bevelling machine, which must have been a great time and labour saving device when dories were being turned out in mass production. It was while I watched with interest, as the three Lunenburgers were completing their dory, that I made another discovery which amazed and delighted me. I was amazed that a large dory could be made with the process they were using. I was delighted for the reason that I had been building model dories for years and those men were employing the same methods of construction on the large dory that I had been using to build their tiny counterpart. For the Lunenburgers, instead of setting up their timbers, stempost and stern on the bottom, as do the other dory builders, they at first fasten three bulkheads to the bottom, one at the forehook, one at the after-hook and the third at amidships. Next they attach the stempost and the stern, after which the bottom is placed upon a low cradle, called a horse in Massachusetts. The top of this cradle has been cut rocker shaped or curved and the bottom is forced down in the curve and is held there firmly by shores or posts which have been jammed between the shop's rafters and the dory's bottom.

The bulkheads, of course, carry the same outward flare as timbers. Commencing with the garboards, the sideboards are nailed to the stempost, then brought tightly around the outside edges of the bulk heads and fastened to the stern. After the dory has been completely boarded up, the timbers, which have been cut to their proper size and shaped beforehand, are put in place. I timed the timbering out operation in the Lunenburg factory. Freeman Rhuland, Charles Beck and Wallace Schnare had every timber in position and securely fastened in thirty-five minutes. The bulkheads were then removed.

I asked Mr. Rhuland if the factory had always used that technique when building dories.

"Many hundreds of dories have been built off these," he said. "Of course, we have a different set to suit each size dory that may be ordered."

Apart from the fact that bulkheads are used in the Lunenburg factory, before dories were timbered out the remainder of the work is performed by the same methods as that which are carried out by the other builders.

The Banks-shore fishing dories were and still are, built right side up or as it is often called, mouth up. By building them when in that position, it is much easlier to clinch the side boards together where they overlap. The clinching being always done with chisel pointed, galvanized nails which are one and one eighth inches in length, these are driven through the overlap of the side boards in holes that have been previously bored. The points of the nails are then bent or clinched by forcing them over with an iron weight pressed against them on the inside of the dory as a hammer is applied, rather vigorously to the heads of the nails on the outside.

Bottom and side boards used in the building of dories varied in thickness, depending on the size of the craft being built. When constructing the 16, 17, 18, 19 and 20 foot sizes, builders use bottom boards of 1¼ inches thick, with side boards measuring 11/16 of an inch thick. These large dories are usually built to accommodate engines as they would be rather heavy to be operated as row dories. In the 14 and 15 foot sizes, lumber of 11/8 of an inch thick serve as bottom boards while the side boards are 11/16 of an inch thick, or the same as those which go into the larger dories. In the 8, 9, 10, 11, 12 and 13 foot sizes, the bottom boards are 1 inch thick, while the side boards are 5/8 of an inch thick.

Contrary to the opinion of some people, there was never a specific rule laid down regarding the exact widths that the bottom and side boards of a dory should be. Most builders, however, preferred to use four boards to each bottom in dories measuring up to fifteen feet. But in the larger motor dories, I have counted five and six. Realistically, the number of boards that went to make up each bottom was often governed by the widths of lumber a builder had on hand. The same condition applies to side boards. Most dory builders preferred to use four to a side, but, if they did not happen to have the stock to reach the required height by using four boards, then they were compelled to build with a larger amount of narrower lumber. Actually, the number of boards or strakes that went into the building of a dory was not important. But the correct height or depth of the boat was. For example, I have seen many dories which had been built with four narrow boards on one side and three wider ones on the other, yet both sides corresponded to the overall width of the three wider boards.

Captain Lawrence Allen of Lunenburg made his first trip to the Banks when he was twelve years of age and celebrated his thirteenth birthday there onboard the Banks fishing schooner *Frank Adams*. Captain Allen admitted to me that he did not like Banks fishing because conditions were too hard and

Captain Larence Allen of Lunenburg, a fishing skipper, captain of rum-runners and a dory-builder for twenty-seven years — (Jerry Kelland Photo).

hazardous. But despite his dislike of the trade, he managed to sail for fifteen years as a doryman.

Then he became captain of a fishing vessel. He skippered a salt banker for one year, then spent two years fresh fishing. Later he took the famous *Bluenose* out on a couple of trips and was her captain when she came home from Boston after her final race against the American fishing-racing schooner, *Gertrude L. Thebaud*.

Like numerous other Nova Scotian, American and Newfoundland fishing skippers, when the bottom dropped out of the salt fish markets, Captain Allen tried his hand at rum-running. For three years he was commander of several vessels engaged in that trade.

"An illicit operation though it may have been," he said, "but it was during the hungry thirties and a man had to do something to make a dollar."

In 1938, Captain Allen decided to remain ashore where he became actively involved in repairing various types of vessels.

When the salt banking fishing industry was at its peak of production, there were two dory factories operating on a full time basis in Lunenburg. But by 1945, when this branch of the fisheries was being supplanted by more modern fishing methods and the big dory carrying schooners were being replaced by powerful, ocean-bottom-ripping draggers, dory building declined to such an extent that one of the factories closed down. The remaining one was managed by Henry Rhuland. When Mr. Rhuland retired in the fall of 1945, the factory was taken over by Captain Allen.

Up to the time he embarked in the dory building business, Captain Allen told me that dories were turned out in three sizes only. Namely, the thirteen foot, known by Lunenburgers as the handline dory; the fourteen foot, which was classed as a single-handed dory, both of these types were used in shore fishing operations; the third size was the fifteen foot, double or two-man Banks dory. Captain Allen stated that during the twenty-seven years he had managed the factory, he developed twelve different sizes which ranged from the tiny eight foot row dory to the huge twenty foot motor dory. He told me, with a grim, that Newfoundland shore fishermen, like the Portuguese were the greatest pests he received orders from.

"As many of them requested half sizes, such as the thirteen and a half foot, fourteen and a half foot, etc. But I was very glad to receive orders from them anyway," he laughed.

The large dories with the twenty-foot bottom measured twenty-five feet on top, many of these were shipped to Newfoundland's south coast, where they were equipped with inboard engines and were used in the shore fishery. But apart from the fifteen foot Banks dory, the largest number Captain Allen sold were the sixteen footers, which he shipped to various points in the Atlantic provinces and the New England states. Many of these were equipped with outboard motors. In addition, the Allan factory supplied dories for lifeboats on fishing trawlers and draggers. He also built them for the international dory races which takes place annually between the dorymen of Gloucester and Lunenburg.

The races which are run over a mile long course in Lunenburg harbour are the main attraction of the Nova Scotian Fisheries Exhibition.

The eight and nine foot dories are used mainly by the owners of small yachts, where they serve as lifeboats. The ten, eleven and twelve foot sizes are usually ordered by duck hunters and sports fishermen.

Wallace Schnare, dory-builder, uses the old drawknife to bevel a dory board in the Lunenburg factory —(Jerry Kelland Photo).

Captain Allen has shipped dories to such far off places as the West Indies, Northern Labrador, Vancouver and the Northwest Territories, and Portugal, besides those which were sent to other ports of Canada and the United States. His yearly output ranged from one hundred and twenty-five to two hundred dories, depending on the number of orders he had received.

Captain Allen, a pleasant faced, stockily built man of medium height, retired from the dory building trade in September, 1972. The business was then taken over by Mr. Robert Cram. I am very glad to be able to state that this exceptionally fine-looking, all-round good boat is still (1975) being turned out by Mr. Rhuland, Mr. Beck and Mr. Schnare the expert dory builders of Lunenburg, Nova Scotia. Enough orders keep pouring in to enable the factory to run on a full-time basis.

When I arrived in the French town of Saint Pierre in August, 1973, it was my first visit there since August, 1923, exactly fifty years. Apart from rather drastic changes which had occurred along the waterfront, I found the place to be the same as it had been a half century earlier.

My main interest in going to the French town was to observe the dory builders in action and to interview them respecting their trade. I had already known that the first dory factory had been set up on Saint Pierre island by the late Monsieur Leon Poirier and later a second factory had been activated by the late Monsieur Dranier. When I was a boy, there was also a dory factory on Dog Island (renamed Sailor's Island) which was owned and operated by Monsieur Amedee Tillard. After his death the work was carried on by his son, Paul.

Then, as I walked along the waterfront seeking the sight of a French row dory, I was very disappointed to discover that resting on the decks of the French fishing vessels in port were not the colourful, Saint Pierre built dories like those of the past, but craft that had been manufactured in Lunenburg, Nova Scotia and Fortune, Newfoundland. I am not suggesting that French fishermen made any mistake in selecting those two fine types, but I could not help wondering what had happened to the French row dory. I recalled the day when three hundred of those had been in use by the shore fishermen of Saint Pierre et Miquelon.

As I walked along I noticed more Grandys (Fortune) and Lunenburgers hauled up on slips where they evidently serve as secondary boats to the large motor flats, erroneously called dories by some people, that their owners moored off from piers and beaches. Continuing on to the sites of the old row dory factories, I discovered that with the exception of a long shed which, formerly had been used as a storage place for dory building materials, both factories were non-existant.

The double doors of the shed were wide open. I could see a young man inside busily engaged at building a large plywood boat. I went in and spoke to him. He stood upright, grinned, then replied in that time worn phrase, "No speak English."

Well, I cannot speak French, so remaining there was a waste of time. I went back outside where I noticed three men lounging near a big motor flat which was hauled up on a waterside slip. I walked over to where they were standing. When I spoke to them I found they could not speak English either. But the language problem was solved a few minutes later when two people with whom I am acquainted happened along. They are residents of Saint Pierre and are bilingual. At my request they kindly consented to act as interpreters.

During the course of the interview, one of the men, Etienne Sarazola who answered all my questions, told me that the boat we were standing alongside of was his. Although he was seventy-five years old he was still actively engaged in prosecuting the cod fishery. He had been fishing cross-handed since 1935. Monsieur Sarazola told me that the dory factories had gradually ceased operations, as the marine engine became more and more reliable and their shore fishermen realized that they would need much larger boats to accommodate both engines and fish.

"The result was," he continued, "That by the mid 1940s, the row dory building factories had been phased out altogether." He pointed a sinewy finger towards the large handsome looking craft anchored in the stream and hauled upon slips.

"All the dories you see there, which you Englishmen call flats, came into being because of the invention of the motor engine. Of course," he said, "that is but one of the reasons why our builders ceased producing the row dory. The other reason is that salt bankers no longer come out from ports in France to engage in the cod fishery. For many, many years past," he continued, "ships from the mother country have not been calling into Saint Pierre to get replacements for broken dories."

The old Frenchman then told me that Monsieur Elie Jugan is the man who has built all the motor dories now in use. When I asked him where I could locate Monsieur Jugan, he informed me that the dory builder was out fishing, but that I would be able to see him the next day.

"The young man," he said, "whom you saw in the shed building the boat, is M. Jugan's son. He assists his father with the dory building."

The following day I met and talked with Monsieur Elie Jugan through interpreters, Mrs. F. Bowring and a genial, co-operative taxi driver, Hubert Plante. Monsieur Jugan informed me that he has been building motor dories for the past thirty years. The number he built each year depended on the number of orders he received, approximately five to twelve. He emphasized that it was only a part-time occupation for him, as there were not enough

Elie Jugan of St. Pierre, expert flat and dory builder —(Jerry Kelland Photo).

orders coming in to enable him to make a living entirely from the operation.

"So," he said, "I fish all summer and build dories during the winter."

Up to three years ago, he told me, he built the boats from pine, which he imported from Nova Scotia, but it is no longer possible to procure the long lumber required to construct those large craft from that source. As an experiment, Monsieur Jugan built a couple of dories using B.C. fir plywood, but he discovered this type of material to be unsuitable for the construction of a large boat, as the grains were inclined to splinter easily. Recently, he informed me, he had imported a supply of plywood from France. He conducted me to a shed on the waterfront and showed me this stock. The sheets were in thirty foot lengths with a width of four feet. When I first viewed them I thought that they were cedar, but a closer inspection proved that they were of a special kind of wood that I had never seen before. Monsieur Jugan was in the same position, he could not tell me the name of it. He told me that he had tested it by bending a sheet around a dory already built and that it appeared to be very good.

This hardy, sixty-seven year old fisherman/boat builder has been hired by the Government of India on two occasions. The first time he journeyed to India, he took along two of his dories which had been purchased from him by that government. His main purpose for going there was to instruct Indian fishermen how to handle a dory properly, also to teach them how to fit out, equip, bait, set and haul trawls.

On his second trip in 1972, he was engaged to instruct Indian boat builders as to the proper methods of constructing the French type motor dory. Outside of his boat shop, he showed me two more of the big dories, packaged securely in wooden crates. These too, were consigned to the Indian Government.

Being anxious to get a picture of a French type row dory for my book, I asked Monsieur Jugan, "Are there none of your row dories left at all?"

"There is but one," he replied. "One which I built four or five years ago, on a special order from a man who is employed apart from the fisheries. He uses her at the spare time hobbies of seabird hunting and cod jigging. But," he added, "I have not seen her around for several days, perhaps the owner has gone to one of the other islands in her."

For the next three days I patrolled the waterfront several times, hunting for that dory, but with no luck. On the morning of the fourth day, I knew that if I did not locate her before eleven o'clock, that I would not see her at all. The coastal steamer, *Petite Forte* was due at that hour and I would be compelled to join her for the return trip to Fortune, as my annual leave had expired. At six o'clock in the morning I left the boarding house accompanied by a reluctant son whom I had persuaded to break his rest and tag along with his camera, for I had decided to have one more try at finding that elusive dory.

As we came to the basements of the fire razed buildings that in my younger days had housed the store of J.B. LaGasse and the Cafe du Middi, I walked to the end of the pier and peeped over. Jason, when he first eyed the *Golden Fleece*, could not have been more elated than I was at that moment, for there below me hauled upon a sloping, concrete slip, sat the little dory which I had been seeking and she was a beauty.

Although not adorned with such a variety of colours like many of the French dories wore a half century ago, she was none the less a fine example of Monsieur Jugan's handiwork. The little boat was painted in two tones, white with bright red trim. Despite the fact that it was a dull morning with fine mist falling, we managed to get some very good pictures of her. I was extremely happy that I had been able to view and photograph the only Saint Pierre built, French row dory in existance on this side of the Atlantic.

There seems to be doubt in the mind of at least one Newfoundlander as to whether dories had ever been built in this province. In February 1973, whilst a man was being interviewed on a regular C.B.C. program, he said in effect, that dories used by Newfoundlanders had always been imported. He further stated that he was sending men to Nova Scotia in order for them to learn the art of dory building. Then after those men had acquired the necessary skill, he would employ them to embark upon, what he termed, was a brand new industry for Newfoundland.

Those statements made by the gentleman in question, caused widespread indignation amongst residents and former residents of our southwest coast, who felt that a major insult had been delivered to Newfoundlanders in general and to our expert dory builders in particular. Those people were fully aware that no finer dories had been built anywhere than by the late Eli Harris, the late Stephen Grandy and his sons of Grand Bank, the late James Tuff of Lamaline and the Monk brothers of Monkstown, Placentia Bay. In naming those men I am only making mention of very few of the great dory builders of Newfoundland.

The furor which was caused by the interview respecting dories, aroused the literary curiosity of Mr. Michael Harrington, editor of The Evening Telegram and able writer of those exciting sagas of our past history. As a result, Mr. Harrington decided to conduct a bit of research in connection with dory building in Newfoundland. He states that he was aided by some fascinating details supplied by Mrs. Bobbi Robertson, energetic secretary of the New-foundland Historical Society.

I wish to say that I too have been the recipient of generous assistance from Mrs. Robertson whilst engaged in conducting research pertaining to this book. I am indebted to both Mr. Harrington and Mrs. Robertson for sup-plying some of the information contained in the following account which appeared in the 'Daily Colonist', dated October 23, 1886, under the heading, 'Our Local Industries: Dory Building'. I now quote from that article.

'Until within the past few years, the dories used here were imported from Canada and the United States. Mr. Thomas Carter of Bay of Islands, commenced the building of dories in the year of 1885 and the last year the Legislature put on an import tax on all imported dories of $2.00 each. Mr. Carter imported the best skilled labour he could obtain.'

The article, however, does not state whether he imported his dory builders from Canada or the United States. But it says that he entered the business quite extensively.

'The boats built by Mr. Carter have been, throughout the past season, supplied to the trade by his agents, J. and J. Furlong and have given general satisfaction. They have been highly approved and have been pronounced, by American captains, to be superior, for their strength, length and buoyancy, to any dory imported here. Mr. Carter's dories are built of native pine, with spruce gunwale (gunnel) and stern piece, all well and carefully selected and well seasoned. The timbers or knees are of natural growth, which are considered much stronger than fastening by clips.' Here I would like to interrupt the article to say that those timber fastenings were commonly called locks on the Burin Peninsula. The item continues: 'When a branch of industry like this, or any other, is fostered, it will not only employ home labour and capital, but the competition which will inevitably arise, may be expected to cause the article to be manufactured at home as cheaply as it can be imported.'

Mr. Carter commenced building dories in Bay of Islands in 1885 and a St. John's firm commenced building them in 1886. The 'Daily Colonist' carried this advertisement on September 21, 1886:

DORIES! DORIES!

These subscribers have entered into arrangements for the building of banking dories on approved American model by a first-class and experienced builder and of the best material.

The trade can be supplied for the next season on liberal terms. A sample of our dories will be shown in a few days.

The notice was signed: Herder and Halleren. Following the article on Thomas Carter's, the 'Daily Colonist' contained the following story.

'A specimen dory of Newfoundland build, is on exhibition in the Hon. M. Monroe's Cove. She was built by Messr. Herder and Halleren at their factory, Hill of Chips, under the supervision of Mr. T. Brown, a gentleman who has had a large experience in dory building in Shelburne, N.S. The boat is fifteen and one half feet long and five feet, four inches beam amidships. She is built of Newfoundland pine and fastened with galvanized nails. The Salisbury dory is only fastened, in many cases, with the ordinary cut nail. There are four strakes of planks on either side of the boat, which number is considered the best by experienced dorymen. At the stem and stern are iron clamps securely fastened beneath the gunwale on the inside. These clamps, which by the way are never seen in an American dory, add considerably to the strength of the boat.' (Most French and Portuguese dories were equipped with iron clamps.) 'The timbers are in parts in the present dory. Meaning four piece frames locked or clipped together at the limbo holes (water channels) but Messrs. Herder and Halleren intend in future, if possible, to have the timbers continuous. That is running from gunwale to gunwale in one piece.' I would like to say here, it was actually meant that they intended to build their dories using naturally grown knee timbers, with the completed frame not being formed by one piece but by two, that is to say with the first part going from the gunnel down two and three quarters of the way across the bottom on one side, with the second part being fitted in a like manner on the opposite side, where the two sections overlapped they were nailed securely together. For it stands to reason that it would be absolutely impossible to locate even one tree root which could make a dory's complete timber frame in one piece. 'The Herder and Halleren dory is wider at the fore and after hooks than is usual which gives her one third more carrying capacity than the ordinary dory. The builders can turn out these boats very much cheaper than they can be imported and there can be no doubt but a ready market will be found for all that can be made in the future.'

In May, 1887, the 'Daily Colonist' carried the following article:

'The Excelsior Wood Factory is situated on the Hill of Chips at the east end of the city, between Duckworth and Water Streets and is approached from either. It is owned and conducted by Messrs. Herder and Halleren. The building is sixty feet long and forty feet wide. It is twenty-seven feet high on the Duckworth side, but is ten feet higher on the Water Street side. The building contains three stories and a basement. The entrance to the latter is from Water Street. On the east side or back of the building an engine house has been built, in which is situated the boiler and engine which runs the whole machinery of the factory. The engine house is forty feet long and fifteen feet wide. It is two stories high. On the top storey over the engine is the drying room in which green material is put to shrink and season before being used in the factory. The basement of the building proper is used for storing purposes. The flat above the basement, the ground flat when entering from Duckworth Street, is called the machine flat, where all the sawing, planeing and moulding of the business is carried on.

'When the work is in full swing there is a great noise in this department. The whirr of machinery and revolving wheels and the buzz of numerous saws make a noise that can be heard for some distance. Look to the ceiling and you notice the revolving bars and the numerous bands extending down from them. Look below and you see a party of keen-eyed workmen. Apparently, heeding not the noise of the machinery, but each carefully directing the part of the work allotted to him. When the work leaves here it is taken up one flat to the carpenter and joiners department. To see the various articles after leaving the machine shop brought to this department, one would think it impossible to get everything in its proper place. Window pieces and general moulding are all mixed up, but everything is known by some distinctive marks or size, and from apparent chaos order soon follows.

'The third flat or the top one is devoted exclusively to dory building, a comparatively new industry to this country. The American and Canadian dory was almost exclusively used here, till about two years ago, when Messrs. Herder and Halleren started in the business. The work was a little up-hill at first, but by superior workmanship and lower rates, the foreign article was driven out of the market. It may be safely said that the Excelsior dory and Mr. Carter's dory of the west coast have supplied the trade for the present year (1887). The dory flat is under the control of Mr. Thomas Brown, a skillful mechanic and a man who has a large practice in dory building both in Canada and the United States. To fill the orders which have poured in this spring, Mr. Brown and his staff had to work day and night, from February the second, when the first order was received until nearly the end of May, one hundred and sixty-four dories had been produced. All this work was done by Mr. Brown, another man and two boys.'

I would like to insert here that Mr. Brown and his helpers must have been workers extraordinary, for at the beginning of the dory building venture, while Mr. Brown was highly skilled in that area of endeavour, the chances are that his assistants, particularly the two boys, were not! The tremendous array of parts which had to be manufactured, with precision, in order for the builders to be able to turn out one hundred and sixty-four dories in just under four months, makes one realize and adequately recognize the outstanding ability and powers of endurance possessed by Mr. Brown and his crew.

According to the description of the Herder and Halleren dories by the 'Daily Colonist', they were what is known as five bed types, meaning they were constructed with five sets of timber frames. As the boat's timbers were fastened together with locks or clips, it means also, that four pieces were required to make up each set of frames or twenty pieces to a dory.

As I am familiar with the names and number of parts which go into the building of boats of this type, I can assert that the number of parts it was necessary to fashion in order to complete the one hundred and sixty-four dories were eleven thousand, six hundred and sixty. When broken down these appear as follows:

Bottom boards	656
Side boards	1,312
Bottom and side strips	1,640
Timber sections	3,280
Gunnels	328
Gunnel cap sections, approx.	1,000
Counters or sterns	164
Nose caps	164
Stern knees	164
Stern strap pieces	164
Stemposts	164
Breasthooks	164
Bollards	328
Gunnel blocks for rollers	328
Risers	328
Rubbers	328
Thwarts	656
Bulkheads	492
TOTAL	11,660

According to a further description given of the Herder and Halleren dories in the 'Daily Colonist', the boats were built with four boards to a side. As they were constructed by the clinker or lap strake method, it was necessary to bevel the two center boards on each side on both edges, while the two garboards (lowers) and the two top strakes had to be bevelled on one edge. Therefore, eight hundred and twenty boards carried bevels on both edges or sixteen hundred and forty all told, while the two top boards and the two garboards meant an additional eight hundred and twenty bevelled edges.

A rather amazing number of separate parts and bevelled boards, I am free to admit. But that is exactly the amount of work Mr. Brown and his assistants were called upon to perform in order to build the one hundred and sixty-four dories. Yet, before the boats were ready for delivery, it was necessary to bore twenty-one holes in each dory, e.g., two in the bow for nose straps, two in the counters for stern straps, sixteen in the gunnels to accommodate the tholepins, rollers and galvanized oarlocks. The latter held the steering oar in place over a dory's quarter when she was under sail. Finally, a hole bored through the bottom, commonly called plugholes, as plugs were inserted into them before the dories were dropped down to the water from a fishing schooner or launched from a beach or slipway by shore fishermen. While it was not essential to have plugholes in shore fishing dories, they were a must in nested Banks dories as with their plugs removed they permitted rain and boarding spray to drain off, otherwise the craft would fill to the gunnels with water which would create quite a bailing out problem on the crowded deck of a schooner.

As the brace and bit and power drill were still in the future, in 1886, it was necessary to do all the boring with an old fashioned auger. It was a task which required great skill and patience, more especially when it came to boring the tholepin holes, as these had to go down at exactly the correct angle. For if they followed a bore which canted the for'ard pins too far ahead, the oars would slip up over their tops and out of the oarlocks when rowing pressure was imposed upon them, especially during a heavy breeze. The holes which were bored in the one hundred and sixty-four dories added up to a total of three thousand, four hundred and forty-four.

Finally, there was the enormous paint job. It took two gallons of hull paint and one pint of gunnel paint to give each dory two coats. So that fleet of dories used up three hundred and twenty-eight gallons of hull paint, plus one hundred and sixty-four pints of gunnel paint.

The fact that Mr. Brown, the other man and the two boys were compelled to work day and night, so as they could fill all orders received, is hardly cause for amazement. How about overtime? Well, I suspect that wishing for a trip to the moon during the 1880s would be similar to wishing for overtime pay.

It appears that after their dory building venture commenced to meet with success, it was the proud boast of Messrs. Herder and Halleren that their dories were as good and could be bought just as cheaply as those which were imported from Canada or the United States. In fact, some American fishing skippers stated that the Newfoundland built dories were even superior to the others.

On April 18, 1888, two brothers, William and Joseph Fleming of Torbay, a fishing settlement situated some seven miles from St. John's, went astray from the Newfoundland Banks fishing schooner *Jubilee*, in dense fog. They were trawling on the Grand Banks. Two days later the dory entered a field of ice. It became very cold and William, the eldest brother, had his fingers frostbitten. They finished the last of their drinking water on April 22. They got soaked to the skin, meanwhile, their hands became so swollen that they were forced to discontinue rowing.

On the 24th, William Fleming lapsed into unconsciousness. Joseph too was in pretty bad shape. He could not use the oars and lacked the strength to blow the foghorn. He fell asleep but awoke when seawater boarded the dory and splashed his face. Hoping he would gain some warmth, the thoroughly chilled fisherman crawled up underneath the fo'ard thwart and lay down, where he too became unconscious.

Five days later on April 30, the brothers were rescued by the British barque

Jessie Morris out of South Shields. The ship was bound to Quebec City. The unconscious dorymen, after being taken onboard the barque, were revived under careful treatment. The *Jessie Morris* landed the Fleming brothers in Quebec City, where they were hospitalized. Joseph recovered with few ill effects, but William lost most of his fingers. Eventually they returned to Torbay where they resumed fishing.

Joseph Fleming was snatched from the very jaws of death by the captain and crew of the barque *Jessie Morris,* only to die a few years later from the effects of a brutal beating he had received at the hands of some ruffians. He was on his way home to Torbay after attending the annual regatta in St. John's when the incident occurred. His murderers were never apprehended, neither was any motive for the crime ever established. The fickle finger of fate sure deals peculiarly with some people.

The dory which the Fleming brothers were using at the time they strayed from the *Jubilee* was a Herder and Halleren craft. For twelve days that little boat had voyaged aimlessly around the northwest Atlantic. She had drifted through a field of ice. For six of those days she was not under control and both her crewmen were unconscious for five days and nights prior to their being rescued. As Joseph Fleming had remarked later, "God knows what our dory did during that time."

What winds and waves assailed the little boat, what boiling tides swirled her about, or the number of ice cakes she bumped against will never be known. But one fact remains very obvious; the dory remained buoyant, stable and generally seaworthy, regardless of whatever unsavory conditions she may have encountered, which testifies most eloquently of the skill and conscientious efforts of her builders. It also fully substantiates the faith which Messrs. Herder and Halleren had in their sea-going product.

So many wood particles must have been flying around from the power and manually operated tools while the various projects were progressing in the Herder and Halleren factory, it would not be necessary to hire a Scotland Yard detective to ascertain why that steep incline down the east end of St. John's, where the mill was located, had been named 'Hill of Chips'.

The Herder and Halleren wood working factory was totally destroyed by fire on November 3, 1891. Nine months before the great fire that wiped out the east end of St. John's in 1892. The Herder and Halleren loss was estimated at twenty thousand dollars. The factory was not rebuilt.

In addition to supervising his shipyard, where he built many fine schooners, including several tern or three-masted vessels, Eli Harris had a dory factory in operation in Grand Bank. The dories he turned out were used extensively in both the Banks and shore fisheries.

I can recall that the Harris dories were patterned after the Shelburne craft and were so similar to them in appearance that it was most difficult to distinguish one build from the other.

Roy Grandy, Fortune, Newfoundland. An expert dory-builder for some forty years, Grandy stands beside one of his masterpieces nearing completion — (Jerry Kelland Photo).

When Mr. Harris closed down his factory, Stephen Grandy, to whom I have already made reference, activated one. Mr. Grandy, who I understand from his son Roy, had been employed as a dory builder in the Harris factory, designed and perfected dories which carried their own marks of distinction already described. Stephen Grandy and his three sons produced upwards of three thousand dories over the years. Following Mr. Grandy's death, his three sons carried on the business of building and repairing fishing vessels as well as building dories.

A few years ago their shipyard and dory factory was moved to the nearby town of Fortune, where one of the sons, Roy, is still actively engaged in the shipyard at Marystown.

I visited Fortune and talked with Roy Grandy, in the fall of 1973. My arrival found Mr. Grandy and his men putting the finishing touches to a dory they had just built. Mr. Grandy told me that during the days of the salt bankers, a time when there was a constant demand for dories, their factory turned them out in mass production. Their modus operandi were as follows: All the separate parts would be manufactured and assembled, until they had a sufficient amount of material shopped to permit them to build two dozen dories. When everything was in readiness, they would set up two dories at a time. Then two crews of builders went to work. They kept fitting, hammering and sawing energetically all day. The factory commenced work at 7:00 in the morning and closed at 6:00 p.m. Those two dories would be totally completed and ready for the painters. The following morning two more would be set up. This process was repeated each day until the two dozen dories were finished. Then the builders would commence manufacturing parts for a further two dozen.

James Tuff and his wife photographed in one of the dories he built. Tuff was an expert dory builder in Lamaline —(Courtesy Louise Harnett, Lord's Cove).

The late James Tuff of Lamaline was building dories for the trade before the turn of the present century and he continued to build them up to 1922. His was a smaller operation than that of Eli Harris and the Grandys. For the reason that he was a part-time builder, as he fished with codtraps all the summer and built dories the remainder of the year.

Jim Tuff was one of the most skillful men with carpenter's tools that I have ever known. He could turn his hand to making anything he chose in the woodworking field. Neatness and perfection were obsessions with him. Whether he was building a dory or turning out an article of furniture, he would always come up with a masterpiece.

A local poet composed verses praising Jim Tuff's dory building. I can remember one stanza only, which went:

> Jim Tuff he builds dories,
> And he builds 'em neat and strong,
> While his brother, Tom hunts rabbits,
> And he hunts them all day long.

I know that on more than one occasion, some of us got a rather severe shellacking from unsympathetic teachers when we turned up late for school after dropping into Jim Tuff's little factory to watch in fascination as he deftly clinched the side boards of a dory together, while time slipped by unnoticed. After all, back in those days in the outports, what else was there to be fascinated with but things like that. There was no radio, television or movie houses to divert one's attention away from the finer, more precious aspects of life.

Mr. Tuff usually built from three to five dories each winter. He did not always confine himself to building from a single type of pattern. Sometimes, he would turn out the boats by using French moulds, on other occasions he would build from Lunenburg or Shelburne moulds. But whatever style he adopted, he experienced no difficulty in making sales. For his dories were quickly bought up, mostly by shore fishermen from his home harbour or from other nearby settlements.

Down in Monkstown, Placentia Bey, the brothers, John and Henry Monk, were part-time dory builders, for like James Tuff they fished all the summer. Those two, energetic, hard working, skillful men, turned out dories for more than sixty years.

While Mr. Tuff was compelled to import his dory building materials, as no suitable timber grew in the Lamaline area, the Monk brothers constructed their craft by using timber and lumber cut from trees which they felled themselves, near their home. During the early days, they shaped frames, stemposts and stern knees with adze and axe. The pitsawed bottom boards, side broads, sterns and other necessary parts, dressing the lot by using hand planes. In later years, a sawmill was established in Monkstown and they got all their material sawn there.

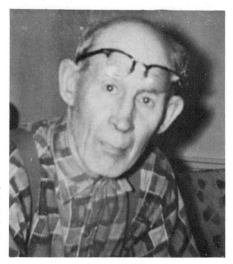

John Monk Sr., Monkstown, Newfoundland, who with his brother Henry spent sixty years building the renowned Monk dory, a craft of their own design —(Courtesy John Monk Jr.).

John and Henry Monk always kept going on the theory that hard work alone never killed any man and their philosophy must have been running on the same wavelength with their physiques, for those two grand old gentlemen are still hale and hearty. Their ages? Eighty-four and eighty-five years (1974) respectively. They no longer build dories. That work is now being performed by John Monk's son, John Jr., who learned the trade from his father and uncle.

I was talking with an aging Placentia Bay, western boat skipper and he paid the two old dory builders this compliment: "I knew a number of men who could build dories in our area, but none could turn them out as good as did John and Henry Monk."

That dories were turned out in mass production in Newfoundland is proven by the true facts contained in this chapter, with regard to sending men out of this province to learn dory making, such a move is by no means necessary. For there were many expert builders in Newfoundland. The dories built by those men have undergone some very severe tests in all sorts of weather and have been pronounced second to none by the men who really know. The skippers and dorymen who manned our vessels. I have no hesitation, therefore, in asserting that Roy Grandy and John Monk Jr. would make instructors, par excellence, in the rather intricate business of dory building.

As we entered the 1950s, salt banking went into decline so sharply that by 1960, with the exception of the Portuguese, men no longer fished from dories on the Banks. Consequently, dory building dropped off proportionately. But up to the present day (1978) it has not entirely disappeared. I am of the firm opinion that it never will. For shore fishermen, particularly those who live on Newfoundland's south and southwest coasts will not exchange their dories for any type of small craft. Some years back a number of them invested in the larger more expensive longliner. But I have been informed that within the past few years, many of them have returned to dory fishing. The faithful, little dories can also be seen today prominently displayed on the decks of modern fishing vessels where they are carried to fill the role of lifeboats. If anything goes wrong with the big ship, as it very often does, and she is getting ready to plummet to the bottom, the dories are there to keep her crewmen afloat until they can be rescued by another vessel or row to land and safety.

The once great white fleet of Portuguese dory trawlers has been reduced through losses by fire as well as other causes, until it now portrays but a shadow of its former strength. Some of the survivors have been converted to a more sophisticated method of fishing. Gone from their decks are the towering stacks of nested dories, which always caught the eye of picture hunting tourists when the big schooners docked in St. John's harbour. The dories have been replaced by a boat of vastly different design. When compared to the colourful Portuguese dory, they are blunt nosed, squat and ugly. But I presume that they are also vitally necessary in order to enable these fishermen to engage in the modern scheme of things.

In 1973, six dory trawlers sailed to the Banks from Portugal. In 1974, only three set out, one of these was destroyed by fire off St. John's. In 1975, apparently, there were none. I did not see any on the waterfront. There is hardly any doubt but what the Portuguese dorymen, like their Newfoundland, Nova Scotian, American and French counterparts will soon disappear into the fogs of nautical history, taking with them their beautiful, sturdy, seaworthy little craft, the cross-handed or single man dory.

The heyday of the Banks trawling row dory has passed, while the greater majority of men who fished, slaved and suffered in her have passed on also.

She must have been considered the Cinderella of the small row boats by nautical historians, for despite her gigantic contribution towards the welfare of the human race, they barely give her a literary glance.

Today in Amesbury, Massachusetts, the dory's birthplace, Ralph Lowell and his son, John, the seventh and eighth generations of Lowells to carry on the family business, still build dories from an ancient plan from which more than one hundred thousand of the reliable little boats have been turned out. But they, like the Newfoundland dory builders, Roy Grandy and John Monk, Jr. build them only on order. The Lowells now concentrate their main efforts on the production of more modern craft like speed boats, motor powered yachts, fibre glass outboards and duck hunters skiffs.

CHAPTER FOUR

Dorymen Astray

BLACKBURN AND WALSH

Fear of going astray from their various vessels during thick fog or in heavy snowstorms was one of the most unwelcome prospects confronting Banks fishermen. Particularly was this to be dreaded whilst they were engaged in winter fishing operations, as the bitter cold could kill men very quickly. It was a grim spectre that haunted them continuously and the following accounts portray quite clearly why their fears in this connection were by no means groundless.

Tales of hardship and death suffered by straying fishermen abounded in the olden days. From my selection of such true stories I have selected seven. I have chosen these for the reason that they vary considerably, not so much perhaps where the experiences commenced, but rather as they progressed and terminated; going from stark tragedy to grim humor.

The American fishing schooner, *Grace L. Fears* was built in the yard of David A. Story, at Pearce Street, Gloucester, Massachusetts. She was successfully launched on July 2, 1874. Her first skipper was Captain Randell McDonald. The vessel, during her twenty-three year life span was used in most all branches of the fishing industry, which included halibuting, Georges Banks handlining, haddocking, mackerel seining and voyaging to Newfoundland to pick up herring cargoes.

Many of Gloucester's greatest skippers commanded the *Grace L. Fears.*

Like all vessels that had engaged in year round fishing, she was battered by many storms. On February 24, 1885, she arrived at Gloucester from a Banks halibut trip. Her captain reported very severe weather. Her cable was parted twice, losing two anchors together with one hundred and forty fathoms of cable. As a result, she was obliged to lay to for nearly a week.

In August, 1883, the *Fears* was struck by a gale on Brown's Bank. She sprang a leak and ran for Liverpool, Nova Scotia. As the vessel entered that harbour, there was over two feet of water covering her cabin and forecastle

The fishing schooner 'Grace L. Fears' on the stocks in Gloucester, Massachusetts, 1872 —(Courtesy Gordon Thomas).

floors. Her skipper decided to run her ashore, where she very quickly filled. Later the schooner was refloated and repaired.

The *Fears*, while under the command of Captain Nathaniel Greenleaf, on August 10, 1881, had two of her dorymen go astray in heavy fog on Grand Bank. One was Charles Nelson, the other Layfayette Greenleaf, brother of the captain. They were picked up five days later by a French barque and landed at Savannah, Georgia. When rescued they had no food and only a small quantity of water.

Not so fortunate, and that's putting it mildly, were two other crewmembers of the *Grace L. Fears*. The vessel on a halibuting trip was anchored on Burgeo Bank, situated twelve and a half miles from the southernmost point of Outer Ramea Island and approximately thirty-five miles from the mainland coast of Newfoundland.

On the morning of January 25, 1883, dorymen Howard Blackburn and Thomas Walsh set out from the vessel to haul their trawl. Rowing over a smooth sea with no wind to hamper them, they reached their gear quickly and commenced hauling operations. Before the task was completed however, the wind came on suddenly, blowing from the northeast, a very bad point indeed, particularly during that season of the year. In a matter of minutes it increased to half a gale, snow came along with it, then a blizzard quickly followed.

Howard Blackburn was a Nova Scotian by birth and a Gloucester fisherman by choice.

But search as I would, I was unable to pinpoint the birthplace of his dorymate, Thomas Walsh. (I have been told that he was a Newfoundlander, a Nova Scotian and a New Englander. I have found his named spelled Welsh, Walch and Walsh. Today, nobody knows for sure the correct way to spell it, which is not surprising, as ninety-two years have passed by since he died. In the story I have decided to use the name Walsh.)

In the blizzard that had descended upon them so suddenly, the men soon lost sight of their schooner in the driving snow. Shipping their oars they commenced to row, but the wind developed such power that it was impossible to make any headway against it. So, they dropped anchor and hoped to ride out the storm. But the dory's bow pinned down considerably by the weight of the anchor rope, commenced to ship water in the high running seas. It grew frosty and ice began to build up all over the dory. Between the ice and the heavy seas breaking over her the little dory was in constant danger of being swamped. So to ward off that menace one man had to keep bailing while the other pounded away at the encroaching ice.

The blizzard kept raging without let-up all through the day and night, the following day and the second night. On the morning of the third day the wind had moderated sufficiently to enable them to resume rowing. Although it still snowed and lessening wind did not drive it so fiercely as the gale had done the first two days and nights.

Now with one of the men rowing and the other bailing out water and breaking off ice, they headed in the general direction of the Newfoundland coast. Severe frost still continued. Blackburn, who was rowing, noticed that his fingers were turning white. He became aware that they were slowly freezing. His hands were uncovered for the reason that he had lost his woolen mittens on the second day out. Deliberately, he curled his fingers around the lums or handles of the oars, permitting them to freeze in that shape, for he knew that if he lost the precious oars their chances of reaching land would be gone, as the second pair of oars and the spare or steering oar had been washed overboard many hours previously.

When daylight appeared on the morning of the fourth day, Blackburn discovered to his horror and dismay that Tom Walsh was dead, his body frozen stiff. Evidently the poor fellow had sat in the stern of the dory to take a nap, a fatal mistake in freezing temperatures, when a man's body has been without nourishment for more than three days.

Now, with the frozen corpse of his dorymate in the stern and his hands curled around the oar handles like whitened claws, Blackburn rowed steadily all day and far into the night, when he decided to put over a drogue or sea

58

Howard Blackburn, super doryman. Note his fingerless hands —(Courtesy Gordon Thomas).

anchor and rest. Meanwhile, the snow had ceased falling. It was still bitterly cold and though the wind continued in blow fairly strong, fortunately, the dory shipped no water.

Blackburn dared not risk going to sleep for fear of freezing to death like his dorymate. So he placed himself back to the wind, then clasping his arm around one of the thwarts and kept moving backwards and forwards without cessation all through the night.

Many old time Banks dorymen astray from vessels who have lost a dorymate either by drowning, freezing or starving to death, have stated that they found it impossible to describe the terrible feeling of loneliness coupled with despair, which they had experienced after suffering such a loss. While astray on a vast ocean with no human aid in sight, assailed by hunger and thirst, surrounded by dense fog, or blasted by driving snow and freezing winds, it was very comforting just to have someone to talk to.

Blackburn's dory had evidently drifted shoreward during the night, for as soon as it became light he could discern land to the north. The wind by this time had died away until it had become nearly calm. Then, by superhuman strength he managed to haul the drogue, get out his oars and row toward the distant shoreline. Slowly but surely the land came closer. In the afternoon he passed, what he later learned, was the Little River Rocks, which are situated approximately seven miles from the coast.

That morning the sun had risen bright and clear, the day, thereafter remained fine.

Just before sunset the weary, hungry, thirsty doryman was close to land which was high and rugged. At first he was unable to see a harbour or entrance of any kind in the towering cliffs. Then on turning his head and looking over his shoulder in the direction the boat was heading he saw a small house, nestled at the foot of a steep hill bordering the entrance of a river. But a closer observation of the dwelling brought only bitter disappointment, for it became obvious to him that it was unoccupied, making the chances of securing food and water there very slim.

Pointing the dory upriver, Blackburn rowed beyond the cabin for more than half a mile, meanwhile keeping an anxious lookout for anything that would indicate the presence of inhabitants. But not a sign of life was seen. By this time he was feeling the strain of pulling against the fairly strong current which finally compelled him to turn back toward the river's mouth. Near the old cabin was a little wharf. Blackburn brought his dory alongside and made her fast.

Clambering upon the wharf he discovered a small shanty or stage in which was a half barrel of pickled cod. Taking one fish out of the brine, he put it in the snow to freshen. He said that he was never able to determine why he did this, for there was fresh fish onboard the dory he and his dorymate had taken from their trawl before the blizzard struck. Most of their catch had been thrown overboard to lighten the dory after they had been surrounded by violent winds and heavy seas. A few fish, however, had been reserved in case they should be needed for food. But this was frozen so solid that it probably would have been too hard to chew anyway.

Blackburn said that despite his hunger he never once reached the point of attempting to eat the frozen fish. Neither did he eat any of the pickled fish, for he recalled that doing so would increase his thirst which was already very intense.

He walked up to the house which had been deserted for some time as it was without windows and doors while the snow lay deep on the floor. After slacking his thirst somewhat by eating snow, Blackburn made a further inspection of the dwelling. In another room he found a bunch of fishing nets hanging on a spike. This room also contained a bedstead or berth having wide boards for the bottom. These boards were covered with snow. The doryman turned them over in order to have their dry side upward. He then arranged a bunch of fishing lines for a pillow and lay down, pulling the fish nets over him for cover. As was to be expected, he now felt the cold more severely than ever and his teeth chattered. Seeing what this man had already gone through, this could hardly be cause for wonder. Blackburn found that sleep was impossible. He reasoned that it would have been dangerous to slumber anyway, so he got up and spent the remainder of the night in pacing the floor, meanwhile eating snow to quench his thirst. Those were the days when people talked frequently of wooden ships and iron men. Howard Blackburn was an outstanding example of what being an iron man meant, even up to this point, and his troubles were by no means over, for at daybreak he went to the wharf intending to start eastward in search of an inhabited harbour, only to discover the heartbreaking fact that his dory was full of water with nothing left on board but the body of his dead dorymate.

Blackburn discovered that a big hole had been knocked in the boat's side. Evidently the plug had been punched out of her bottom when she pounded upon some rocks, the same rocks which holed her. To add to his discomfiture, the doryman noticed that the thwarts and oars were floating around in an eddy near the wharf, liable to be carried far beyond reach at any moment.

The situation seemed hopeless, but after great effort, despite his frozen hands, he contrived to reach the stern strap or becket. Then near the wharf he noticed a rocky shelving ledge, reaching this with considerable difficulty with the dory's sternline nipped over one of his arms, he dragged the stern of the dory to the ledge. Then passing both arms through the becket with three or four heaves, he managed to pull her upon the rocks, he kept her there until all the water ran out. As soon as possible he got the body of Walsh in his arms, making a valiant, but futile attempt to place in on the wharf, but it slipped out of his grasp and sank in several feet of water, which lay between the ledge and the wharf. It was impossible for him to recover it.

The plug which had been tied to the dory's riser was put back into her bottom. Blackburn was greatly relieved to note that the large hole in her side would be above water now that she was empty.

Again calling on hidden reserves of strength, the doryman managed to recover oars and thwarts, after which he launched the dory. Then slipping the oar handles through his curled up fingers he rowed eastward, first passing a cape on the eastern side of the river, later he entered a little bay, learning afterward that it was known as Gulch Cove. There were two houses at the head of this cove, but he could see no sign of life. It became increasingly obvious to him that no one lived there except during the summer fishing season. Keeping on to the eastward, Blackburn sighted two becalmed schooners lying about three miles distant. They looked to be heading in the direction from which he had come. New hope surged through him, with all his strength the nearly spent fisherman rowed in an attempt to intercept them. But an unkind fate decided to deal him another bitter blow, for the wind suddenly breezed up and the schooner took off without anyone on board noticing him. The wind now favoured his return to the river. Consequently, there was nothing left for him to do now but row in that direction. Upon entering the stream close to the land on the eastern side about a mile and a half from the outer headlands, he observed a small cluster of dwellings. The sun had gone down and in the deepening twilight Blackburn rowed toward these. It was no easy task for a man in his condition to cover the distance from the river's mouth to the cove, particularly as there was a number of ice blocks floating around with the current coming against him fairly strong.

Putting every effort into the task, he forged ahead slowly, but surely. Then, when nearing the houses, he suddenly came to a standstill, for his dory had bumped into ice. Turning around he discovered that the river at this point was frozen solid from bank to bank, so further passage by boat was impossible.

It was then that Blackburn got his first break, for while he had been rowing, the moon had risen over the surrounding hills and was shining brightly on the river. This brilliance enabled three men who happened to be crossing the ice at that moment to see the dory and the lone occupant. They instantly came down and hauled the battered little boat with the distressed fisherman upon the ice.

These men were eager to hear the story of Blackburn's experience. In the fewest possible words he gave them an idea of what he had gone through, but to impress them with the thought that his suffering was less acute than is appearance indicated, he requested two of the men to get into the dory and go down river with him to get his dorymate. He did not tell them that Walsh had died. But they told him to go to one of the houses, saying that they would pick up Walsh. As they shoved off, Blackburn told the men where to find him, whereupon all three exclaimed, "Oh, he is dead!"

Apparently, the Gloucesterman was under the impression that if he told the men that his companion was dead they would not have gone down to recover the corpse. It was the wrong impression, of course, for Newfoundlanders are a race of people who would not reject the dead any more than they would desert the living.

The three men set out immediately, recovered Walsh's body and brought it back to the settlement where it remained until spring when it was taken to Burgeo and interred in a cemetery there.

Blackburn learned that he had reached the settlement of Little River, situated twenty-one miles to the east of Burgeo, he was also told that if he had continued rowing eastward around the cape, instead of trying to head off the schooners, he would have reached the settlement of Cape La Hune, where the residents were generally in comparatively comfortable circumstances.

Blackburn was taken to the home of Frank Litchman. This family made no effort to conceal the fact that they were very poor, but eagerly and generously signified their desire to do anything possible to aid him.

The doryman related that one of the first acts of these kind people was to try and save his hands and feet which were badly frozen. Therefore, his boots, socks and clothing were cut away from the lower parts of his body. His feet and hands were then immersed in cold water to remove the frost from them. A quantity of salt was then thrown into the water. Having had experience with frozen limbs before, the Litchmans had learned that brine would more readily remove frost from frozen flesh than fresh water. Blackburn's hands and feet were kept in water for an hour, and the doryman had become as weak and helpless as an infant. He was lifted into a bed and covered with all the quilts that the family could spare from their poorly furnished house.

It is necessary for me to explain here that the people who resided on that coast depended solely on the fishery for a livelihood. Their prosperity or destitution was governed absolutely by that resource. In short, no fish: no food or other vital necessities.

While going through the files of the 'Evening Mercury', a St. John's newspaper that was operative in 1883, I came across a letter that had been written late in the winter of 1883, by the Reverend L.P. Quinton to the Anglican Bishop Jones. Reverend Quinton, who was in charge of the mission of Channel and Rose Blanche described the terrible conditions that existed on the coast, which included Little River, the place where Blackburn landed. The clergyman stated that the people had nothing to drink but cold water or spruce tea, without molasses or sugar to sweeten it, they had very little flour and have been living on dry bread. Men, women and children were miserably clad. In a number of cases they had neither beds or bedding and many suffered from frostbite.

Never in all his life, the clergyman continued, did he witness such destitution. The reason he gave for the terrible plight of the people was that the fishery had been extremely poor the previous summer. The winter fishery was a total failure. The destitution of the Litchman family spoke audibly of those fishery failures.

Back in 1883, so unlike the present day, there were no foreign draggers criss-crossing the waterways, literally ripping the guts out of Newfoundland fishing grounds and seriously depleting fish stocks. Yet, there were years when the cod simply did not come. Silvery little caplin, the favorite food of the codfish, never failed to show up. They always arrived and still do arrive in countless millions early each summer to deposit their spawn on our beaches.

But occasionally for some unexplained reason the cod fail to follow them in. The result partial or whole destitution for many fishing families.

After being put to bed, Blackburn fell into a deep sleep, the sleep of utter exhaustion. He awoke late the following morning, feeling somewhat better, but still very weak. When the poultice was removed from his hands and feet the day following his arrival, the little finger on his right hand, wich had been badly mutilated when frozen, dropped off. This did not surprise him, but he hoped that his remaining fingers and toes could be saved. Four days after he had arrived at Little River, a boat from the settlement succeeded in reaching Burgeo, where the pertinent facts concerning his experience and condition were reported to the Reverend John Cunningham, Anglican minister there. The clergyman immediately telegraph'ed the information to the American Consul in the capital city, St. John's. A reply from that official requested Mr. Cunningham to supply Blackburn with everything he might need, consequently, enough provisions were sent to feed one man for two months. But as the Litchman family was on the verge of starvation, Blackburn shared his food willingly with them, for as he said later, they had freely and willingly shared their all with him.

As was to be expected, the Gloucesterman suffered agonies of mind and body during the long weeks and months that he lay helpless at Little River. Dry gangrene set in and he was forced to watch his fingers as well as his toes drop off, one by one. The question may well be asked, why the man was not taken to some place where he could receive the services of a doctor, or why some medical man was not brought to Little River to treat him. The answer to the first part of that question is that Blackburn, in his terribly weakened and ill condition could not be moved. Secondly, as far as I can ascertain, there were no doctors on the coast at that time. In addition, the only means of transportation between settlements in 1883 were comparatively small open row or sail boats. During the winter months in those far off days, even the twenty-one mile voyage to Burgeo would entail major risks for men in top physical condition. In Blackburn's case, such a journey was unthinkable.

The doryman stated the excruciating physical pains with which he was afflicted bore less heavily on him than the prospect of facing the uncertainties of the future with fingerless hands and toeless feet. On April 23, after spending nearly three months at Little River and having improved considerably in health as well as strength and with better weather in the offing, the men of the settlement took him to Burgeo at his own request. He related that they took him to the boat, laid him down carefully, then covered him over with quilts and boat sails. All the people in the place bade him farewell as the boat shoved off. Indeed, the entire population, men, women and children, followed him to the mouth of the river, some of them in boats, while others walked along the banks, shouting goodbyes and best wishes until his craft reached the open sea. Burgeo was reached that evening without incident. Blackburn was taken to the house of Mr. James Payne where he resided until May 3. By this time he had regained his strength. Meanwhile, his mutilated hands and feet had become completely healed.

He arrived back in Gloucester on June 4, having made the trip via Saint Pierre, Halifax and Boston. The whole town of Gloucester turned out to greet him, he was welcomed as a hero. Later a public subscription was raised on his behalf which enabled him to enter the saloon business on Main Street, where he poured drinks and deftly scooped up change with his half hands and the stumps of two thumbs.

But Howard Blackburn was not finished with the sea by a long shot, despite his harrowing experience, suffering mutiliation in the winter of 1883. He had a thirty-two foot sloop built, then departed from Gloucester in her alone on June 18, 1899. Hauling ropes and holding the tiller lines by nipping them with his thumbs, he arrived in Gloucester, England, sixty-two days later, achieving world fame.

Two years later, in a twenty-five foot boat, once again sailing alone he left Gloucester, Massachusetts, on June 9, 1901, making Lisbon, Portugal in the record time of thirty-nine days.

As for Blackburn's old schooner, the *Grace L. Fears,* she sailed on her last voyage on December 9, 1897. She was bound for Newfoundland for a herring cargo in command of Captain John Aiken. The vessel was sighted on the morning of December 17, by the schooner, *Columbia One,* Captain John Campbell, approximately thirty miles from Saint Pierre et Miquelon. She was never seen again. The *Fears* was supposed to have gone to the bottom in a gale that arose on the day following the sighting.

Her master, Captain Aiken, fifty-six years old, was a native of Barrington, Nova Scotia. He left a window and six children. The schooner carried a crew of seven. In August, 1901, a young man named William DeWinter picked up a bottle on a beach near Gloucester. It contained a message which read: 'We are sinking, whoever finds this hand it to my wife.' The note was signed, 'John Aiken, Captain'.

The message was given to the captain's wife. If it was a genuine note, it was indeed a fantastic discovery, that bottle had been floating on the sea for four years.

The super doryman, Howard Blackburn died in Gloucester, on November 4, 1932 at the age of seventy-three. He probably would not be too pleased if he were around today to see that his old saloon on Main Street has been turned into a laundromat.

REID AND KEEFE

For a number of dorymen who went astray from vessels on the Banks, it proved to be a traumatic experience. It often left those who had survived long enough to be rescued and who lived for a number of years thereafter, scarred in both body and mind.

John Reid and James Keefe of Marystown, Newfoundland were amongst the lucky ones in that respect. For after they had gone astray from their vessel in pea soup fog and bitter cold, they were buffetted around for five days and four nights before they managed to reach land. Yet they came through the experience unscathed, either mentally or physically. In fact, they were in such good shape that they were able to rejoin their schooner immediately and resume fishing.

John Reid and James Keefe were crewmembers of the Banks fishing schooner *Carrie and Nellie,* which was owned by G.A. Bartlett of Newfoundland. The schooner carried ten dories and was under the command of Captain Jacob Thornhill of Grand Bank. It was in March, 1946, that the *Carrie and Nellie* sailed on her first voyage of that year.

The weather was unusually boisterous even for March, a month which was never known to be placid or kindly disposed toward Banks fishermen, or anyone else for that matter. In due course the *Carrie and Nellie* arrived on the western peak of Quero Bank, where the captain put over his dories and the men set their trawls. The wind never seemed to settle down to blowing from one direction for very long, but shifted back and forth to every point on the compass in a matter of hours. The dorymen were being treated to the varied types of weather that each wind brought along. For example, a cold nor'wester which froze the wet woolen mittens on their hands, made it difficult for them to rebait hooks. Those winds were usually accompanied by heavy snowsqualls which reduced visibility to a minimum. Then there was the sou'wester which very often brought along a cold rain, followed by the nor'easter with its raw biting cold that could almost shave the beard off a man's face. Finally, the sou'easterns with their dense fogs.

One bitterly cold, Tuesday morning the captain of the *Carrie and Nellie* eyed the high running swells with misgivings. The big seas were criss-crossed by a nasty lop which had been created by the rapidly shifting winds. He decided it was too rough. But fishing was good and his energetic young dorymen made an earnest appeal to him to be permitted to go out and underrun their trawls. He finally relented and off they went. The wind at the time was blowing from the nor'west. A few minutes later it veered around from the south, bringing with it a thick blanket of fog.

Reid and Keefe thought that they could easily locate their trawl with the aid of the dory compass, but it turned out that they missed the keg buoy markers completely. They listened intently for some sound from the other dories or blasts from the schooner's foghorn, but could hear nothing beyond the noise of the restless waves surging and roaring around them. It was 6:00 a.m. when they had set out from the ship. When they couldn't locate their trawl they rowed around at intervals all that day hoping to find some trace of the *Carrie and Nellie* or of their shipmates, but met with no success. By late afternoon they were reluctantly forced to admit to having gone astray.

Quero Bank is situated some one hundred and sixty-eight miles from the nearest point of southern Newfoundland. One hundred and sixty-eight miles is a long distance, more especially so when the only means of transportation is a row dory. But John Reid and James Keefe were hardy, courageous dorymen. So despite the fact that they had been riding over wild seas and beset by chilling winds all that day, they decided to try and reach the Newfoundland coast. As it was possible for them to row around for five or six days without locating their vessel or another craft, then in all probability, they would not be in any condition to row to land. The men had a small quantity of sea biscuits and a gallon of water. They were aware that they could not hope to retain their strength for long on that type of food, so they headed for the coast.

They had no light in the boat, so when darkness fell in addition to the fog, they both had to remain awake and alert to listen for approaching ships which might run them down. To their intense relief, shortly after it became dark the fickle wind veered around from the nor'west again. This change proved to be a blessing, as it whisked away the fog and enabled them to steer by the stars which shone very brightly. They scanned the ocean all around them with the hope of sighting a steamer or a schooner which might rescue them. But no ship appeared, so they settled down to the task of rowing and a heartbreaking task it was, as the wind was against them and the seas were still running high. One moment their dory would be riding the crest of a big comber and the next she would be at the bottom of a trough with two dark walls of water tipped with white, towering over her. But they toiled on, substained by the thought that their little craft had been designed and built to withstand such heavy weather and with the help of God would bear them up.

After back-breaking labour that lasted all Tuesday night, Wednesday, Thursday, Friday and until 4:00 p.m. Saturday, when John Reid identified the towering cliffs in the distance as Penguin Island. It took them a further two hours of strenuous rowing to bring them alongside the island and to the little fishing settlement of Cape La Hune.

The incoming dory had been observed by the people there for some time, but as Reid and Keefe appeared to be rowing strongly and not in need of assistance the residents did not deem it necessary to row out and meet the strangers. As the dory entered the harbour, she was identified by her markings as having come from a banker which fact told the Cape La Hune men that her occupants were either astray from their ship or else the vessel had foundered and Reid and Keefe had made their escape as she went down. The people of Cape La Hune greeted the weary men warmly when they discovered that the fishermen had been astray for such a long time. All the men and women crowded around, all eager to be the first to offer them hospitality.

The first duty required of Reid and Keefe as they themselves saw it, was to go to the telegraph office and wire the news of their safety to their families and the vessel's owners. As they reasoned by then the captain would have reached port and reported them missing. Meanwhile, they inquired from the owners as to when they could rejoin their schooner. Their messages were delivered on Sunday. As it happened the *Carrie and Nellie* had reached Burin a short while before.

The captain had reported that Reid and Keefe were missing, presumed drowned. The skipper informed the ship's owners that he had conducted an extensive search for them, without success, before coming into port.

On Monday a message arrived from the owners instructing the men to proceed to Harbour Breton, via the coastal steamer, where the vessel would pick them up. When they reached Harbour Breton they received a rousing welcome from their shipmates who greeted them as men back from the grave.

WILLIAMS AND MAY

The Lunenburg Banks fishing vessel, *Donald R. Creaser,* in command of Captain Allison Creaser, took on a caplin baiting in Fortune Bay, Newfoundland, in June 1927 and promptly set sail for the Grand Banks. The schooner carried seven double or two-man dories, which meant that in addition to her skipper, cook and catchee, she had onboard fourteen fishermen.

Amongst her crewmembers were two Newfoundlanders, George Robert May and Charles Williams. May, fifty-four years old, of medium height and slightly built, while Williams, fifty-three years old, was over six feet and heavily built. May's birthplace was Point Rosie and Williams hailed from Pools Cove. Both settlements are located in Fortune Bay.

On June 17 the *Creaser* arrived on the Bank. The weather being favorable, Captain Creaser shouted the customary order issued by Lunenburg skippers, which was 'Dories in the air!'. One would imagine that the order would have been, dories in the water. But as the dories had to be hoisted out of their nests into the air before they splashed down into the water, the skipper who coined the phrase must have gotten his inspiration from seeing a dory danging high over his head, after she was plucked out of her resting place, to pause momentarily before making her descent into the water.

In any case, Williams and May set off with the other six dories, each one going in a different direction. When the Newfoundland dorymen had reached a point, approximately one mile from their schooner they set their trawls. After waiting for a while on their outer buoy they commenced to underrun the gear, hauling back towards the *Creaser*. In that operation at least, Lady Luck smiled upon them, for they succeeded in loading their dory with fine, fat cod. Rowing back to the vessel, they threw their fish onboard, then after having a 'mug-up', they went out to underrun their trawl again. The time was 3:00 p.m. when they boarded their dory. They had only gone a quarter of a mile from the schooner when a fog, that insidious enemy of Banks fishermen, arrived with deceptive speed and density, for which it is famous. It settled down around them like a thrown blanket reducing visibility to nil. As often was the case, their dory compass could have been a little off from true north or when rowing through the wooly-like vapour they could have misjudged both directions and distances. Whatever the cause, they missed both the inner and outer trawl buoys. Then, despite a search that extended for more than an hour, they failed to locate them, whereupon they decided to return to the *Donald Creaser*. But the vessel like the trawl buoys appeared to be non-existant, for although the dorymen rowed and sailed around for upwards of five hours hoping to hear the welcome sound of the mother ship's foghorn, no such pleasant sound greeted them. Suddenly, they felt awfully deserted and alone upon the vast, heaving fog shrouded ocean.

But Charlie Williams and George May were hardy, experienced fishermen. During their many years on the Banks, they had faced possible injury and death more than a score of times. There was one thing which neither man lacked and that was courage. They were fully aware of the fact that they had gone astray, but they did not panic. Therefore, those two brave men calmly lowered their sail and stretched out on the bottom of the dory to get a night's sleep, hoping that with the appearance of dawn, the weather would clear enabling them to find the schooner. No such luck was in store for them, however, for when daylight broke it revealed the same foggy conditions of the previous day. The only food in the dory was a handful of biscuits, while there was not one solitary drop of water.

When the dory was introduced to the Banks fisheries during the middle 1700s a period of trial ensued, wherein the testing of various sizes of dories was carried out with a view to ascertaining which size would prove to be the most suitable to accommodate two fishermen and their trawl gear. In the meantime it was essential that the boats be of such dimensions so that as much deck space as possible would be reserved. Those tests and trials with their attendent errors resulted in the fifteen foot type being finally selected. The fourteen and fourteen and a half foot were discarded as being rather too small, while the fifteen and a half and the sixteen foot were considered too large, as well as unweildly to manoeuvre. Furthermore, they were heavy to row and very weighty to hoist outboard and inboard, a chore which had to be performed quite frequently onboard a salt banker. In addition, their wider beams and greater lengths would occupy too much space on fishing ships that were much smaller in the 1870s than those built after the turn of the century. I should emphasize that when dory sizes were given it was the bottom lengths only which were recognized, so that a fifteen footer would measure approximately twenty feet on top.

By June, 1927, or at the time of the Williams and May incident, the fifteen footer had become established on ships for all nations who used two man dories on the Banks, while fishing for cod or haddock. It is true that in the halibut fishery the sixteen foot dory was used as those fish were so big and heavy that it required a larger dory to boat them safely. As the banker *Donald R. Creaser* was engaged at fishing for cod, it is safe to assume that her dories were fifteen feet and of the Lunenburg construction, for the home port of Captain Creaser was Lunenburg. It was also the port of registry for his schooner and no self-respecting Lunenburg skipper that I ever heard of would nest any dories that were not returned out in the factory in his beloved home town. As a matter of fact, if one were to even suggest in the presence of a Lunenburg fisherman that dories constructed by Shelburne, French, American, Portuguese or Newfoundland builders were superior to those produced in Lunenburg, he would be inviting a punch in the mouth.

In view of the foregoing, there is little doubt in my mind but that the dory crewed by Charles Williams and George May was a fifteen foot Lunenburger. I go a little off course in making that statement for the reason that some years ago, when I was reading an article which recounted the story of those two fishermen, I noticed that the writer mentioned the fact that they were using a sixteen foot dory. If that meant her bottom size, the type was dispensed with long years previously to 1927, for the reasons I have explained. On the other hand, if the writer had been informed that she measured sixteen feet on the top, it would mean that her bottom length was only about eleven feet, which would make her entirely unsuitable for even a cross-handed or one-man Banks dory. As the thirteen foot bottom size was the smallest carried on a single dory banker.

Taking a sane view of their situation on that dreary morning and realizing that it was possible for them to roam around for many days and nights in a quest for their vessel, which could prove futile, Williams and May decided to try and make St. John's. Using the small dory compass they set a course which they supposed would take them to Newfoundland's capital city. As luck would

70

have it, the wind happened to be blowing in the right direction, so stepping their mast, they set sail and jib. All that day they sped along before the breeze when darkness descended they decided to tie up the sail and take another night's rest.

An alarming situation developed shortly afterwards however, when the wind freshened to half a gale which caused a heavy sea to rise. Then one comber, larger than its fellows, broke partly into the dory, sweeping away two of the oars. They were now assailed by grave fears that the lively gale would develop into a major storm, but very fortunately, their fears were proven groundless, for with the coming of dawn the wind died away, which automatically had the effect of calming the waters. Meanwhile, the new day made them acutely aware of the fact that they were suffering greatly from hunger and thirst. George May discovered a plug of tobacco in his jacket pocket and he shared this out with his dorymate. As everyone knows, tobacco is a very poor substitute for food, but it was the only thing available for them to chew on. Under those circumstances they drove on and on before the wind with dense fog still surrounding them.

As darkness settled down at the end of the third day, the sickening realization came to them that if they had been heading in the right direction, they should have by now made a landfall. They realized too, that the compass which they had relied on must have been out of kilter, for instead of leading them shorewards, it had actually caused them to go further out to sea.

On the fourth day, the fog remained as thick as ever, but the sea had dropped down to almost a calm surface. By then the ravages of hunger and thirst combined with exposure caused both men to weaken rapidly. Charlie Williams' feet were causing him considerable pain and he removed his long rubbers only with great difficulty owing to the distressing fact that his feet had swollen to twice their normal size.

The next day came and went, which meant that a full five days had gone by since a drop of water had passed their lips, causing them to suffer horribly with thirst. The last crumb of their biscuits had been consumed and the final piece of tobacco was shared out.

As they advanced into the sixth day the fog thinned, enabling them to see ahead for a much longer distance. That afternoon, as they raced along under sail, an object came into their range of vision. It was always considered to be a menace to all seagoing men, particularly was it dreaded and avoided by Banks fishermen, but it was welcomed joyously by the thirsty, nearly exhausted dorymen, for what they had sighted was the tip of an iceberg, which showed up glistening through the thinning, lowering vapour.

The berg was a big one and the weakened fishermen felt new hope surge through them for they knew that huge hunk of ice was composed of fresh

71

water. Being expert dory handlers, they brought their craft alongside with all the speed they could command, which in itself was a risky business, for icebergs often are poised in a hair trigger position and have been known to roll completely over at the slap of a diminutive bow wave coming from a small boat. Fortunately, for Williams and May the berg remained upright. Breaking off pieces of ice, they took them onboard and biting off small chunks, they allowed them to melt in their parched mouths. They stated later that after suffering from intense thirst for so long a period, the coolness of that icy lunch was nothing short of heavenly. They continued to suck ice for more than an hour, until they were filled to capacity with fresh water from its melting. Now, with their thirst completely slaked, they loaded a tin with ice also, then shoved off from the giant berg. Greatly refreshed they again set their sail and continued on their journey. As to how that journey would terminate of course, they could not form an opinion.

Two more dreary, hungry, monotonous days and nights dragged slowly by, but now they were facing the thirst problem once more. A small amount of water remained in the tin from the melted ice, however, when they proceeded to take a drink, it smelled and tasted so horribly bad that even though their wasted bodies were weak and crying out for more water, their willpower remained strong enough to hold them back from partaking of it.

Then the wind veered around from the southeast and it piped up into quite a blow. The ocean became rough, but the change of the wind brought them another blessing. A downpour of rain. They used their woolen mitts to soak this up from the bottom of the dory, then sucked them dry and repeated the process. Despite this refreshment, their strength was draining away. Only a grim determination to survive at any cost kept them alive.

On the evening of the ninth day, Charles Williams' once powerful grip could no longer maintain a hold on the steering oar. It slipped from his fingers and disappeared astern.

On the tenth day a towering wave smashed into the dory, sweeping away their remaining pair of oars. The two men were so weak by this time that they did not have the strength to row, so the loss of the oars did not make any difference. They were now at the mercy of wind and tide, having no choice but to go wherever those moody elements fancied to take them.

Then on the afternoon of the eleventh day, when they were nearing the very verge of death, the British steamer *Abuera*, under the command of Captain Georgeson, came over the horizon and sighted their dory. The steamship, with much difficulty, edged alongside the frail craft and rescued them.

Once onboard the *Aburea*, the distressed dorymen were treated with every kindness and consideration by the officers and crew of the big ship. When he rescued Williams and May, Captain Georgeson had been bound for London.

A few days after their rescue, the dorymen were landed at Tillbury Docks. They were hospitalized and when they recovered sufficiently, were sent back to their homes in Fortune Bay.

The little settlement of Point Rosie, where George May was born and from where he set forth on so many occasions to man a dory on the great offshore fishing Banks was literally wiped off the map of Newfoundland during the resettlement program. The program was introduced and put into effect during the 1960s. Its residents were absorbed mostly by the towns of Harbour Breton and Garnish. Pools Cove, the home of Charles Williams, presents a different picture. That community of fifty families did not obey the resettlement call, they unanimously decided not to move.

Some of Newfoundland's finest fishing skippers and foreign going captains came from Pools Cove. An outstanding family in those areas of endeavour was that of Captain John Henry Williams and his five sons, master mariners all. The most widely known of the sons was Captain Clarence Williams. As a Banks fishing skipper and a foreign going captain, he had no peer. Mr. Andrew Horwood in his book, 'Newfoundland Ships and Men', assets that a whole book could be written on the thrilling and dangerous exploits experienced by Skipper Clar. Having known Captain Williams since early boyhood, I concur most heartily with Mr. Horwood on that point. Incidentally, Captain John Henry Williams and his five sons were uncle and cousins of the straying doryman, Charles Williams.

Charles Williams did not live too long after his harrowing experience. But, I was informed by one of his close relatives that his death was not caused by the suffering he had endured while adrift for eleven days in an open dory, far out on the broad Atlantic, but by cancer of the stomach.

Williams' dorymate, George Robert May had reached the age of eighty-two when he passed away on June 6, 1955. Normally he might have attained a greater age, but he contracted a case of severe influenza which caused his death.

As the resettlement program had not been activated up to the time of his death, Mr. May was interred at Point Rosie.

FRANK KNICKLE AND JOHN GREEK

Banks fishing in the days of dory trawling was no place for soft men or soft words. It embodied violent, hard and gruelling work. It was abrupt, dangerous, too often profane and it took real men. Men with the bark firmly on to live through it. That is if they managed to stay alive.

There were always a few reckless men who took unnecessary risks to show those around them what they believed to be courage. The bitter part was that they all too frequently took with them to their deaths, the more careful men.

Frank Knickle of Lunenburg, former doryman, survived a nine-day ordeal in an open dory during bitter winter weather —(Jerry Kelland Photo).

A courageous and careful man was Frank Knickle, of Lunenburg, Nova Scotia. He made his first trip to the Banks when he was thirteen years of age. I interviewed Mr. Knickle in his comfortable home on Green Street, Lunenburg, June, 1973. He was seventy-one years old but could pass for a man in his fifties. In 1930 he was a crew member of the schooner, *Ina Hazel*, Captain Basil Knickle commanding, when she ran ashore on Seal Island, Nova Scotia and became a total loss. The crew rowed ashore without difficulty.He was a doryman on the banker, *L.W. Lohones* in 1932, when she was lost by striking Renews Rock, Newfoundland. The crew took to their dories, all hands rowing safely into Renews harbour. From there they proceeded to St. John's, then were returned home to Lunenburg.

Now with two shipwrecks under his belt, Frank Knickle was ready to try again, so he signed on the Lunenburg banker, *Ocean Maid,* a knockabout (no bowsprit) type vessel, under the command of Captain Arnold Park. One day while the schooner was heading for Burin to procure bait, she sprang a leak and sank. As the craft was settling into the water, Knickle and his shipmates took to their dories, rowing safely to land without any noticeable incident occurring. In between his numerous Banks fishing trips, Frank served on several steamers without mishap.

He recalled a time when he was serving as mate or second hand on the Banks fishing schooner, *Jean and Shirley* under Captain Shorley, when they came upon a dory with two men who had been astray from another vessel for a couple of days. As they came alongside, one of the men on the *Jean and Shirley* recognized one of the dory's occupants, a sixty-year-old man named Billy Yarn.

"How are you feeling, Billy?" The doryman who recognized him called out.

"I'm feeling fine, just fine, replied Billy.

Two of the *Shirley's* men then reached down, seized his hands, pulling him up to the vessel's deck, where to their amazement, they discovered that he was stone dead. The man had actually died on his feet as he uttered the words, 'I'm fine, just fine.'

Frank Knickle had served for twenty-four years on various Banks schooners and a number of steamers, meanwhile surviving three shipwrecks without running into trouble of a noteworthy nature. At the end of two and a half decades on the ocean during all types of weather conditions and not having suffered from hunger, thirst or frostbite during all that time, it finally happened.

In January, 1941, Frank joined the fishing schooner *Lila M. Boutilier.* The vessel sailed out of Halifax harbour in charge of Captain George Himmelman. They arrived and anchored on Ambro Bank, which is situated ninety miles from Halifax. The weather was not too bad for that time of year. The trawls were set and fish was discovered to be fairly plentiful. Early on the morning of January 28, all twelve dories put out from the *Boutilier* to haul their trawls. Knickle and his dorymate John Greek, a fellow Lunenburger, had their task partly completed when with little warning, it commenced to snow very thickly. In a short while the wind rose to half a gale. The water became so rough they were forced to let go of the trawl. They immediately decided to try and locate their schooner. The snow thinned out for a few minutes, which enabled them to sight a banker in the distance. Although they could not be sure it was the *Boutilier,* they were determined to try and reach her. They stepped their mast as the wind was blowing more or less toward the schooner. They unfurled their sail and headed their dory in that direction. Then, unluckily for them, the snow came on again thicker than ever, and the wind increased in volume until the weather attained blizzard proportions. It became severely frosty, causing the two men to suffer from the driving snow and biting cold. Their woolen mitts which had become soaking wet while they were hauling the trawl, froze on their hands.

Fearing that their dory would capsize with the sail up, they managed to get it down with great difficulty, but owing to their hands becoming stiff with cold, they could not hold on to it, so it went overboard and disappeared. They got the oars out and started to row but they never did find the ship they were seeking. They figured that either they had missed her in the blizzard or she had moved on to another location. By this time their hands were paralyzed with cold, so they could not grip the oars properly. These too, finally slipped out of their grasp and went the way of the sail. Now, without oars they could only sit tight and let the dory drift. As night descended, John Greek stood up for a moment. As he did so, the dory gave a violent heave and toppled him into the water. Knickle managed to get a grip on his wrist and with desperation managed to get him back onboard, to set him down on the after midshiproom thwart. Of course Greek's clothing was saturated from his immersion in the icy water. A half hour later he did not answer when Knickle spoke to him. When daylight broke, it was still snowing though the wind had moderated and it was still very cold. Slipping aft to where John Greek was sitting bolt upright Frank found that his dorymate was dead and frozen stiff. Knickle decided to let the corpse remain where it was, with the hope that he would be rescued. Then John's body could be taken ashore and given a decent burial.

An hour after making his gruesome discovery, Frank said that the wind increased again, coming on stronger every passing minute, which caused the flat-bottom dory to scud before it like a scalded cat. In the afternoon the little boat was belted by a particularly heavy sea, she lurched so violently that the corpse of John Greek was torn loose from the thwart. It stood against the gunnel for a moment then toppled overboard. When it reached the water, the body again assumed an upright position and Frank watched it drift rapidly off before the wind, like a man sitting on the water being towed by a motor boat. It finally disappeared in a welter of snow and foam.

Now alone, Frank Knickle suddenly realized that he was hungry and thirsty. He searched in vain for the boat's emergency food and water containers. He concluded that either someone had forgotten to place them in the dory's riser, or they had been bounced overboard when the craft had made one of her violent lurches. He started to knaw on frozen fish, which they had taken onboard when hauling their trawl. He slaked his thirst by eating snow, a plentiful supply of which had drifted into the dory.

Knickle drifted about in his unmanageable little boat for nine days before being rescued. A lot of water came into the dory when rough seas boarded her, with the result that he was forced to keep bailing and breaking off ice continuously as it formed on the dory. He remembers praying for rescue many times, but he felt that he dare not indulge in taking a nap for fear that if he should do so he would freeze to death. He stated that if he slept at all he was not aware of it.

On the evening of the ninth day he was picked up on George's Bank by the

Boston trawler, *Breakus*, commanded by Captain Olsen. He was not aware that he had been rescued, however, for when the trawler reached his dory he had lapsed into unconsciousness. A short while later the *Breakus* met up with the vessel *Argo* which was inbound for Boston. Knickle was transferred to this ship and was taken to port with all possible speed.

On her arrival in Boston, he was quickly conveyed to a hospital, where under treatment he soon regained consciousness. His fingers, toes and face were badly frozen, but he is extremely grateful today that owing to the expert medical care he received he did not lose any part of the digits. He can use them just as actively today as he could before he went astray from the *Lila Boutilier*. His finger and toe nails came off, but they all grew back again. His face does not show any scars in the slightest degree.

When I visited him in his home, I found him propped up in bed.

"I presume, Mr. Knickle," I inquired, "that you are now bedridden as a result of those terrible nine days you spent thirty-two years ago?"

"Hell no, boy," he replied with disgust. "A couple of weeks ago I was walking through my stage when a plank broke in two under my feet and I fell into the water, breaking three of my ribs as I went down."

I asked his permission to take his picture, but he flatly refused to have it taken whilst he was lying in bed. Against my protests and those of his wife, he got out of bed, dressed himself and posed out in the garden.

"This is the proper place for a man to have his picture taken," he said. "Not lying down like an invalid."

William Dodge, Pool's Cove, Fortune Bay, was astray from his vessel entirely without food or water for sixteen days in August, 1951. Mr. Dodge is shown at age eighty-seven in 1976 —(Jocelyn Kelland Photo).

DODGE AND BISHOP

In the days of dory trawling on the Banks, the survival of two Newfoundland fishermen for sixteen days without sustenance, either liquid or solid, constitutes what I believe to be a record in time length for fishermen who have gone astray from their vessels.

In August 1951, the banker *Lucy Edwina* out of Belleoram, Newfoundland in command of Captain Ralph Skinner, sailed for the Banks. Amongst her crew members were William Dodge and George Bishop, both of Pools Cove, Fortune Bay.

On August 11, the schooner was anchored on Grand Bank. Early in the morning of that day, dorymen Dodge and Bishop set out from the parent ship to haul their trawl. Bishop was only eighteen years old and was his first trip to the Banks. As they rowed towards their gear, a thick blanket of fog rolled up enveloping them completely and cutting off their view of the *Lucy Edwina*. It also caused them to miss the key buoys which served as markers for the trawls. For several hours they rowed around endeavouring to locate those markers, but met with no success.

A rather stiff breeze blew in from the south, but luckily, it did not develop strength enough to endanger them. Late in the afternoon the wind died out. So, for half an hour they were in a dead calm. Then the wind breezed up once more. This time it came from the northwest. That proved to be a blessing, for the nor'west wind quickly dissipated the gloomy fog. The two men became overjoyed as they watched it disappear. Their elation quickly turned to dismay, however, for as they scanned the ocean an all sides, they failed to sight their craft or any of the other dories. Neither was there a craft of any description visible to the horizon. William Dodge was now fully aware that they were totally astray. He was well aware of what that could mean. During his thirty-odd years of Banks fishing it had never happened to him, but he was familiar with stories of what happened to other men who had gone through harrowing experiences whilst astray in dories on the Banks. He had witnessed the irreparable damage that had been done to the minds and bodies of some of the men as a result of terrible, prolonged suffering. Then he knew of others who had gone astray, never to be heard from again.

As he gazed about, he got the feeling that he and his dorymate were sitting on a tiny chip on that vast expanse of water. Then he prayed for rescue.

The ocean looks so mighty,
While the dory feels so small,
Where the northern gales blow flighty,
When you're huntin' a Grand Banks trawl.

You already know the stories,
Of men who went astray,
In those flimsy, little dories,
Now, you're not ashamed to pray.

Dodge, at the beginning of the voyage, had requested permission from Captain Skinner to take young Bishop as a dorymate and the skipper had complied. Dodge stated that he had chosen Bishop as a dorymate for a variety of reasons. To begin with, the young man was his nephew, his sister's son. In addition, he was tall, powerfully built, was a strong as an ox and very eager to learn the trade of deep-sea fishing. He really possessed the qualifications which make a good Bank's fisherman. Dodge said he felt more comfortable when the captain permitted him to take George as a dorymate. As being such a close relative, on his first trip to the Banks he felt himself more or less responsible for the younger man's safety while at sea. But grim fate decided to take a hand; ironically, if George Bishop had not gone in his uncle's dory, he would in all probability be alive today.

For fifteen days and nights Dodge and Bishop roamed the waters of the Atlantic amid unusually unsatisfactory weather conditions. Gales of wind, with the resultant mountainous waves, plagued them. When the winds died out and the seas went down, they would encounter periods of flat calms and dense fog would lie like a huge, wooly grey blanket all over and around them. The fog of course always lessened their changes of being sighted and rescued by some passing ship. It was the type of weather that's dreaded and feared by every man who has been compelled to wrest a living from Banks fishing.

On the second day out, with no sign of rescue in sight, Dodge decided to open the emergency food rations which were held in two metal containers. One was filled with hardtack and the other with water. Upon opening the containers, Dodge found to his dismay that both hardtack and water were contaminated. It became clear to him that the tins had not been opened for inspection for a long time. It was quite evident, also, that they had not been properly sealed. Although by now the men were hungry and thirsty, they decided against partaking of the spoiled food and water; for if they had done so, serious illness or death could have been the result. So Dodge threw both containers overboard in case that later when their hunger and thirst increased, they would find it impossible to resist the temptation to use the contents.

They kept on through the dreary, weary days and nights that followed, ever buoyed up by faith and hope that a rescue ship would come. Dodge valiantly tried to keep the younger man's spirits up by talking about every subject, except the one concerning their being adrift. Very often the old doryman resorted to singing songs and hymns, hoping to relieve their terrible distress and monotony.

On the morning of the fourteenth day, Dodge, on looking aft toward his nephew, could in no way recognize him as the tall, well-built, handsome man he had set out with such a short while ago. Bishop was now reduced to a mere skeleton of his former self. Then Dodge realized that he too, must be in a similar condition. When the morning of the sixteenth day broke, despite his maddening thirst and clouded mind, Dodge became aware that his young dorymate was sinking fast.

On the previous afternoon an empty bottle had drifted close to their dory. Dodge picked it up and filled it with salt water, with the hope that by drinking a small quantity it would alleviate their thirst. They were not the first sea-bound men to make such a mistake. And a mistake it was, for drinking the salt water only increased their misery. Although they had been visited by every change of wind known to man, not once did a single drop of rain fall upon them. They had become so weak that they had given up rowing several days before. Allowing the dory to drift where it would, they decided on this measure in order to conserve their remaining strength.

In the early afternoon, Dodge, who was gazing about, noticed that a low mist was hanging over the water in the near distance. Suddenly he caught sight of a schooner's top masts towering above the vapour. The old doryman decided not to get too excited about it too quickly. To use a modern expression 'he kept his cool'. After all they had been astray for sixteen days, so a few minutes more would not make any difference. The sight of the schooner's top masts could be a cruel mirage, for he knew that those strange phenomena sometimes appear on the ocean as they do on the deserts. In this respect, his main concern was for Bishop, for he had no intention of raising hopes in the boy only to have them shattered later, if he discovered the ship was non-existent.

But the more he studied the top masts, the more he became convinced that they were the spars of a real vessel. He felt new strength surging through his weary, parched body. He shouted to Bishop to cheer up, that a rescue ship was near. On hearing this the young man raised himself up, then fell back. When Dodge bent over him, he knew that the ship had arrived too late to aid Bishop; he was dead.

To witness the young man's demise was a bitter pill for William Dodge to swallow, for through all the days and nights that they had been astray, he never lost hope that he would eventually be able to return him safely to his parents. Now he felt that it was incumbent on him to do something proper and respectful with his nephew's body, but he was unable to decide what.

Gathering his remaining strength, he shipped a pair of oars. Then with his dead dorymate lying on the dory's bottom, he rowed toward the schooner. He was fortunate in one respect at that time, for a light breeze was blowing straight in that direction, which aided his advance greatly. He reached the side of the ship after rowing for about twenty minutes. She turned out to be a Portuguese fishing craft anchored on the prolific fishing ground known as the

Virgin Rocks. William Dodge had reached her in the nick of time, for she was fully loaded and was about to haul up her anchor preparatory to departing for Portugal. A half hour later and she would not have been there, and no other ship was in sight.

Dodge, despite the long period he was astray, totally without food and water, in addition to being cramped up in a small boat, was able to step up on the vessel's deck and walk to the fo'castle unaided. Truly another ironman of the sea. Portuguese sailors hoisted the dory with the remains of Bishop aboard their schooner.

A group of Portuguese dorymen stand near their single-man dories nested on the banker 'Creoula' —(Robert Kelland Photo).

The Portuguese are a devout Christian race of people, so out of respect for the dead, the captain announced that he would delay his departure until the following day. He had the young man's body sewed up in a stout canvas bag and weighted. The next day, August 28, he sailed his vessel out to deep water and then while the entire ship's company assembled on the quarter deck with heads bared, he conducted a simple but impressive burial-at-sea service. At its conclusion all that remained of Bishop was committed to the deep.

After the burial, the Portuguese captain turned his vessel about and steered a course for the nearest Newfoundland port for the purpose of landing William Dodge, who was showing good signs of improvement under the kind, tender care of the ship's cook and crewmen.

In the late forenoon of that day, August 29, the Newfoundland banker *Dorothy P. Sarty,* hove in sight. Acting in response to signals from the Portuguese ship, she came alongside. Dodge was transferred to her. A short while later he was landed at Grand Bank, where he was immediately conveyed to hospital there. After a month's rest under expert medical care, he was almost completely recovered. He attributed his survival to his unshaken faith of eventually being rescued.

Always a man with a healthy appetite, used to getting his meals regularly, he stated that he had no idea that he could survive so long without food or water. While lying in a hospital bed, he was asked if he would ever go to the Banks again. He replied, "T'is my way of earning a living. I will go out again next year if I am able."

And go he did, for several years after the tragedy that claimed his nephew dorymate.

In 1975, Mr. Dodge took up residence in the Pentecostal Home for senior citizens at Clarke's Beach, Newfoundland. At this writing, 1978, Mr. Dodge, at the age of eighty-seven years remains in a reasonably good state of health.

MATTHEWS AND THOMAS

After reading a few stories of the suffering Banks dorymen endured when they went astray from their vessels and of those who died before they could be rescued, you would hardly imagine that an experienced fisherman who must have been fully aware of the dangers surrounding him and who was adequately conversant with the stories of disaster which had overtaken other dorymen under similar circumstances, would stubbornly refuse an offer of rescue on two separate occasions, from passing ships. Then to top it off, after he and his dorymate had made it to land would slew around and reject the kindly offer of a lighthouse keeper to put them up for a night. But such a case actually did occur back in 1921.

On June 16 of that year, the fishing schooner *Florence E.,* commanded by Captain John Hickman Matthews, anchored on Banquereau (Quero) which is part of the fishing area known as the Western Banks. The vessel which was owned by a Grand Bank firm had gone out on a caplin trip, that is to say, she had onboard caplin for bait. She also carried ten dories. At 3:00 a.m. the following day, all the dories left the vessel to set trawls. It was a fine, calm morning with a smooth sea. Two of the dorymen, Charlie Thomas and Leonard Matthews, both residents of Grand Bank, returned to the *Florence E.* after running out their trawl, to have breakfast. When the meal was over, the two young men loaded their bait jack with caplin and went out to underrun their gear.

On that voyage, the elder and more experienced of the two, Charlie

Leonard Matthews Sr., Grand Bank, Newfoundland. He experienced most unusual circumstances while astray from his schooner in 1921 —(Courtesy Leonard Matthews Sr.).

Thomas, had been appointed as dory skipper. But not in every case was it the older and more experienced man who got that job. Many of them declined to accept the position because they had no desire to assume the responsibility that went with it. So very often, in the days of the two-man dory salt banker, it was the younger man who took charge when dories left the vessel to tend trawls. This, despite the fact that dory skippers enjoyed certain privileges which their dorymates did not.

When a fishing schooner was carrying ten double dories, she also carried twenty dorymen. The messroom table in the fo'castle of those ships was much wider near the companionway or after end than it was at the for'ard end, as it was necessary for it to follow the contours of the ship, which narrowed as the bow section closed in. For if the table was of equal width at both ends, it would obstruct the men from climbing into their bunks. By the same token, it would prevent them from sitting at the for'ard end of the festive board.

On schooners the size of the *Florence E.*, the table was not of sufficient length to accommodate twenty dorymen and skipper, who usually took his meals with the crew. Therefore, the cook was obliged to set two tables. At the first table on the starboard side would be seated the captain and the five dory skippers, while the mate, who was also a dory skipper, sat with the remaining dory skippers on the port side. Being seated with the captain and the mate at the first table was one of the privileges enjoyed by dory skippers, while their

83

dorymates had to wait hungrily for the second sitting. So it appears that even onboard grimy fishing vessels there was class distinction. But, after all, I guess that was the way it had to be, for rules made in connection with the perilous business of deep sea fishing were drawn up for the benefit of all hands.

Once the dories departed from a schooner, their skippers automatically took on the same mantle of authority which the captains carried on board the mother ship. In other words, their dorymates were obligated to obey all orders without question, whether they agreed with them or not.

The fact that Charlie Thomas possessed the authority accorded to dory skippers and that Leonard Matthews was duty bound to carry out his orders, caused the latter to experience some very disquieting hours during the days ahead.

When they made the first underrun, Thomas and Matthews were lucky for they loaded their dory down to the gunnels with a fine fare of large cod. Rowing back to the *Florence E.* they discharged their catch then went below for a 'mug-up'. Figuring that they might collect another load of fish from their rebaited trawl, they rowed out once more. Picking up at the handy end of the gear, or the one nearest the ship, they hauled off toward the outer buoy. While they were so engaged, a stiff, southerly breeze blew up, bringing with it a dense fog. When the men reached the last tub of trawl they could hear the vessel's foghorn blowing. Apparently their captain was endeavouring to guide his dories back aboard. When the outer buoy was reached, the dorymen noticed that a strong tide was running to the east'ard. But they did not know just how strong it was. Meanwhile, the wind had risen to half a gale. Shipping their oars, they started to row in what they believed to be the direction of the vessel. They could no longer hear her foghorn, and with the wind and the tide against them, they did not seem to be making any progress. The heavy squalls would lift the oars clear out of the oarlocks. In view of this Thomas decided to anchor. They remained anchored until complete darkness had settled down. The wind continued to blow as strongly as ever. The fog had not thinned and the seas were rising higher with each passing moment.

The dory began to ship water. The skipper decided to pull in the anchor and run before the wind to Grand Bank, approximately one hundred miles away. Shortly after they set out, an electrical storm broke over them, lightning flashed all around, followed by the loud crash of thunder, while rain descended in torrents. This made it imperative for one man to bail constantly while the other steered. The storm kept hounding them until daylight, when it flashed and grumbled off in the southern distance. In the meantime, the wind lessened appreciably and the sea had gone down, so the men hoisted their sail and ran under a goose wing, which means that the high peak of the sail was lowered. The fog was still thick, but it was not so dense as it had been the previous day.

Around 9:00 a.m., they heard the whistle of a steamer blowing dead ahead. So they doused their sail and got out their oars in order to check the dory's speed, as they certainly had no desire to become involved in a head-on collision with a steamboat. A few minutes later the ship broke out of the fog a few yards off their starboard bow. Leonard Matthews instantly tied his oil jacket to an oar and held it up. The steamer's lookout spotted them, whereupon the ship changed course and came over to them. As she neared the dory, the officer on watch manoeuvred her to the win'ard of the dory so as to give the fishermen shelter under her side. The ship was the British steamer, *Crescent*, bound from Liverpool, England to Quebec City.

Her captain appeared on the bridge and offered to take them and their dory onboard, then land them when he reached his destination. Leonard Matthews eagerly agreed to this kindly proposal, but unfortunately for him, Charlie Thomas had other ideas. Matthews could scarcely believe his ears when the dory skipper said to the steamer's captain, "No thank you, sir. I don't want to be carried all the way to the city of Quebec. We're going home to Grand Bank in our dory."

"But Charlie!" expostulated the flabbergasted Matthews. "We'll be gettin' a free trip in solid comfort to a big city where we can see all the sights, maybe visit General Wolfe's Cove and the Plains of Abraham, where the British and the French fought that big battle. After all, we've gone though a rough day and an even rougher night." But Charlie was adamant.

"To hell with Wolfe's Cove and the Plains of Abraham," he said. "We're headin' for home right now."

The steamer's captain upon hearing that statement, had a generous supply of food and a large pot of hot coffee sent down to them. Very welcome gifts indeed, as the two men had not partaken of food or drink in twenty-four hours. Before she set them adrift, the steamer towed them eight miles and put them on the proper course that would hopefully take them to Grand Bank. It was with mixed feelings that Leonard Matthews viewed the big ship as she disappeared into the murk to resume her voyage. The wind continued to blow in the right direction fairly strongly.

So the dorymen ran before it once more under a goose wing sail. All through that day and through the hours of darkness, the little boat drove on. When daylight broke, the fog thinned out which enabled them to see quite a distance ahead. Then at 10:00 o'clock they discovered that they were heading straight for a large schooner. One of the crewmen sighted the dory and the vessel hove to. When Matthews and Thomas reached her and were taken onboard, they were informed that the craft was a rum runner, the *M.M. Gardner*. This time the dorymen were wined and dined for the schooner was loaded to the hatches with assorted liquors.

After they had downed a couple of shots of much needed rum and while they were having breakfast, the captain of the rum runner informed the dorymen that he was bound to New York City. His cargo, he stated was consigned to that port for trans-shipment.

The term trans-shipment, during the days of the rum runner, was a loophole, provided by law, through which the largest ship on rum row could be driven through without fear of interference from government officers. Provided of course, that the vessel's papers were perfectly in order, which they always were. The high-ranking gangsters connected with the rum-running business and who owned most of the ships engaged at the trade would never overlook such an important detail.

The captain of the *M.M. Gardner* informed Thomas and Matthews that he would be more than delighted to take them along. Matthews quickly accepted the invitation, he was overjoyed at the prospect of getting a free trip to another big city, New York, a place he had often hoped to visit but never expected that such an event would become a reality. Yes, a free trip to one of the largest cities on earth, aboard a staunch, well provided schooner would be exactly to his liking. This time he did not have the least doubt but that Thomas would readily go along after spending a second twenty-four hours cramped up in that little dory, accompanied by miseries and potential dangers.

But Leonard Matthews was dead wrong regarding his feelings as to what Charlie Thomas would do, for the stubborn dory skipper once more rejected the offer of rescue.

"I thank you, Captain, very much for your kindness," he said. "You are free to go if you want to Matthews, but me, I'm going home to Grand Bank in the dory."

That statement put young Matthews in a rather bad spot. Although he had his dory skipper's permission to remain on the ship, he was faced with the grim spectre of Thomas never reaching Grand Bank or any other place. So that if he himself arrived home safely to discover that Thomas had not turned up, he would never be allowed to live down the fact that he had deserted his dorymate, leaving him to make his way alone in a small open boat far out on the Atlantic. He therefore, decided it was far better for him to remain with the dory skipper, supposing he drowned, rather than face the accusing eyes and gibes of the people back home. Accordingly he rejoined Thomas in the dory. Then with the schooner's crew lining her rail wishing them all the luck in the world and with a generous supply of food from the ship's stores, a rum jar full of water and a bottle of Haig and Haig whiskey, off they went.

The fog had been replaced with a light mist and the visibility was reasonably good. The brisk wind was still blowing in their favour, but it was not strong enough to endanger them, so they hoisted the sail to full peak. For the remainder of that day they raced on with the little dory remaining watertight and bearing up beautifully.

They continued on through the night and all the next day. Then as sundown was approaching, they came to land at Green Island, one of the Saint Pierre group, which is forty miles from Grand Bank, where the lighthouse keeper met them. A few minutes later they were enjoying a tasty meal with the keeper and his family. By the time the meal was over, darkness was closing in.

The hospitable keeper and his wife urged them not to continue on that night and offered to put them up until morning. Once again Leonard Matthews accepted generosity with alacrity. He was aware that the forty miles of open water could become extremely rough in a few minutes should a sudden storm blow up. To make the crossing in daylight would be risky enough, in an open dory, but to attempt such a journey during the hours of darkness would be utterly foolish. Matthews was pretty sure that by this time Thomas would prefer sleeping in a warm, comfortable bed to sitting upright all night in a spray-drenched, tossing dory. He guessed wrong again, however, for it appeared that Charlie Thomas was not yet finished with tempting 'Mother Fate'.

"Come on, Leonard," he ordered, briskly. "We're leaving for home right now!"

Seeing that the dory skipper was determined on taking his departure, Matthews knew that any objection on his part would be useless. So he boarded the dory without a word.

They shoved off, hoisted their sail at full peak and with the kindly wind still in their favour, they were on their way once more. When they were about five miles out from Green Island, the wind hauled a little more from the south'ard. As the wind changed it freshened. In about twenty minutes it was blowing great guns. Then their old enemy, the electrical storm descended upon them again in fury, while rain cascaded down in sheets. Matthews had to keep bailing, while Thomas steered. They were obliged to reduce sail to a goose wing again, as the wind came on stronger and the seas rose higher. Leonard Matthews thought of that nice bed back at the lighthouse where at this time they should have been slumbering like infants. But he knew that they would never be able to return to the lighthouse against the wind and sea.

Although the distance from Green Island to Grand Bank is forty miles, it is only eight miles as the crow flies, to Point May, situated to the north on the mainland coast of Newfoundland. The shore along there is bleak and inhospitable. It is a wild shore (no Harbour) and almost impossible to land safety in rough weather. Between Point May and Fortune lies a place called

Danzic Cove, which is only a small indentation in the shoreline. Back in 1921, a few fishermen from nearby settlements occupied shacks in this cove where they resided during the summer fishing months only, as it was near to a good fishing ground. It would be safer to attempt a landing there, than on the coast leading to Point May.

Now with the sudden change to unfavourable weather, which had brought along high winds, a thunder and lightning storm, torrential rain and heavy seas, Mr. Thomas voiced the opinoin that they would never make it to Grand Bank.

"Our only hope," he continued, "is to land in Danzic Cove and take shelter in one of the fishin' shacks until daylight or until the wind and sea goes down."

The mention of landing in Danzic Cove caused Leonard Matthews to 'freak out', as the saying goes.

"Looka here, Charlie," he screamed. "You refused a free trip to Quebec City, you refused a free trip to New York. You denied me the chance to see all the wonderful sights in those places. We could have enjoyed both trips on boats that were luxury liners compared to this dory. Then on top of that, you rejected the lighthouse keeper's kind invitation to spend the night sleepin' in a cosy bed. Now you want me to go ashore in Danzic Cove to sleep on hard boards in a miserable stinkin' fishin' shack. Ah no, Charlie,me b'y, you wanted to go to Grand Bank and that's exactly where you're goin' now. Either to Grand Bank or to the bottom of the sea, dependin' on our luck. I'm takin' over as dory skipper from now on in," raged Matthews. "Though you might get me hung for mutiny on the high seas!"

Then reaching back, Leonard took the steering oar out of Charlie's hand and ordered him to change places. Very much taken aback by his dorymate's outburst of anger, Thomas meekly obeyed.

Miraculously the dory did not swamp, but raced before the wind around the toe of the Burin Peninsula's boot like a devil to wing.

Once more their good luck did not desert them and they drove their dory ashore in Grand Bank Gut one hour after midnight. Those two men had covered one hundred miles of ocean in an open dory, plagued by dense fog, wild winds and towering seas to safely enter the snug haven of their own harbour. This despite the fact that the dory skipper had spurned the offer of rescue from passing ships and rejected the invitation of a lighthouse keeper.

The case of Matthews and Thomas constitutes what must be the most unique case of survival in the annals of straying Banks dorymen.

Matthews and Thomas nearly caused massive heart attacks amongst their relatives when they presented themselves at that graveyard hour in soggy oilskins and dripping sou'westers. The said relatives in their sleep-befuddled state, imagined for a moment or two that the boys had been drowned on the Banks and were appearing before them as ghosts.

The following morning the schooner, *Florence E.* entered Grand Bank harbour with her mast fluttering at half mast from the main rigging. Charlie and Leonard on observing her approach, went down to the wharf and hid behind some puncheons (large barrels). When the vessel had been tied up, Captain Matthews came ashore, his face drawn and haggard. He told the crowd assembled on the wharf, "It is my sad duty to report the loss of two men, my nephew, Leonard Matthews and Charles Thomas." He added, "We've covered many miles of ocean searching for them. I am sure that they didn't survive, as the weather has been pretty rough since they went astray." At this juncture, Charlie and Leonard popped up from behind the puncheons, "Who didn't survive?" they chorused.

The look of intense relief which spread over the captain's face when he discovered that they were safe remained there for only a moment, when it was replaced by a wolfish grimace.

"Ah no," the skipper ground out. "You weren't drowned during the past few days, but you're goin' to be drowned right now, over this wharf."

As he advanced toward his grinning dorymen, with hands extended and fingers curled like the talons of an eagle, Charlie and Leonard scampered off and escaped in the direction of the hills.

Charlie Thomas has long since gone to his eternal rest. His dorymate, Leonard Matthews passed away in September, 1978 at the age of seventy-six. Mr. Matthews was best known around the Burin Peninsula for his skill in turning out model ships and dories, as well as other beautiful replicas of items which portray our past history in miniature.

AMERICO FLORES DaSILVA

In the month of July, 1970, a young Portuguese fisherman, Americo Flores DaSilva, went astray from the schooner, *Capitoa Joal Filarinho*, on the Grand Bank. For five days and nights DaSilva wrested with wind, wave and loneliness. Hope for his survival was all but gone. His parents and relatives in Portugal were notified that he was missing. Word came back from them that everyone was praying for him, praying really hard.

Their prayers must have been answered, for on the early morning of the sixth day he was sighted and picked up by the Newfoundland vessel, *Newfoundland Eagle.*

Considering that he had spent such a long time on a boisterous ocean, in a tiny open boat and having spent the final two days without food or water, he was in good mental and physical condition.

DaSilva's dory was the smallest of the Banks fishing dories, known as the cross-handed or single man, thirteen foot type. His five days and nights of unplanned ocean wandering, coupled with the fact that he lived through it, proved that dory fishermen are still one hardy breed of men.

It also proved that present day dory builders are constructing the little craft sturdy and seaworthy enough to make them capable of covering a large expanse of rough water, without capsizing or becoming swamped.

CHAPTER FIVE

Dories, Flats and Skiffs

Some contemporary writers in describing certain types of small boats, have referred to the dory-flat, dory-skiff and the semi-dory.

Well, I contend that the use of such terms is a lot of hokum. They make about as much sense as if you were to strap a bridle and saddle on the back of a bison, then called it a horse-bison or a semi-horse. There are no such boats as dory-flats, dory-skiffs or semi-dories, for there is no halfway mark as far as

A 'to-scale' model of an 18-foot (bottom size) motor dory built by the author for the Biafran Government, West Africa —(Photo by John Fallon Jr.).

the true dory is concerned.

Amongst members of the older generation when the word dory is mentioned, all minds flash to that little boat, the flat bottom of which is sharp pointed at both ends, has straight, outward flaring sides, with a rather heavy rake at the stem and stern. This craft is endowed with a feature not found in the construction of any other type of row boat with the exception of the Swampscott dory. For the true dory possesses a distinctive individuality. The mark which so distinguishes her being the 'V' shaped stern or counter, known in New England as the tombstone stern. The flat and skiff being boats that are broad of stern, both at the bottom and top, are as unrelated to the dory as is a modern speed boat.

Furthermore, I am absolutely sure that if you were to request a man from Grand Bank, Lunenburg or Gloucester, thirty years of age or older to go down to the harbour and bring back a dory, he would arrive back with a sharp-nosed boat that carried flared sides, flat bottom and a 'V' shaped stern, because that is the boat they have always called a dory.

Then there is another point to be considered in connection with the naming or identification of various boats and a lot depends on in what part of the world a man is born and raised. For example, the broad sterned, flat bottomed row boat which is called a skiff in Nova Scotia and New England, is known as a flat in Newfoundland.

My friend, Ted Harper, an Englishman and one of the senior lecturers in the department of Naval Architecture, Newfoundland College of Fisheries, told me that over in the old country, they use a broad sterned, flat bottom boat, which is known as a westway boat. Her name is derived from the fact that she had her origin on the west coast of England. According to Ted's description of this craft, she could easily pass for the Newfoundland flat or the Nova Scotian and New England skiff.

Eight years ago, Ted Harper built a boat in the Fisheries College boat shop. According to traditional designs, it could neither be classed as a flat, skiff, westway boat or dory. For while it was not constructed with a keel, it did not have a flat bottom either which rose upward from the center forming what I would describe as a depressed 'V'. The sides had a moderate outward flare. The bow was sharp somewhat resembling that of a dory, but the stern was broad and only slightly raked.

When he constructed this craft, Ted Harper had the idea that the type would replace the dory as a lifeboat on modern fishing vessels. It appeared to have a length of approximately seventeen feet on top, was well proportioned in breadth and depth and was constructed of lightweight marine plywood which, compared to the dory's bottom of inch plus board and its solid side boards of 11/16 of an inch in thickness, coupled with heavy hardwood timber frames, stern and stempost, would be lighter to row, as well as easier to hoist outboard and inboard than the dory. However, the idea did not catch on. The dory still reposes in the chocks of longliners and draggers.

But, Mr. Harper has no need to feel upset or disappointed that with his new idea he failed to replace the unyielding, stubbornly persistent dory.

Over the years several naval architects and boat builders have attempted to do the same thing. I will set forth a couple of examples. The Gloucester boat building firm of Higgins and Gifford, who gathered world wide renown for turning out its batten seam seine boats, also built fishing dories for a period after setting up its boatshop in 1873, including the dory that Captain 'Centennial' Johnson sailed single-handedly to England in 1876. Also the nineteen-foot dory that the Andrew brothers of Beverly, Massachusetts, crossed the Atlantic in two years later. Their voyage was completed in forty-five days.

This firm patented what they termed an improved fishing dory. In its construction, they emloyed batten seams, the same style they used in building seine boats. In their new dory, they also added a special gunnel rein-forcement. But like Ted Harper's boat, it was doomed to failure. For neither Banks nor shore fishermen would desert their regular reliable dories that had served them so well for such a long period of time.

During the 1890s, the Higgins and Gifford firm apparently gave up building dories altogether, for in their catalogues of that period they referred those interested in procuring dories to the dory building shop of Hiram Lowell and Sons in Amesbury.

Another new venture in dory building was brought forward by Guildford's Limited in Dartmouth, Nova Scotia, when the firm introduced a moulded, fibreglass dory in 1965. Its shape conformed to that of a Shelburne dory and was designed specifically as a six-man lifeboat for modern fishing vessels. In this boat there were no joints or seams to come apart, it was tough and was expected to outlast the three- to six-year lifespan of a wooden dory. In 1965, the wooden dory cost $125.00. The Guildford's built forty during the first year, but they cost three times as much as the traditional wooden dory.

Whether it was the high prices which had to be paid for them or some other cause, they never did replace the old, indefatigable dory. I saw a couple of them in the summer of 1967 on the deck of a Lunenburg fishing vessel that called into St. John's to take on supplies. In the summer of 1968 I saw the same vessel lying alongside a pier on the St. John's waterfront. Her fiberglass boats were missing. They had been replaced by Lunenburg type wooden dories. I inquired from a couple of crewmen as to why this had been done. One of them, a grizzled, middle-aged seaman, grinned and then patted one of the old dories affectionately, I thought, like one would pat the faithful family dog, saying as he did so in accents handed down to him by his German forefathers, "The vooden dory is a werry good boat, a werry good boat in-deed. There had never been inwented or ever will be inwented a craft to take her place as far as general efficiency is concerned."

In any case, the fiberglass dory seems to have disappeared from the waterfront scene entirely, while the wooden dory is still very conspciuous there.

A full-sized Swampscott dory rests on the floor of the Salem, Massachusetts museum.

THE SWAMPSCOTT DORY

If I remember correctly, it was on a summer day in 1917 that the coastal steamer, *Argyle,* delivered to Mr. Cyrus Pitman, the Customs Collector at Lamaline, a boat that differed considerably in style from those which our fishermen had always been used to seeing.

That it was a dory of some sort was plainly visible in her clinker built sides, sharp bow, raking ends, flat bottom and 'V' shaped stern. There the similarity to the ordinary dory ended, for though the sides flared somewhat, they did not rise straight up from the bottom but were rounded in the bilges, like a trapskiff or punt. The bottom was pointed at each end but was much narrower than that of the regular dory, approximately eighteen inches in the center.

In answer to inquiries from curious fishermen, Mr. Pitman proclaimed his new boat to be a swamp-bottom dory. I do not recall that he ever named her place of origin.

Many years later I developed considerable interest in this close relative of the ordinary dory. I learned that the attractive looking boat had become very popular with shore fishermen in the Burin area, also that several men who

The so-called swampbottom dory built in Epworth, Newfoundland —(Courtesy Randell Roberts).

lived in Epworth, about six miles from Burin proper, had been building for many years the craft that Newfoundlanders called a swamp-bottom dory.

I felt reasonably confident that the type did not have its origin in Newfoundland. In talking with my friend Edwin Dicks, a former resident of Burin, now residing in St. John's, I brought up the subject of the swampbottom dory and her birthplace. Mr. Dicks could not enlighten me as to her place of origin, but suggested that I contact Mr. Rendell Roberts of Epworth, who, he said, had been building swamp-bottom dories for several years. I telephoned Mr. Roberts. He informed me that the boat of that type which appeared in the Burin area during the days of World War One was brought in from Nova Scotia. The first one to arrive came in on a Newfoundland Banks fishing vessel that had occasion to call into a Nova Scotian port. The captain took such a fancy to them that he purchased one. Others were imported later and the fishermen of Epworth found them to be ideally suitable for use in shore fishing operations. They were light to row and handled better under sail than the traditional Banks-shore fishing dory. With the introduction of the gasoline engine, however, their days of sail were soon over, for in a short space of time they were all motor equipped. However, Mr. Roberts was unable to tell me if the swamp-bottom was the brainchild of some Nova Scotian or otherwise. So I decided to trail the charming little boat back to her cradle if it were at all possible.

I discovered in Nova Scotia that the swamp-bottom had been in use in that province before the oldest inhabitant of the present day had been born. Of course, I could not talk with everyone in Nova Scotia, but those I did interview possessed the vague idea that the boat originated in the United States, possibly Massachusetts or Connecticut. I might say at this point that I was doing a double take in research, in that I was endeavoring to locate the birth-place of two types of dory. You have already read of my discoveries respecting the origin of the Banks-shore fishing, straight sided variety. Well, regarding the swamp-bottom, the trail eventually led to and terminated in the town of Swampscott, Massachusetts. Enroute in the seaport towns of Marble Head, Salem, Gloucester and other places, I saw dozens of boats that could have been twin sisters of the swamp-bottom acquired by Cyrus Pitman so many years before. Everyone I interviewed on the subject in the various places as I went along, were unanimous on one point. The craft was invented sometime during the latter part of the eighteenth century by a boat builder of Swamp-scott. Recently, I was walking with Mr. Robert Cram, managing owner of the dory factory in Lunenburg. He told me that boat in his home province is and always has been known as the Swampscott dory.

There are a good many miles stretching between Swampscott and Epworth, Newfoundland. Somewhere along the way, the original and rightful name underwent a change or became corrupted with the word bottom, replacing that of scott. However, one thing remains certain, the swampscott and the swamp-bottom are one and the same type of boat. What is in a name anyway? For when all is said and done, it is a boat's stability, coupled with her powers of performance during all varieties of weather, that really counts.

Mr. Rendell Roberts, the dory builder, informed me that in recent years, he, as well as other builders of the Swampscott dory, have been putting in wider bottoms, extending them to two feet in the center in comparison to the eighteen inch widths formerly in use.

Said Mr. Roberts, "The wider bottom not only increases the boat's seaworthy qualities, it also enables her to bear up a much heavier load."

There is hardly any doubt but that the name of this dory was changed after she made her debut on the Newfoundland scene. Newfoundlanders always had a habit of changing names which did not appeal to them. The change from Swampscott to swamp-bottom could have taken place when one of our countrymen, eyeing the boat's narrow bottom for the first time, expressed the opinion that she would swamp easily. Pure speculation, of course, but one guess is as good as another.

MOTOR DORIES AND MOTOR FLATS

One fine August day in 1916, a group of us youngsters were standing on the beach at the western end of Lamaline Harbour. A big, two-masted schooner was anchored offshore. We were watching several of our relatives, who were fishermen, loading their dories with salt bulk fish, then ferrying it out to the vessel. The craft did not belong to our section of the coast and was known as a trader. Her captain, who represented some Newfoundland firm, was paying

A fleet of French motor flats, often erroneously called dories, on the beach at St. Pierre —(Jerry Kelland Photo).

the undreamed of price of $10.00 per quintel for codfish in salt bulk, or as it was taken out of the stages in an unwashed condition.

Made fish, or that which had been washed and dried in the sun brought higher prices. On the other hand, fishermen by selling their fish salt bulk, were eliminating the time and labour it took to wash it, which incidentally, had to be done by hand one fish at a time. Then several days were spent going through the tedious, back-breaking process of getting it sun cured, provided that the sun was obliging enough to show its face. It could be disastrous if it rained for a week or more, for the newly washed fish could become utterly spoiled, resulting in heavy losses to fishermen.

Furthermore, selling their catch salt bulk left the men free to prosecute the fall fishery. Both squid bait and codfish were very plentiful so all hands were reasonably sure of rounding off a good season's work.

While we stood around or played in the sand, and a few seventy to eighty year old, retired fishermen sat around watching their sons and grandsons ferrying salt bulk off to the schooner, an incident occurred which had the effect of causing us youngsters to experience a feeling of considerable alarm. It also caused the younger men to suspend their dory loading and the older men to become visibly excited. For suddenly, there had arisen a terrible ungodly sound, which came from the direction of the harbour entrance. We could observe an object moving toward us, surrounded by a huge cloud of blackish smoke, tinted with blue. The object seemed to be some kind of boat and standing in its center was a figure which, though dimly seen, appeared rather inhuman. As the apparition drew closer, the noise became deafening. It was equal to that which could be made by a giant whacking on an iron door with a sledge hammer. One ancient fisherman leaped to his feet with all the sprightliness of his bygone youth and shouted in my ear, "Here she comes, right out of Hell's fire with the devil heself drivin' of her."

Well, you could imagine the feelings of us kids on hearing that statement. After a brief consultation we decided that, 'The time had come', had come for us to disappear, for we certainly had no desire to make the acquaintance of the gentleman so raucously described by the oldtimer and who was approaching us at an uncomfortable rate of speed.

Before seeking refuge in flight, however, we stood and risked one more glance seaward. We noticed, too, that our fathers were standing their ground. Though while they were staring at the sinister appearing craft and her occupant with utter disbelief, they had not budged an inch, even the old men were moving down toward the water's edge. This display of courage on their part had the effect of expelling our fear to the point where we decided to stay put. A few yards from the beach now, we saw the figure in the boat bend over, then making a quick motion with his hand, the deafening noise instantly ceased as if by magic and the heavy cloud of smoke was quickly whisked away by the smart little breeze that had arisen a short while before.

With the clearance of the smoke, the mysterious craft could be identified as a plain, ordinary dory, her lone occupant, a Frenchman from Saint Pierre, and several of our men knew him, having met him on the fishing grounds several times before. Here I would like to repeat that our close proximity to Saint Pierre caused us to have many contacts with the men from that town. The fishing grounds covered the area between Lamaline and Saint Pierre, where the men of two nations fished side by side freely offering assistance to each other if occasion demanded it. To those Frenchmen were we known as Englishmen, never as Newfoundlanders or Lamaliners. I have heard Frenchmen make such remarks as, "I was talking to an Englishman from Lamaline, today. He told me squid were plentiful down there."

By the same token, we did not call our neighbours from the French islands St. Pierrais or Miquelonais, always they were referred to as Frenchmen.

During the many decades that those two groups of men rubbed dories and crossed trawl lines, I have never known or heard of one solitary incident that caused trouble or ill feeling. Occasionally, I have known our men on coming home from the fishing grounds to remark casually, "A bloody Frenchman sot his trawl across mine today. Of course, it was very foggy and the poor man probably couldn't see my buoys. He apologized when he found out and moved his gear."

I have not the least doubt but that there were occasions also, when French fishermen on returning home passed the same remarks concerning some bloody Englishman. But that was as far as it went. Over such a lengthy period of time, regardless of any differences that might have existed between their mother countries, those two fine groups of men set a glowing example of peaceful co-existance.

Many of them on both sides were totally illiterate, yet they achieved and maintained an ideal of perfect harmony which the greatest brains in today's world are finding it mighty difficult to duplicate.

The Frenchman in the dory spoke English very well. In answer to queries from our men, he explained that the brightly painted hunk of iron bolted to the bottom of his dory, which bristled with rubber tubes, wires and what appeared to be flat topped brass knobs, was a motor engine, an import from France.

"A couple of our fishermen," he continued, "had installed engines in their dories in the summer, as a result they were spared a lot of hard rowing. I had my engine installed yesterday and for a test run I decided to make a trip here."

He explained that the dense smoke, which issued from his exhaust pipe was caused by the fact that he was using kerosene for fuel. The loud noises erupted when his engine backfired. He also informed our men that the invention of a gadget called a muffler was in the process of being perfected and would soon be available. The attachment of this device to the exhaust system would eliminate all excessive noise.

"In addition," he continued, "an improved type of carburetor is on the way. When it is installed it will permit dorymen like me, to burn gasoline instead of kerosene and that eye-stinging smoke will disappear, also."

Anyway, that was our introduction to the motor driven dory. I guess that you cannot blame us children for being a little bit scared, for this thing which none of us had seen before was sprung upon everyone so suddenly. By the end of 1916, most shore fishing dories, particularly those which operated from the Placentia and Fortune Bay settlements were equipped with gasoline driven engines.

Those engines were of the inboard type and came from various manufacturers. With their installation, fishermen who had been used to toiling and sweating at the oars, often being required to force their dories against adverse winds accompanied by short lumpy waves known as lops, could then, as one fisherman put it, sit on a thwart, fold their arms and watch her go.

They soon discovered, however, that even the largest dory then available, which was the five bed, could carry only a comparatively small quantity of fish. For the weight of the engine, coupled with the accessories reduced the boat's freeboard capacity. To combat this problem, dory factories immediately started to build larger dories. Meanwhile, many fishermen who had always built their own row dories soon went to work and built their own motor dories.

At first they turned out the sixteen foot, carrying seven bed of timbers. Sometime later, they increased the size to seventeen foot, using eight or nine bed of timbers. Then came the eighteen foot, equipped with ten bed of timbers. This meant that the eighteen foot bottoms measured nearly as much in length on top as the average trapskiff of that period.

The Saint Pierre French motor dories were equipped with keels during 1915, as was the craft operated by our unexpected French visitor. The keels were necessary to take the propeller shaft and had to be of sufficient depth at the after end, so that the propellor blades could not come in contact with the dory's bottom. Luckily our fishermen escaped having to use that appendage, which had proven itself to be such a cumbersome nuisance to French dorymen, who like so many of our fishermen were accustomed to hauling their dories up each night on a beach or slipway. Men who fished from a wild shore (no harbour) were forced to keep up this practice owing to storms which often suddenly blew up, and the resultant heavy seas would either swamp dories on their collars or cause them to break adrift from moorings and send them reeling ashore to be smashed to splinters on the rocks. Back in those days fishermen guarded their dories well, for there was no generous government around then to replace lost boats, fishing gear or other equipment that happened to be on board them. There was another factor, too, regarding keels. Men who had fished from late boyhood to middle age and elderly manhood in flat bottomed dories entertained a great love and respect for the little boats. Consequently, they could not bear to see them suffering the indignity of being converted into keel boats. It was downright distasteful to them. That was expressing sentiment at its best. But the main, practical objection to the keel was that it would make the task of hauling up a heavy dory a heartbreaking, muscle-tearing chore as the big dories were manned by only two men, who even with the aid of a manually operated capstan, would not find a keeled dory nearly so easy to haul up as when she was flat bottomed. The keel would cause the boat to heel over permitting her side to dig into the sandy beach or stick on a wooden slipway.

The reason our fishermen escaped having to attach the dreaded keels to their dories was that just prior to the arrival of engines in our section of Newfoundland the universal joint had been invented and was in use. In order to make this blessed contrivance workable, a section of the dory's bottom had to be sawn out, this opening taking the shape of the letter 'T'. The long section of the 'T' ran aft from the engine, the length of which was governed by the size of the dory being outfitted. This opening was walled in with wooden sides and roofed over with the same material, forming a tunnel.

A box that had to be of sufficient dimensions to allow the propellor free access to its interior was built into the cross section of the 'T'. A slot was cut into the lower part of the forward end of this box, opening it into the tunnel. Of course, it was essential to have the slot large enough to permit the propellor to be raised and lowered without obstruction. The box, too, was roofed over. Meanwhile, both the tunnel and box were made watertight.

Then the forward end of the propellor shaft was connected to the engine with the universal joint acting as an intermediary, while the after end of the shaft was fitted with the propellor. A second shaft, which was fastened to a coupling encircling the main shaft, ran upwards through a hole previously bored in the box top and was permitted to protrude above it for approximately fifteen inches. The upper end of this shaft was fitted with a stirrup type handle. The box was called a haul up box; the perpendicular shaft, a haul up shaft.

The universal joint enabled a doryman to raise or lower his propellor whenever he had need to do so. For example, when he found it necessary to beach his dory or put her on a slipway, he could haul up his propellor shaft, and it now being out of harm's way or above the lower edge of the dory's bottom, the boat could be hauled up or launched out without fear of causing damage to propellor or shaft. Moroever, if a doryman had occasion to run over an area of shoal water, where he was apprehensive that his propellor, in the down position, might come into contact with the sea bed, again, he could pull his propellor up into the box and with his engine still running, navigate the shallow place in safety. For even with the propellor in such a position, a dory can move ahead at a reasonably fast rate of speed.

With the advent of the longliner and other types of modern fishing vessels, a number of fishermen deserted their motor dories to man these craft. As a result, motor dory building declined. But within the past few years the motor dory has made a comeback. I was talking to an old fisherman from Garnish, Fortune Bay, in November, 1976. He told me that there were more motor dories in operation on the south coast now than ever before. My guess is that like their little sisters, the row dories, they will still be around for a long time yet to come. A spry, hardy fisherman, who has spent sixty of his seventy-one years dory fishing, told me recently that he would not exchange his motor dory for all the longliners in existance.

"That dory," he said, "has been my constant companion for a great number of years. There were times when I was caught out in some mighty rough water but she always brought me home safe and sound."

A number of men who earn their living in avocations far removed from the fisheries, use the motor dory today as a safe dependable pleasure craft. They use her in a number of spare time occupations, which range from taking their wives and children off to some quiet cove for a picnic, to the more pleasurable one of getting their mothers-in-law out for a spot of cod-jigging.

As far as I can learn, the motor dory was never used on the Banks in the same capacity as the row dory. Although I have been informed that Captain John Thornhill, sailing out of Grand Bank, did carry one of these craft to the Banks for a few trips, its purpose being to tow row dories back and forth when tending trawls.

The required number of motor dories could not be successfully accommodated on fishing vessels, for it would be impossible to fit them into one another as in the case of row dories, owing to the fact that the engine house and haul up box caused obstructions.

The beautiful crescent shaped motor boats, at present in use in the Saint Pierre et Miquelon area, are erroneously called dories by many people. A broadside view of them passing by or lying at anchor certainly gives that impression. For at least up to a year ago, they were clinker or lap strake built, having the raking ends and flaring sides of an ordinary dory, although their sheer is considerably more crooked.

The feature which disqualifies these fine craft from being classed as dories, lies in their sterns, for where they join the bottoms, they do not end in a sharp point or true 'V', but range in width from ten to fourteen inches.

They are now and always have been called flats by our south coast fishermen, which is exactly their correct classification. Skiffs, as Newfoundlanders know them, were the large keel boats used in the operation of codtrap fishing.

Before the marine motor was introduced, they were usually twenty-five or twenty-six feet in length. But like the motor dory, they gradually increased in size after the arrival of the engines. I do not know the exact lengths that some of them attained, but I have measured codtrap skiffs, which ranged from thirty to thirty-six feet on top.

I am, of course, referring to the open boat variety, Bow design in those sturdy craft varied. Many of them were plumb stemmed, others carried a raking dory type stem, more were round bowed. They were built off single-sided wooden models that had been carved by hand, in most cases by the men who actually built the larger craft. Their sides were rounded and the deadrise amidships varied according to the fancy of the men who carved the models. Their hulls were not clinkered or lap straked, as is the dory's, but their planks were fastened to the timbers with one plank fitting down on the previous one, edge to edge style, as it is known in Newfoundland, or batten style, as the New Englanders call it. These boats were hardly without exception, beautifully, strongly and expertly built. They sat well in the water, were excellent seaboats and handled easily either empty or loaded during foul weather.

There were and still are in use in many parts of Newfoundland, a boat similar to the trapskiff, only very much smaller. Newfoundlanders called this type a punt. I have been informed that in the Kelligrews area of Conception Bay, these craft are used in two sizes; with the larger being known as a punt, the smaller a rodney.

Boats of this type were used all along the northeast coast of Newfooundland during the heyday of the row boat. In addition to the part they played in the shore fishery, they were carried on Labrador fishing vessels as well, where they served as lifeboats and as secondary boats to codtrap skiffs.

If there are some people today who are classing the dory and the flat as one and the same boat, there was at least one nautical minded lady, in the olden days, who unmistakenly identified the dory and the flat as two distinct types. That lady, also, during the course of her seagoing wanderings evidently met up with a lad who was as amorous as a tomcat in the spring of the year and who possessed just as many ideas. For she wrote:

Oh, I went up in a dory,
And I come down in a flat.
I'm a dacent married woman,
Take yer hand outta that!

CHAPTER SIX

Dory Pick-ups

THE FRENCHMEN WIN A VICTORY

It was June, 1913. The morning was sunny and calm. So the shrill young voice could be plainly heard by everyone in our section of Lamaline Harbour, when it announced, "Mr. Joe Pitman picked up a dandy dory this mornin' when he was out fishin'. He's towin' her into the barisway now."

After that item of news had been delivered, busy men laid down their tools, women deserted their clotheslines and children abandoned their play, with all hands converging on the barrisway waterfront led by that inborn curiosity which is possessed by cats and humans.

Back in 1913, all fish caught on the Banks, in the shore fishery and in the Labrador fishery had to be put under salt to preserve it. Later it was washed and dried on beaches or flakes, preparatory to shipping it to foreign markets. The price paid for fish was low, three dollars per quintal (one hundred and twelve pounds). A quintel of fish could not purchase a barrel of flour which cost five dollars. Like the words in that famous, old Newfoundland folk song, where the author bemoaned the fact that 'Fish is low and flour is high'. Then, if in addition to the low price, fish was also scarce and fishermen made a poor voyage, which often happened, they had to depend on the merchant to carry them over the winter and outfit them again in the spring. The result being, the majority of men ended up deeply in debt and remained that way until the end of their days.

Taking all things into consideration, lucky indeed was the fisherman who picked up a dory, unmanned and without a visible or known owner. If such a boat was identified as belongong to a man in our settlement or to one of a nearby place, it was returned to the owner. If, however, the craft was not recognized as the property of some person who the finder knew, then he obeyed the law as it was propounded by Mr. Cyrus Pitman, Customs Collector, Justice of the Peace and notary public, which was: 'Any person picking up a dory or any other kind of boat would report his find to the

Customs Officer. That official in turn would report it to his superior in St. John's, who would pass it along to the local newspapers. Then at the end of three months if the property was not claimed, it became the possession of the man who picked it up.'

Joe Pitman was a good fisherman and a hard worker and he was lucky on that fine, June day. For when he was rowing out to haul his trawl, he took a shortcut that lay over Diana Rock. He espied a dory resting bottom up and high and dry on the nearby Diana Bar.

The Diana Rock was a small underwater reef, which on more than one occasion had proven that it could be extremely treacherous, even when a very low sea was running. Men had drowned there when broken, boiling waves overtook them as they were over the Rock, filling their dories and capsizing them. The Diana Bar is a sandy, rocky strip which lies exposed with the falling tide.

As the dory did not carry a schooner's name, nor a bow number, she obviously had not broken adrift from a banker. Therefore, she must have drifted across from the French Archipeligo, fourteen miles to the west. In any case, she was quite a welcome prize.

I was present when Joe landed on the south side of the barrisway. After the dory had been hauled up, all the men and boys quickly surrounded her, admiring the boat with glances that probably contained not a little envy. Although that dory was identical in size and shape to hundreds of other French dories, which had been used and observed by our fishermen over the years, if a stranger were present, then he would have imagined from their enthusiastic comments and the noting of the boat's fine points, that it was the first dory they had ever seen. Favorable remarks concerning her sheer, flare, rake and paint scheme poured in from all sides.

"You got one hell of a fine dory there, Joe," observed an aging fisherman.

"A handsome little brute," commented another man.

"By cripes, Joe," ventured a third, "she'll be a sweet little bastard to go gunnin' in next winter."

"What are you goin' to do with her, Joe?" queried one of the men.

"Well," Joe replied, "this is the tenth of June, so if nobody turns up to claim her by the tenth of September, she'll be mine according to the law around here. In the meantime, I'll just moor her off the barrisway there, until the time is up."

The dory swung back and forth on her mooring the remainder of the summer. She had been built with five boards to a side. Whoever owned her had followed the usual custom of French fishermen of that period by painting each individual side board a different colour, which to say the least was very eye catching. By the middle of October nobody had appeared to claim the handsome, little craft, which fact made Joe Pitman her rightful owner. However, Mr. Pitman was destined never to use that dory.

Around the end of October, Joe built a strong, four-legged stand in his garden. Then he had the dory hauled ashore and placed upon the stand, in a capsized position where he lashed her down securely in order to prevent her from being blown away and possibly smashed to pieces when vicious winter storms arrived. A few days later, Joe left for Gloucester, Massachusetts, to engage in the fall and winter fishery.

A week or so following his depature, the little steamer *Saint Pierre* arrived in our harbour from the town of her anchorage. The boat landed a party of eight Frenchmen. They were equipped with shotguns and were accompanied by hunting dogs. The object of the Frenchmen's visit was to take part in the partridge hunting on the nearby barrens, which teemed with birds in those days. It was a sport which had been enjoyed by many residents of Saint Pierre for a number of years before the dory incident. As the group were passing along by the Pitman residence, one of the Frenchmen spotted the dory in the far end of the garden. Evidently calling upon his companions to halt, he commenced pointing to the boat and jabbering excitably. In a few seconds bedlam broke loose, as all eight men got into the act, yelling and screaming, gesticulating and pointing with much shoulder shrugging.

The Pitman property on which the dwelling and the dory were situated was completely surrounded by a picket fence. It could be entered only by a solitary gate, which opened on the road where the Frenchmen were standing. Henry Pitman, younger brother of Joe, who happened to be at home, came out of the house to find out what all the ruckus was about.

Henry Pitman was an imposing figure. He was twenty-four years of age, stood six foot, three inches in his stocking feet and he weighed one hundred and ninety-five pounds, all of it bone and muscle. He had been rowing dories from the time he was twelve, while working with his older brothers at the shore fishery. By the time his brother, Joe, had picked up the dory, five years as a Banks fisherman was behind him also and he was in top physical condition.

When Henry arrived on the scene he remained inside the fence with both powerful arms resting on top of the gate. Probably imagining that he was the man who had picked up the dory, two of the Frenchmen, who could speak English, walked over to him. One of them with some assistance from his friend, told Henry that he owned the dory and demanded that the young fisherman open the gate to permit them to enter the property and take possession of her. Henry explained to them that his brother, not he, had picked up the dory, also that Joe was then in the United States. He pointed out that Joe had left the dory in his care.

"Unless," Henry told them, "you can show me proof that you really own the dory, you will have to wait until my brother returns in the spring, then you can make your claim to him."

On hearing this statement, the two diminutive Frenchmen became very aggressive and for a moment it appeared as if they would rush the gate and attempt to enter the garden by force. However, on taking a second glance at the towering young giant inside, they wisely decided that any such rash action on their part might prove to be extremely unhealthy. So, grumbling and sputtering, they rejoined their fellows who up to this point had remained aloof. Then, as if the whole bloody show had been staged for a movie, who should appear on the scene, but Joseph Benning, Est., Stipendiary Magistrate in and for the said district. Journeying by horse and carriage from this home in Lawn twenty miles to the east, he unwittingly arrived just in time to take part in the dispute over the dory. He was accompanied by Constable Thomas Kelly of the Newfoundland Constabulary. It seemed that the magistrate and the constable had been making a routine visit around their jurisdiction, which they did every two months, to hear complaints and deal with legal matters that required their attention. Magistrate Benning was pushing sixty, his head was crowned by a mass of snow-white hair, in addition he sported a silvery goatee and he bore a remarkable resemblance to General Jan Christian Smutts of South African fame.

Now if some other magistrate had shown up, matters might have ended differently. But as far as those Frenchmen were concerned, Mr. Benning just was not some other magistrate. He was the Lord's answer to a distressed Frenchman's prayer. For the very good reason that over a period of twenty years previous to his being appointed to the position of magistrate, Mr. Benning had conducted a business in the town of Saint Pierre, which business premises had been razed to the ground by fire.

According to the magistrate the destructive fire was caused by one of his hired help. A rather careless fellow in the magistrate's opinion, who after lighting a cigar had, very thoughtlessly, thrown the still burning match into an open barrel of kerosene oil. Shortly after collecting the insurance on his levelled store, he was advised of the death of his elder brother, Henry who for several years had held the position of Stipendiary Magistrate in the St. Lawrence, Lawn, Lamaline jurisdiction. Seeing that he was at a loose end, Joseph Benning promptly applied for the vacant post and received the appointment almost immediately.

That Magistrate Benning was well acquainted with all eight Frenchmen standing outside the Pitman property soon became obvious. No sooner had he alighted from his carriage than they crowded around him, greeting him with a display of effusiveness that almost bordered on violence. As a matter of fact they implanted so many kisses into the center of the magistrate's goatee that for a few moments he appeared as if he were going to become ill. When he finally managed to get the emotional Frenchmen to calm down, he held an earnest conversation with them in their own language. When that talk concluded, Mr. Benning strode over to Henry Pitman and ordered him to open his gate to permit the Frenchmen to enter the garden and take possession of the dory.

"If you disobey an order from me, you will find yourself in serious trouble," concluded the magistrate.

Young Henry Pitman was a law-abiding citizen and as such he had no desire to disobey a legal order from the magistrate. Before he complied with the order, however, he protested to Mr. Benning that the man who laid claim to the dory had produced no positive proof that the dory was his. Furthermore, Henry called the magistrate's attention to the fact that the dory had been in his brother's possession for more than four months while three months, without a claimant, was all that would be required under the law as he understood it.

"Look here, young man," snapped the magistrate, "I know this Frenchman. He is absolutely honest, so when he says that the dory is his property his word is good enough for me."

"Well, it's not good enough for me," chimed in Constable Kelly, who was never known to remain silent when he thought an injustice was being perpetrated.

Leaving his home in Placentia at the age of seventeen, Constable Kelly had gone to the United States. He remained there working in various cities in New England before returning home to join the ranks of the Newfoundland Constabulary. For not only had Mr. Kelly been around, he was the type of individual who would not permit himself to be pushed around. It was an open secret that Magistrate Benning and Constable Kelly did not get along. In this case, Kelly opened with, "Mr. Benning, as far as this matter is concerned, in my opinion you are assuming an authority which you do not legally possess. For to repeat what Mr. Pitman just said, these Frenchmen do not have proof positive that one of them owns the dory. I think you should at least obtain sworn affadavits from the supposed owner and his friends in order that his claim may be supported. For," added the redoutable policeman, "what's to stop any man from claiming he is the owner of a certain piece of property. Is it the usual practise to give it to him on the strength of his word alone? I am sure that such is not the case, Magistrate, and you are fully aware of it."

By the time Kelly had stopped speaking, the magistrate had turned livid with rage.

Dame Fate must have been in a mischievous mood that day for Constable

Kelly's words had scarcely died away when a half dozen large mongrel dogs put in an appearance. Several of those animals were kept by the men of the community, the dogs' main purpose in life to retrieve salt water ducks which had been shot by their masters from dories or from the beach during the winter months. They would plunge into the icy water without the slightest hesitation as a shotgun boomed to bring down a duck, then swimming swiftly out, they would seize the dead bird in their powerful jaws returning it to the dory or the beach. They were commonly called water dogs, a name which suited them very appropriately.

Previous to the arrival of the water dogs on the scene of the dispute over the dory, the purebred hunting dogs of the Frenchmen had been tied to leashes held in the hands of their masters, and had been lying down fast asleep or sitting peacefully idle. When the big mongrels showed up, however, their canine peace was woefully shattered. For with the same lightning speed and energy that they leaped from a dory, but with an added show of ferocity, the water dogs promptly attacked their more refined cousins. Some of the purebreds fought back and a genaral melee followed. The Frenchmen tried valiantly to rescue their beloved hunters from the certain destruction and became so entangled with their dogs' leashes that they went down in a heap amonst the fighting, snarling animals. In the cloud of dust which arose, it was most difficult to distinguish dogs from men. One of the Frenchmen broke out of the tangle, dragging his setter along with him, but just as he was free of the mess, a water dog dived in to attack. The frightened purebred in attempting to escape from the larger adversary, circled the magistrate twice. Now with his distracted master holding tight to the free end of the leash and his fear-crazed setter tugging frantically on the collar end, the double circle of rope tightened around the magistrate's ankles, his heels clicked together, like a soldier's when he snaps to attention. The next moment Mr. Benning's feet were jerked out from under him and he crashed down on his back into the dust of the roadway.

Order was quickly restored when the owners of the local dogs arrived. Wading into the fray, the men seized their animals and dragged them off home where they were securely tied up. Constable Kelly and another man disentangled the magistrate's ankles and helped him to his feet. His worship, with his once immaculate grey suit covered with dust and grime and the dogs' blood was trembling with rage, he yelled at the policeman, "You are the cause of all this. How dare you have the gall to dispute any order that I give."

"Well," replied the undaunted Kelly, calmly, "I still maintain that you are doing wrong if you permit the Frenchmen to trespass on Mr. Pitman's property and remove that dory without a legal court order."

Ignoring Kelly after those remarks, the irate magistrate turned to Henry Pitman.

"You release that dory to her owner immediately, Mr. Pitman," he raged, "or I will take action against you in court."

He omitted to mention just what charge he was placing against the young fisherman.

Maybe Henry Pitman by this time was becoming a little fed up with the dispute or perhaps he decided not to take the chance in offending the magistrate too greatly, for wisely or otherwise, he opened his gate and permitted the Frenchmen to ender the garden and take the dory. Quickly unlashing the boat from her stand, they raised her to their shoulders, still bottom up. Then with four men to a side, they marched through the garden gate and down the road to the waters of the harbour, with their faithful, but mussed up and blood bespattered dogs following at their heels.

As they strode along with their free arms swinging, they sang the 'Marseillaise' at the top of their voices. For they had won a victory and must have reasoned that their national anthem was a very fitting number to sing.

MY FATHER'S GREAT DISAPPOINTMENT

With regard to men picking up stray dories, apart from the practical uses to which they could be put, there was a special thrill experienced by fishermen at receiving such a fine gift from the sea.

There was a time when many hundreds of row dories were used by Newfoundland's shore fishermen when they sallied forth from villages along that great stretch of our south coast, which extends from Bay Bulls to Port aux Basques. Then thousands of dories were nested on the decks of vessels which made up the various Banks fishing fleets.

Dories often snapped their painters and drifted from the bankers or washed overboard and were lost during heavy weather. Shore fishing dories would break free from their moorings or be swept off beaches and slips to be carried out to sea, when blinding storms fretted our shores.

During the heyday of the fishing row dory, there must have been dozens, perhaps hundreds of the little boats drifting around on the North Atlantic. When I was a crewmember of the SS Sable Island, from July 1923 until November, 1924, we picked up several dories which we came across drifting on the Bay of Fundy. We were not exactly wandering around looking out for lost dories, for we were steering straight courses all the time. When the fishermen from our place were out to sea, always they kept a weather eye lifted for stray dories. I guess it was every man's ambition to come across such a boat. To fully understand the reason for harbouring an ambition of that nature, a man would really have to be born in a fishing village and raised as a fisherman.

My father was born and raised in the community of Winterton, formerly called Scilly Cove, Trinity Bay. Like most young men of his time, he did a trick at fishing and spent a few springs at the icefields. But up to the time he was transferred to stations on the Burin Peninsula as a member of the Newfoundland Constabulary, he had never seen a dory. For the favorite boat of Trinity Bay fishermen who lived in such settlements as Winterton and Old Perlican was a round-sided, keeled craft known as the punt. Later as the codtrap was invented and put into popular use, a larger keeled boat commonly called a trapskiff was built to accommodate that type of fishing equipment.

Trinity Bay fishermen had heard of the sharp-nosed, flat-bottomed boat with the 'V' shaped stern, which men of the south coast were using, but the stories they had heard concerning the dory were all bad. This boat they had been told, was built with frail timbers, spaced too far apart. She was cranky and capsized too easily. It was impossible to carry sail on her. In short, they had been led to believe that the dory was a totally unseaworthy, unreliable craft. Consequently, those Trinity Bay fishermen assumed that the south coast fishermen must indeed be crazy to venture out to sea in such a boat. For many, many years, fear of using the dory did not apply to the fishermen of Trinity Bay alone. In Bonavista Bay, as well as in other bays and inlets all along the northeast coast, the little boat was strictly shunned.

Whoever had spread the insidious propaganda in those areas concerning the finest and safest small row boat ever devised by man, must have done his work well, for the fear of the the grudge against the dory persisted there until about twenty-five years ago, when the men of northern Newfoundland commenced to buy schooners from the southern men. As all those vessels were equipped with dories which were thrown in with the bargain. The thrifty northern men could not bring themselves to the point of condemning the dories and casting them ashore to rot or to break them up for firewood. Their very natures rebelled against wasting such free gift items. To advertise the boats for sale would also be a useless venture, there was no market for dories in the localities where they resided. Subsequently, although they feared and disliked the little boats intensely, a determination to make use of them was born. Yes, they decided to learn how to handle those dories, even though there was a possibility that they might be drowned during the process.

In a short space of time the dory was accepted by the men of the north, who operated vessels in the coasting trade. They had learned by using dories that those craft were not as bad as they had been led to believe. They discovered too, that the dory was everything that people had been saying for years, she was not. The result is that today one rarely sees a keel boat resting on the deck

111

of a northern coaster or fishing vessel. The once despised and dreaded dory has replaced them.

A fine, sturdy, courageous, hardworking race of men were our northern Newfoundland fishermen. The greater majority of whom were actively involved with the Labrador fishery, where they voyaged to their fishing destinations along that forbidding coast in schooners or by coastal steamer each spring, reaping the harvest of the sea mainly by the use of codtraps. The men who fished from premises set up on the land were called stationers and those who fished from schooners were known as floaters. They would set their trawls from trapskiffs which measured in length from twenty-eight to thirty-odd feet.

Now, whereas the codtrap fishermen of the south coast used the dory exclusively as the secondary boat to the trapskiff, the Labrador fishermen apparently decided not to push their luck too far. Their choice being the keel boat or the punt. I presume that they felt safer and more at ease in the broad beamed punt when they were setting out or hauling up heavy trap anchors. However, trap anchors could be safely hauled up from a dory, if a man knew how to do it properly.

To attempt to haul up any heavy anchor from that type of boat with the buoy-rope leading over her quarter was inviting disaster. For the weight of the ascending anchor would cause the dory to tip over at such a dangerous angle that two thirds of her bottom would be out of the water. The only thing then that would be required to dump her crew into the ocean and possibly drown them was for a husky windlop to roll up and give the exposed bottom a hearty slap, then she would turn completely over. The safe way to haul up an anchor from the dory is to pass the buoy-rope through the scull hole situated at the top of and in the center of the stern. By using this method, the chances of a dory capsizing are very remote. For pinned by the rope over her stern she will swing end on to whichever way the wind is blowing or the tide is running. She cannot turn broadside and will rise upon the tops of the seas that approach either from the bow or stern while a heavy weight is being raised.

My father, after serving in the Newfoundland Constabulary from October, 1875 to October, 1883, on the handsome salary of $23.00 per month, decided that he had had enough. He was the first member of the force to be stationed in Bay of Islands, the first to be stationed in Bonne Bay, the first to be stationed in Lamaline and the second to be stationed in Burin. Those eight years had been crammed with strenuously overloaded, long hours on duty. He was called upon to enforce laws amongst people who before his arrival were a law unto themselves, and who found it most difficult to understand why this man in a strange appearing garb kept telling them that they were not allowed to do this or that, and who locked them up if they persisted in disobeying what he termed were laws.

My father was stationed in Lamaline when he resigned from the force. He liked the place and decided to settle down there. He built a house, opened a store and got married. The firm of Bowring Brothers in St. John's had advanced him the credit which enabled him to open the store. Later he was appointed as the agent for the firm in connection with the purchasing of salt fish and raw codliver oil. In the meantime, he had acquired some waterfront property and became engaged in the codtrap fishery. Like a number of other men who had learned to handle a dory after having been used to keel boats for several years, my father was completely sold on her. I heard him declare on more than one occasion that in his opinion, the dory was the queen of the small row boats. As time marched on he was no different from other fishermen when it came to keeping a sharp lookout for a drifting, unmanned dory. I suspect that he, like all the others, possessed the hope that some day one would cross his bow.

On a July day in 1910, that hope was realized, for he did pick up a dory. It transpired that he and his crew were busily occupied in hauling a codtrap. Their task had advanced to the point where they were able to see fish swimming around in the trap and could judge that they would have a thirty quintal haul. Suddenly my father glanced up from his work and observed what appeared to be an empty dory, driving down before the smart westerly breeze about a half mile above his trap. At the same time, Thomas Tuff was hauling his trap to the south of him and Thomas Collins was engaged in a similar operation to the north. My father yelled to his men, "Look boys! See that dory drifting down there?"

They looked and saw. My father on glancing over his port and starboard sides, noticed that neither Tuff nor Collins had sighted the dory, for they showed no signs of moving, whereupon he ordered the men to let go the twine, move out and intercept the dory.

"But skipper," protested one of the men, "is we goin' to let all that fish go?"

"Never mind the fish," snapped the old man. "Let's get movin' before those other fellas see the dory and make a try to get her."

Now those were the days when heavy trapskiffs had to be propelled by oars in the hands of men who possessed great strength. So they dumped the twine overboard, shoved off from the trap and the four oarsmen got out their fifteen foot sweeps, then bucking against the breeze they headed towards the oncoming dory. When they neared her, one of the men glanced over his sholder, glimpsed the dory for a second or two, then remarked, "It seems that you're gettin' a real beauty, skipper. She 'pears to be brand new."

When the skiff had come to within a few feet of the dory, my father seized a boathook and ran for'ard.

"Keep the skiff steady, boys," he cautioned.

Then reaching out with the grab, he hooked it into the dory's nosestrap and drew her alongside. She was a fine looking dory and brand new as the man had surmised. Her crooked sheer, high stemhead and brightly painted three-toned sides, branded her as a French type.

Old dad was grinning broadly when he latched onto his prize, but his grin soon turned to a black scowl when he looked into the dory, for there lying down on the bottom, with their arms around each other, and fast asleep, were a young man and woman. That their dreams must have been sweet and pleasant was evidenced by the fact that heavenly smiles were plainly visible on their countenances. My father's disappointment was so great at finding the dory occupied by two living, healthy bodies, that he evened the score when he woke up the slumbering couple by letting out a gigantic roar.

The young man, rather sheepishly explained that he and his girlfriend had decided to spend the weekend down in the main harbour. Then he said, as the wind was blowing fairly towards their intended destination, he had rowed out to the center of the Bight, but did not see the sense in rowing the twelve long miles which separated their home settlement from the harbour to which they were going. So they decided to lie down and take a nap while the friendly breeze did the work. At that point, one of our crewmen remarked, with an evil smirk, "I don't 'low you was napping all the time though."

While the young man was doing his explaining, our codtrap crew were enjoying my father's discomfiture immensely, by making snide remarks and laughing uproariously.

"Ya know, skipper," observed one of the men, "ya could have bought two or three dories from the value of all that fish ye let go."

The skipper answered that brand of logic with two words, uttered with all the venom a disgruntled man could muster, "SHUT UP!"

Old dad really hit the jackpot two weeks later, though. Once again he was busily hauling his codtrap. That time too, the wind was blowing from the west'ard, visibility was rather poor as a fog had rolled in some hours before. One of the crew noticed an American seine boat scant yards away, drifting out of the murk, and heading straight for the trapskiff. As my father hooked her and drew her alongside, he peered into the boat with apprehension. But this time he need not have been worried, for not only was the craft un-manned, she was also unwomanned.

114

CHAPTER SEVEN

The Walsh Tragedy

On August 20, 1935, Captain Patrick Walsh, skipper of the little fishing schooner *Annie Anita* out of Marystown, Newfoundland, had taken on a full baiting and was ready to sail to the Cape St. Mary's fishing grounds.

For two weeks prior to the above date Skipper Paddy, as he was more popularly known, had been trying to locate squid bait, but in this quest he was unsuccessful, as apparently the squid had struck off for other areas. He was therefore, obliged to pick up a baiting of lancelet, commly called lance by Newfoundland fishermen. This diminutive fish which somewhat resembles a female caplin, only it is tinier, is described in one dictionary as a small fish-like animal.

Captain Walsh's widow, Mrs. Lillian Walsh, graciously consented to grant me an interview. Before my visit, I talked with her on the telephone. I informed her that I certainly had no wish to open old wounds as I knew that she must have suffered great mental agony on the blackest day of her life and probably up to the present time (1975) for even the space of forty years does not always heal the type of wounds that were inflicted upon the mind and heart of Lillian Walsh.

I asked Mrs. Walsh if such an interview would in any way upset her, but she quickly assured me that I need have no fear on that score, for she said since that awful day the tragedy has remained with her.

"I think about it in the morning when I wake and it stays with me when I fall asleep at night. I find it comforting to talk about it to anyone who will listen, so your interview in that respect will not upset me."

Mrs. Walsh related that when her husband was ready to sail on the night of the 20th. he came up from his vessel to say goodbye to her, their three daughters and their four-year-old son, who was the baby of the family. She recalls that she was having a cup of tea with her husband when a shower of sand and grass flew up and struck the window where they were sitting. It startled her, she said, and she could not help wondering how sand and grass could blow around on an absolutely windless night. Accompanying her

115

Captain Paddy Walsh as a young
doryman sailing out of Boston —
(Courtesy Mrs. Lillian Walsh).

Lillian (Mrs. Paddy Walsh) just prior
to her marriage to Captain Paddy —
(Courtesy Mrs. Walsh).

Lillian Walsh in her eighty-sixth year, 1976 —(Jocelyn Kelland Photo).

husband to the door a few minutes later, Mrs. Walsh remembered vividly how she had noticed a large cloud, black as ink, hanging in the eastern sky on an otherwise clear night. She gazed at the cloud with apprehension and she was seized with a terrible feeling of impending disaster.

When a fisherman's wife, who has been watching, waiting and worrying for her husband's return from the unpredictable ocean over a period of twenty-five years, it is quite understandable for her to become alarmed at occurrances which a landlubber's wife would not even notice.

Mrs. Walsh called Paddy's attention to the dark cloud and asked him if it portended a coming storm, she also reminded him of the sand and grass which had blown against their window so violently. Did he think it meant ill? Skipper Paddy laughed and assured her that the cloud did not mean a thing for there are always clouds like that floating around. The sand and grass blowing up was caused, in his opinion, by one of those whirlwinds which came along occasionally even during calm weather. Despite her husband's assurances, however, Mrs. Walsh said that such a presentiment of calamity assailed her that she begged Paddy not to set sail that night.

"All right," he said, "if it will give you any comfort, I will not leave port until after daylight."

He then departed to go onboard his schooner.

Captain Patrick Walsh was a fine seaman, a good fisherman and an exceptionally competent skipper. Above all he was a good husband and father. He commenced his career as a fisherman, accompanying his father, when he was only twelve years old. Later as a doryman he fished from various vessels, sailing out of the port of Boston, Massachusetts. Coming back to Newfoundland at the age of twenty-three, his first command was the five-doried banker *Gannet*. For the next twenty-five years he skippered many vessels, usually with success.

Then on the morning of August 21, 1935, Captain Walsh piloted the *Annie Anita* out of Marystown Harbour. It had turned out to be a beautiful, sunny day with just the right amount of wind blowing from the southwest to comfortably fill out the vessel's sails. Captain Paddy's eldest son, James, twenty-three years old, sailed at the same time. He was the skipper of another little schooner, *Mary Bernice*. Seeing the fine weather, the fears which Mrs. Walsh experienced on the previous night disappeared. The storm which she had imagined, the flying sand and grass and the ugly looking cloud had forecasted, did not materialize.

She had worried over the safety of her husband and her eldest son, but what had caused her the greatest worry was the fact that two of her younger sons, Jerome, aged fourteen and Frankie, aged twelve, were accompanying their father to the fishing grounds. The boys had been out on previous occasions and Frankie had always suffered from seasickness. Skipper Paddy had decided to take the little fellows on one more trip before their studies began. Jerome was eager to go, but owing to the miseries he suffered from seasickness, Frankie was probably not so eager. The brave little fellow went along in any case to keep Jerome company.

Mrs. Walsh said that the previous night, her eldest son, James, had dropped in to say goodbye to her shortly after his father had left. Mrs. Walsh requested him to go onboard his father's vessel and bring back his two younger brothers, as she wished for them to sleep at home that night. They could rejoin their father in the morning. James returned a short time later to inform her that he had found the two boys asleep in the after cabin and decided not to disturb them.

The weather continued to be fine throughout the next three days. Then before midday on the 25th., a great storm, which had not been forecast, struck suddenly from out of the northeast. It quickly developed such power, as it swept along over the coasts of Newfoundland, that huge trees which had withstood the buffeting of mighty gales for a hundred years were uprooted. Fishing stages, fences, fish stores and telegraph poles were levelled. Houses were lifted clear of their foundations to crash in ruins. In the areas where winds were raging off shore, roofs were ripped off and sent planing out into the Atlantic never to be seen again.

On August 26th. detailed reports of storm damage which included loss of life, crops and other property filtered into St. John's from magistrates, members of the Newfoundland Constabulary and the customs officers stationed in various places around Newfoundland's coast. The schooner, *Jane and Martha*, captained by James Bruce, reported sighting and passing a western boat type fishing vessel on her beam ends and partly submerged, two miles northwest of the Virgin Rocks. Owing to the vicious wind and gigantic seas, Captain Bruce stated he was unable to get near enough to the craft to identify her, but he had not the least doubt but that her entire crew had perished long before he came upon her.

A message from Trepassey on the southern shore of the Avalon Peninsula, stated that a schooner on her beam ends was observed, drifting around Cape Pine and another which had been dismasted was sighted driving apast Powell's Head. That message also stated that the schooner, *Walter,* out of Kingwell, Placentia Bay, commanded by Captain Boutcher, was missing and it was feared that the captain, his four brothers and another crewman had been lost.

Three motor boats were lost at Witless Bay on the southern shore and Magistrate Green at St. Mary's Bay reported extensive damage to fishing dories, fish flakes and crops.

The schooner, *W.R. Power* was driven ashore at Marystown and the schooner, *Gimball,* from Harbour Buffett was wrecked at Riverhead, St.

Mary's. Both crews landed safely.

From Musgrave Harbour on the northeast coast came a report that the schooner, *Laura Jane,* was driven ashore near that place with the loss of three hundred quintals of fish. From Lamaline came a message stating that four trapskiffs and six dories had been destroyed, also that the Banks fishing schooner *Norman Wareham,* Captain Blandford, drove ashore at a place a few miles east of Lamaline bearing the appropriate name of Wreck Cove. After great difficulty her crew succeeded in reaching land safely.

Six other vessels which hailed from various ports in Placentia Bay were unreported and presumed lost. On the Cape Shore, forty dories and six motor boats were swept away crippling the earning power of her hundred fishermen.

On the afternoon of August 26, a message was received from James Hayden of Petite Forte in Placentia Bay to the effect that one of his crewmen, James Wareham, married, had washed overboard and drowned on the afternoon of the 25th, six miles west of St. Mary's Quays.

Messages reporting destruction by the storm continued to pour in from points as far north as Quirpon on the tip of the Great Northern Peninsula to Port aux Basques and back around to Seldom Come By on the northeast coast. Which meant that the storm was felt country wide. The Portuguese fishing schooner, *Senhora de Saunde,* Captain Jose Pinto, arrived in St. John's from the Grand Bank to land two of his men who had sustained broken legs after the ship had met the full force of the storm. Captain Pinto reported that the gale raged with hurricane force and was the worst that he had experienced in his twenty-five years of Banks fishing.

On the morning of August 27, Captain Phillips of the *S.S. Argyle* and Captain Burgess of the *S.S. Malakoff* were dispatched with instructions to try and locate, pick up and identify wreckage of the vessels and bodies of drowned fishermen. After making a widespread search both steamers returned to St. John's with the *Malakoff's* captain reporting that he had picked up a waterlogged dory marked, *Annie Anita,* the name of Skipper Paddy Walsh's schooner. Neither steamer found anything else. On the afternoon of the 27th., the stern section of a schooner was driven ashore at St. Shotts, on the southern shore. For a while the men of that settlement could not venture near the wreckage because of the big seas which were breaking over it. When the waters receded with the falling of the tide, a group of fishermen boarded the severed section, noting as they went the name, *Annie Anita* painted across the stern. Some of the men knew that the ship had belonged to Captain Paddy Walsh of Marystown.

On entering the cabin, which was still intact, they discovered it to be half filled with sand, which meant that wherever the *Annie Anita* had met her doom the seas must have been breaking right from the bottom of the ocean. When their eyes became more accustomed to the darkness in the little cabin, one of the men espied a small human hand protruding up out of the sand, as if in a final appeal for help. The St. Shotts fishermen dug frantically for there was always hope. They were too late, many hours too late. The body they unearthed was that of Frankie Walsh, the twelve-year-old son of the skipper. The boy who was always plagued by seasickness. Further digging uncovered the body of a man, which the St. Shott's men were sure was the remains of Captain Walsh. Accordingly they dispatched a telegram to Father McGettigan, parish priest at Marystown, the gist of which was: 'Have recovered the bodies of Captain Patrick Walsh and one of his sons in the wreckage of the schooner *Annie Anita*. No sign of other crewmen.'

When the little vessel had sailed from Marystown on August 21, she carried three double dories. Her crew besides the skipper and his two sons were Dominic Walsh, nephew of the captain; John Brinton, also the captain's nephew; Edward Clark, Charles Hanrahan and George Mitchell. With the exception of Dominic Walsh all those men were married with sizable families and they were all from Marystown.

It naturally fell to the lot of Father McGettigan to break the sad news of the drownings to the widows and orphans of the deceased fishermen. Sergeant Larry Dutton (retired) of the Constabulary, who had been stationed at Marystown when the tragedy occurred told me that Father McGettigan had requested that he accompany him on the unnerving and distressing mission. Mr. Dutton said that he had willingly complied. The police officer and the clergyman had become fast friends over the years and both men were well acquainted with the drowned fishermen and their families.

Father McGettigan delivered his sad message on the morning of August 28. Mrs. Walsh said that on learning of the death of her husband and young sons she collapsed in a dead faint. Doctor Harris was called in; after reviving her the doctor placed her under heavy sedation.

Then the following morning she suffered another severe blow, for Father McGettigan arrived at her home again to inform her that the schooner *Mary Bernice* which had been skipped by her eldest son, James, was found floating bottom up in Placentia Bay. Mr. Alberto Wareham of Harbour Buffett had sent out motor boats and the capsized vessel was towed into the harbour of Haystack, where an inspection of her disclosed that she contained no bodies either living or dead.

When the *Mary Bernice* had left Marystown on August 21, she carried two double dories. In addition to her skipper she was crewed by dorymen Dennis Long of Fox Cove, Placentia Bay, married; Dick Hanrahan, married; Michael Farrell, married; and Billy Reid, single, all from Marystown. Mrs. Walsh told me that the *Mary Bernice* was Jimmy's first command. He had sailed for the fishing grounds on that fateful day filled with all the pride, exuberance and enthusiasm a young man could feel having been entrusted to skipper a fishing boat.

The little schooners commanded by the Walshes and several others on the day of the great storm had been dubbed 'western boats' by the fishermen of northern Newfoundland. Those craft differed considerably in design from the northern built vessels. But the reason they had earned the soubriquet, western boats was simply because they were built, owned and captained by men who lived west of St. John's. The materials which went into their construction would be manufactured from timber felled in the deep woods during late fall and winter, by men who later built the vessels. At one time western boats were being built in nearly every harbour from Bay Bulls to Port aux Basques. In most cases the skipper-owner acted as master builder with his crew serving as shipwrights.

Those sturdy, little schooners were good sea boats and excellent carriers. I suspect that in the early days they came from designs which were brought over from England and Ireland by our forefathers. Despite the fact that they carried apple style or buff bows until recent years, they were surprisingly fast under sail. After the turn of the century, the western boat model makers (the vessels were always built from wooden models) commenced to depart from the apple-bowed, flat-bottom plumb-stemmed style to a craft that was much sharper at the bows. They carried considerably more deadrise amidships and a decided overhang for'ard, being patterned after the style of American fishing schooners which appeared between 1900 and 1910. Although the greater number of them were built with the rudder hung on the counter, or rudder-out-of-doors, they were right smart looking little ships, with their green painted hulls, red copper bottoms, white and yellow trims and tanned sails, presenting colourful, beautiful pictures especially when sailing into the eye of a setting sun, which lit them up, enhancing their appearance. Typical 'Red Sails in the Sunset'.

The skippers of western boats were noted sail carriers. Some of them may have been a little reckless on the point. But I never heard of one of them who was downright foolhardy, because they knew exactly what their little vessels could take and acted accordingly. It was when fish happened to be scarce on the home grounds that the daring western boat skippers sailed their little craft to the Grand Banks and other far-flung areas where they performed feats of seamanship that left the crews of Portuguese, French, Spanish fishermen, gazing down from their huge ships, literally gasping and chattering in open admiration. It was of such men that Sir Winston Churchill, Prime Minister of Great Britain during World War Two said, 'Newfoundland fishermen are the finest small boat men in the world.'

The two bodies found in the cabin of the *Annie Anita* were coffined in St. Shotts and sent home to Marystown for burial. On arrival there they were placed in Captain Paddy Walsh's living-room where relatives, friends and neighbours, including the captain's brother positively identified the remains as those of Skipper Paddy and his son, Frankie. But Mrs. Walsh told me that when she gazed upon the faces of the dead (they were not disfigured) she could easily recognize Frank but she knew instantly that the man's body was not that of her husband, and she emphatically said so to the people gathered around her. On hearing her make that statement, her well-meaning relatives gently told her, "Lillian, you have suffered a severe shock and have been under heavy sedation. This man has been positively identified by everyone, including his own brother, as Paddy."

Her reply, she recalls, was, "I don't care what everyone says, surely to God I should be able to recognize my own husband and that man in the casket was the vessel's mate, Thomas Reid. It is definitely not Paddy."

Sergeant Dutton told me that Captain Walsh and Thomas Reid were close relatives and in life they bore a striking resemblance to each other. Mr. Dutton said that he had been well acquainted with both men and after viewing the body of the man, that was about to be interred very shortly, he could have sworn that it was Skipper Paddy Walsh.

Later on the evening following the burial, Mrs. Walsh said that friends and relatives told her she had attended the funeral services both in church and at the graveside, but up to the present day she can not remember being there.

Despite that fact that she was still under sedation, Mrs. Walsh recalls that she spent an entirely sleepless night, following the funeral. Then as daylight approached, she remembered something which, if she could secure the co-operation of Father McGettigan and certain officials of the Government, could prove once and for all if the body of the man interred the day before was that of her husband.

What she remembered was that a few years before, Skipper Paddy had received a severe blow from a pin on the flywheel of an engine he had just started which inflicted a deep gash below the right knee. The wound when it healed left a scar that was prominently visible. In addition she also remembered that while Thomas Reid had been working in Montreal a couple of years previously, he became the victim of an accident which left a scar across his shoulders.

Mrs. Walsh sent for Father McGettigan.

"Father," she said, "I told you all yesterday that the man you buried is not my husband. That poor fellow should be interred in his own family plot, not in ours. For that is where his parents are resting."

She informed Father McGettigan how she had suddenly remembered how both men were victims of accidents and of the resultant scars. She told the priest that in her distressed state of mind she had forgotten those facts prior to the funeral. Mrs. Walsh then told Father McGettigan, "Father, I want you to make the necessary arrangements to have the body exhumed, if you do not, then as soon as I am well enough I will have it exhumed myself!"

Father McGettigan complied with her request and the man who had been buried twenty-four hours earlier was brought up into the light of day once more. The casket was opened and the right trouser leg of the corpse was rolled up. There was no scar on the knee! Next the jacket and shirt were removed from the body. There, plainly visible to all present, was a livid scar that ran from shoulder to shoulder across the back.

Those revelations proved beyond a doubt that Mrs. Walsh had been right. The corpse of the vessel's mate had been interred in the Walsh plot in a grave which had been prepared to receive the remains of Captain Patrick Walsh.

Following the discovery of that rather bizzare, but certainly unintentional mistake the experienced fishermen of Marystown could easily deduce what had actually happened onboard the *Annie Anita,* on the day of the storm. To their logical way of reasoning, Thomas Reid, on that ill-starred morning, had been sick, too sick to go out with his dorymate to tend trawls, with the result that Captain Walsh had taken the second hand's place in the dory. It was quite possible that Skipper Paddy had taken the hardier boy, Jerome, along with him, as, like it has already been stated, Jerome did not suffer from seasickness. It was also very possible that before he left the schooner, the skipper had instructed Thomas Reid to move back to his quarters in the after cabin to keep Frank company and to look after him generally, or Reid might have made his way from the fo'castle to the after cabin on his own initiative as the storm had descended on the vessel in violent fury.

The bodies of Captain Walsh, his son Jerome and the other crew members of the *Annie Anita* were never found. Only one body belonging to Captain James Walsh's vessel was ever recovered. It was identified as that of doryman Richard Hanrahan, when it washed ashore at Spencer's Cove, Placentia Bay.

Today, Mrs. Lillian Walsh is approaching her eighty-eighth year. She is still youthful appearing despite the great sorrow which has burdened her life.

Following her husband's death, this very courageous lady raised her three daughters and her young son without receiving assistance from Government or from any other source.

Her daughters and son are married and have raised families of their own. Mrs. Walsh is justifiably proud of the fact that she is now a great-great-grandmother.

Patrick Walsh, Jr., who was four years old when his father and three brothers died in the savage storm off Cape St. Mary's on that day forty-eight years ago, decided not to look to the sea to earn a living, a decision for which he can hardly be blamed. He is now a stockbroker and is residing in Calgary, Alberta.

CHAPTER EIGHT

The Black Doryman

When we were youngsters we used to play a sport we called 'folleyin' the seas'. About a quarter of a mile above the settlement of Lamaline was a high, pebbly beach that fronted on the open Atlantic. The seaward side of this beach sloped down to a narrow ribbon of sand that led out into the water. The particular section where we played was known as Back-O-The-Beach. The water off this strip of coast was rather shallow for several yards out, so after a big storm with the wind blowing from the west or southwest, the incoming waves would build up to a tremendous height before their tops curled over and they broke, crashing down on the sand to spread far up on the beach behind with vigorous fury.

Our game was to follow each receding wave out until it melted back into the ocean, then race madly to safety ahead of the next comber that rolled in.

While we enjoyed this form of sport immensely, we were also living dangerously, for if we had lost our footing on the return run or if a wave caught up with us and knocked us down, we would have been written off as a complete loss, for the water which was filled with churning sand could smother a person in seconds.

Our mothers were fully aware of what we were doing and they had become extremely worried. They called us all together one day and patiently pointed out just how dangerous 'folleyin' the seas' could be. Aunt Clarie Pitman, mother of the oldest boy in our group, Rod, told us solemnly, "If the seas don't get you, the black doryman will. Some day you'll be sorry, for that black monster comes right up from the bottom of the ocean, so when he lands in that black dory of his, he will catch you and eat you all alive."

Well, once we were out of sight of their concerned faces, we certainly did not take our mothers' advice. In fact, we hilariously ridiculed their words of wisdom and that bit about the black doryman. What did they think we were, little babies to believe such trash?

So we promptly did what we ought not to have done. We went up to the beach and started in 'folleyin' the seas'. The time was on an afternoon during the middle of February. It was an ideal day for the sport. The weather which had been severe up to that time had turned mild. A rather heavy gale had blown in from the west a couple of days previously, which caused big seas to build up. As we raced in and out, we especially enjoyed our contest with the three traditional giant combers, which would put in an appearance with delightful regularity.

All men who have fished from the Newfoundland coast are familiar with those three seas. For a period the waves coming in will be of uniform size. Then three seas, towering away higher than the previous ones will run ashore. After they recede the ocean will become flat as a tennis court for several minutes. Fishermen who have been compelled to land on a wild shore, will keep their craft well outside the breakers when heavy seas are running, until the three gigantic waves have passed and expended their energy. Then during the ensuing lull they will drive for the shore with all their might in order to reach safety before the next waves build up and catch them. On the day in question, we had been following our risky pastime for about an hour. The incoming waves were making so much noise that we could barely hear each other speak.

Suddenly, a hand gripped my arm so tightly that I winced with the pain of it. It was Rod Pitman who had seized my arm so violently. I glanced up and noticed that he was pointing seaward with his free hand, which was shaking like an aspen leaf. He was also jabbering words that were unintelligible to me. Anyway, my gaze followed his outstretched arm and instantly, the sight I beheld gave me the shock of my life, for there riding the waves, about a gunshot off the beach, was a black dory. But that was not the worst of it. The boat was manned by what appeared to me to be a most fearsome looking being. Attired in black from the crown of his head and down as far as I could see, he was standing up in the dory facing us. He held an oar in either hand and was dipping the washes or blades of them up and down into the water. A beard that nearly covered his face which was as black as the soles of the devil's galoshes swept just about down to his waist. His lips were drawn back, exposing in sharp contrast to the rest of him, two rows of snow-white teeth. He also appeared to be very huge and grotesque. The horrible thought occurred to me that if a black doryman really existed in our world or in some other region, either man or devil, then surely this must be he.

Our three companions had eyed our unwelcome visitor shortly after we did and all five of us were standing, staring at the apparition with mouths agape, rooted to the spot with sheer terror. It seemed to me that he had halted offshore to make a leisurely survey of us before deciding as to whether he should eat us one at a time or swallow the whole group in one gigantic gulp. Unfortunately for me, I was the stoutest boy in the bunch, so I became dismayed by the feeling that I would be his top priority, should he decide to partake of his meal one boy at a time.

Abruptly, the creature turned about and sat down, then digging in his oars, he headed for the land at top speed. This action on his part had the effect of breaking the spell which held us so enthralled. For all of a sudden we remembered we had legs and feet. Putting these into instant use, we sped up over the crop of the beach and down the road. On reaching the nearest house, which happened to be where Rod Pitman lived, we raced pell-mell through the back porch and into the kitchen, driving all doors before us. Rod's father, William, enjoyed the liking and respect of everyone. Affectionately he was known as Uncle Billy. When we burst so unceremoniously into his kitchen, it was to find him busily knitting codtrap twine. His wife, Aunt Clarie, was puttering about the stove. Two sturdy fishermen, Charlie Hooper and Albert Purchase, were also seated in the room.

After we had managed to brake to a stop, Rod gasped out to his father, "He's come, skipper, he's come!"

Without pausing in his twine knitting, Uncle Billy calmly enquired, "Who's come, b'ys?"

"The black doryman!" we all shouted in chorous. "He's up there, just like ma said he would," added Rod.

Before the last words were out of Rod's mouth, Charie Hooper and Albert Purchased leaped to their feet and darted out through the door. Then Uncle Billy dropped his twine, got up and hauled on his mackinaw and promptly took off after the other two men. Aunt Clarie, speaking up from her duties, said, "Thought I was tellin' you a pack of lies, didn't you? When I told you that the black doryman would come after you, ha! Now I guess you realize that I knowed what I was talkin' about." Shamefaced and silent, we filed out through the door.

By this time Charlie, Albert and Uncle Billy had disappeared over the crop of the beach to the west and it dawned on us then that the three men had bravely gone up to face the terror which we had run away from and that fact made them number one heroes in our thinking. We held a little confab, then decided to go up to the beach also. I suspect that the inbred curiosity which all humans possess to a greater or lesser degree, coupled with the fact that three able-bodied fishermen now stood between us and the monster, had caused our fear to diminish considerably. So we set out. On reaching the point opposite the place where we had seen the black doryman making his wild dash for the shore, we crept up to the crop of the beach and cautiously peeped over. There a few yards away, we observed our three men hauling the dory up out of the water. When they had placed her well above the high water mark, they stopped. Of the black doryman there was no sign. As we arrived where the men were standing, we heard Unble Bill remark, "Now, where in hell did that Frenchman go to?"

"Frenchman, is that all he is?" asked Rod.

"Yes, b'y," replied Uncle Billy, "a harmless Frenchman, no doubt from the island of Saint Pierre. If he gave you fellas a good fright, you deserved it," finished Uncle Billy, grinning broadly.

We all felt terribly disappointed, for despite a boy's fear of monsters, ghosts and hobgoblins, somehow, he likes to believe they exist. By this time we had noticed also, that the dory was not black as her first appearance showed, for she was actually painted a dark shade of green. Then Charlie Hooper spoke up, "By's, we've got to find that Frenchman and try to discover why he runned away from Saint Pierre. As you know, crossin' that fifteen miles of water in an open dory at this time of year can be very dangerous."

Uncle Billy and Albert agreed. They immediately started to walk up the sloping beach while we trailed along behind. As we went over the crest, there standing on the road on the opposite side of an intervening pond, apparently attempting to converse with another man, Tom Haley, was our black doryman. He was wearing a black sou'wester and a suit of oilskins. Then, of course, there was his long black beard. He did not appear quite so big and tall standing there beside the six foot, powerfully built Tom Haley. In fact, he was only five feet, seven inches in height, but he loomed up a hell of a lot taller than that when he had first appeared off that beach.

That Frenchman had been fully aware of the calm period which invariably occurred after the three giant seas had passed. So when we had discovered his presence, he was simply holding his dory off in the deeper water, waiting for the opportune moment to make a dash for the shore. We were so scared at the time, that we did not even see those three seas coming, but he did and drove hard for the shore when the water levelled off. Of course, he had not been interested in us in the least, but was only attempting to reach safety before the next rollers caught up with him.

Now all hands landed on the horns of a dilemma, for our men could not speak French, neither could the Frenchman speak English, with the result that all the hand gestures, shoulder shruggings and words spoken by both sides simply were a waste of time.

Then Uncle Billy told us, "You fellas run down and get Pierre."

Pierre Souis was a Frenchman who had emigrated to Lamaline from Saint Pierre some thirty years before. He had become a good citizen, an industrious fisherman and a fine and co-operative neighbour in the land of his adoption. Pierre was a short, rotund man with a jolly face and he was always in good humor. We youngsters called him Mr. Pierre or Uncle Pierre, but as he came originally from Bretagne, a province in the northwest of France, he was also

127

known as Mr. Bret.

Shortly after his arrival in Lamaline, he had married one of the local widows. She was the owner of a dwelling and other buildings, besides a sizable piece of land, a dory and fishing gear that had been used by her former husband. The couple were thrifty as well as hard working. They had no children. So that by the time the black doryman arrived on our beach, Pierre and his wife were very comfortably well off.

When Pierre arrived to where the strange Frenchman was, they held an earnest and rather lengthy conversation in their native tongue. At its conclusion, Pierre explained to us that the man's name was Andre Bouchard and he was only twenty-two years old. He informed Pierre that he had come to Saint Pierre from St. Malo, a seaport town in France, six months before, where he had apprenticed himself out to a merchant there. The merchant had treated him very shabbily, he said, keeping him working extra long hours, with only half enough food to eat and equipping him with inadequate clothing. He had become obsessed with the urge to escape to the coast of Newfoundland and take his chances from there. He informed Pierre that sometime before midnight on the evening previous to his arrival at Lamaline, he had slipped away from his sleeping quarters, but when he reached for his outer clothing which the merchant had always insisted that he should deposit in the hall outside his bedroom door, he discovered, to his dismay, that they were missing. The wily merchant must have suspected that he would sometime attempt to escape, and removed the garments.

In continuing his story, he related how he had crept out of the house clad only in his underwear with his feet totally bare. He entered a shed a short distance from the dwelling where he found a suit of blue denims and an old pair of sabots. Donning the denims and slipping his feet into the wooden shoes, he made his way to the waterfront. In a fishing stage, he located the sou'wester and the oilskins. Pulling these over the denims, he boarded the first dory he found that was equipped with oars, tholepins and scoop. Slipping as quietly as he was able out of the harbour, he rowed steadily eastward all through the night and into the afternoon of the following day, until he had appeared before us off the Back-O-The-Beach, unwittingly spoiling our fun of 'folleyin' the seas'.

He was a very fortunate young man on that February day, for although the wind was blowing against him during his long row, it was very light and did not hamper him too greatly. In addition, the weather had remained very mild, unusual indeed for that time of the year. If it had turned frostly, his mittenless hands and sockless feet encased only in sabots, would have become frozen solid in a matter of minutes. Therefore, it is not too difficult to imagine what his fate would have been had the weather turned cold.

Mr. Pierre very kindly and generously took complete charge of Andre Bouchard. First, he conducted him to his new home and had his wife furnish him with a much needed meal. Next, he took him over to a store and bought him a complete new outfit of clothing, which included two suits of underwear, two heavy shirts, several pairs of woolen socks, a pair of woolen mitts, a winter cap, a mackinaw and a pair of thigh-length rubber boots. In doing so, the shrewd Uncle Pierre foresaw a way of turning that investment back towards himself, for he said, "As I have no sons of my own, I have decided to adopt this young fisherman. As I am getting along in years, he will be able to relieve me of much of the burden of hard work."

Unfortunately for Mr. Pierre, young Bouchard apparently had a few ideas of his own, for he did not content himself to work hard for very long for the man who had adopted him, not was he satisfied to take the place of the sons which Pierre and his wife never had. Pierre Souis was an early riser, both in winter and summer. At four o'clock five days after the young Frenchman's arrival, the old man called out to him to get up. After repeating the call several times without receiving any response, he climbed the stairs and entered Bouchard's room to discover that the bed had not been slept in. The black doryman had vanished.

Two years later it was learned that he had made his way to Burin where he had joined a schooner that was loaded with salt cod, destined for some foreign market. When Bouchard arrived at the wharf where the vessel was lying, he made the discovery, somehow, that she needed one more crew member. He applied for the berth and the captain joyfully accepted him, then cast off his lines and promptly set sail. Our black doryman was never heard from again.

Uncle Pierre's comments when learned of his loss were, "After all de tings I do for dat Frenchman, he go off and leave me like dat. I tell you, he will regret it one day."

CHAPTER NINE

On The Banks And Ashore

The Banks are a large submarine plateau, which follows the United States coast up to New England then skirts off the shores of Nova Scotia and Newfoundland. They are the supposed accumulation of deposits of rocks, gravel and sand which have been brought down, adhering to enormous masses of ice pushed along by the Arctic current, where here is met by the warm waters of the Gulf Stream. Natually, the ice on coming in contact with these warm waters, melts with a certain degree of rapidity thereby releasing the rocks, gravel and sand, to spread over the ocean's floor. After surveys of the Banks were made in more recent times, however, the opinion was voiced that it is probable that this plateau at a very remote period formed a part of the island of Newfoundland, which has since been rubbed away by continuous action by ice, over the centuries, until it has assumed the form of these submarine islands.

The meeting of the unequally heated waters of the Gulf Stream and Arctic current also has the effect of producing the fogs which have plagued Banks fishermen for nearly five centuries.

The Great or Grand Bank which lies approximately one hundred and fifty miles off the southeast tip of Newfoundland covers an area of thirty-six thousand miles and was one of the world's most productive fishing grounds. In recent years, however, fish stocks have been seriously depleted due to over-fishing by foreign fleets. The depth over the Grand Bank varies from twenty-five to ninety-five fathoms. The warm Gulf Stream washes its southern side where it falls in a rapid slope to three thousand, one hundred and thirty fathoms.

Outer Bank, or Flemish Cap, appears to be a continuation of the Grand Bank, at a lower level. The soundings on it range from one hundred to one hundred and sixty fathoms.

Saint Pierre Bank, off southern Newfoundland, has depths of from fifteen to twenty fathoms. Other areas in the great chain of Banks are Green Bank, Whale Bank, Mizzen Bank, Banquereau (Quero), Virgin Rocks, Burgeo

Bank, Rose Blanche Bank, Brown's Bank, La Havre Bank, George's Bank, etc.

The fisheries on the Banks were an object of contention for centuries. France, Spain and England quarrelled for their possession from the time of their discovery, until the Treaty of Utrecht in 1713. Even today Canada and the United States are contending for the fishing rights on certain Banks.

The total measurements of the Banks cover more than seventy-five thousand square miles. Owing to the fact that they teemed with fish in former times, they contributed a great deal towards the development of North America.

An inscription appears on a huge granite boulder in Fort State Park in Gloucester, Massachusetts, which gives a description of the birth of that great fishing port. The inscription reads: 'On this site in 1623, a company of fishermen and farmers from Dorchester, England, under the direction of Reverend John White, founded this Massachusetts Bay Colony. From that time the fisheries, the oldest industry in the Commonwealth, have been uninterruptedly pursued from this port. Here in 1625, Governor Roger Conant, by wise diplomacy, averted bloodshed between contending factions, one led by Miles Standish of Plymouth, the other by Captain Hewes.'

In all probability, Governor Conant settled, by arbitration, North America's first dispute.

Banks fishing was often proclaimed to be the sea's most dangerous occupation. One has to agree with that opinion for in its hazardous, difficult operation, there were such a variety of ways in which men could suffer injury and death. There was a time when Banks fishing took a greater toll in human lives than did war. For example, during the American Civil War, one hundred and forty-two men from the Gloucester area died in battle, while within the same period and from the same area, three hundred and seven men were lost on the Banks. Back in 1862, during the great gale of February 24, one hundred and twenty Gloucester fishermen lost their lives in a single night. Thirty-one Gloucester fishing vessels were lost at sea during 1873, taking with them one hundred and seventy-four fishermen. Twenty-nine Gloucester fishing vessels went to the bottom in 1879; they carried two hundred and forty-nine men to their deaths. Here it can be observed that between 1873 and 1879, fishing schooners had been increasing in size, consequently, they were being manned by larger crews which obviously accounts for the exceeding increase in the number of casualties occurring between those two dates.

Covering the period between 1800 and 1897, Gloucester lost two hundred and sixty of its fishing vessels with one thousand, six hundred and fourteen men. Since the founding of Gloucester in 1623, ten thousand of its fishermen have been lost at sea.

In addition to the men who died during fishing operations, a large number of Gloucester vessels were lost with all hands while voyaging to and from Newfoundland ports in connection with picking up herring cargoes. As those voyages took place during late fall and winter, the period when severe storms very often occurred, it was a hazardous and gruelling occupation in the days of the all-sail schooners.

Banks dorymen, in the ordinary course of every working day, were called upon to perform many strenuous tasks, during the process of which they were forced to endure a variety of hardships that were pregnant with potential injuries and death-dealing dangers. Then, besides going astray from vessels and becoming lost forever or suffering mutilation from frostbite or some other cause, men were washed overboard to disappear when giant waves swept across decks. Others were torn from bowsprits when schooners nose-dived during savage weather whilst they were busy at stowing jibs. In fact, such a large number of men were drowned from that protruding spar, that Banks fishermen had a mighty good reason for saddling the bowsprit with the name, 'widow maker'.

Other men were belted to their deaths by wildly flailing booms and slatting sails. Many fishermen were killed by heavy gear falling upon them from aloft. A large number died whilst they were attempting to leave vessels that had been grounded on offshore rocks and shoals, as their stricken craft was being pounded to splinters by ponderous waves. Overloaded dories and capsized dories contributed also to the list of tragedies. Then there have been cases where schooners, in running down their own dories have caused loss of life.

In the spring of 1943, the banker *L.A. Dunton* out of Grand Bank was fishing on Quero Bank in command of Captain George Follett. The vessel carried twelve dories. One morning Captain Follett made a flying set, putting over eleven dories.In one of these were the dorymen, Horatio Brown and Clayton West. When the *Dunton* commenced to pick up her dories and came up to the one manned by Brown and West, she rose high on a towering lop, and, coming down, the heavy vessel collided with the dory, capsizing her. Both men were tossed out of the boat. Quickly launching the spare or submarine dory, the cook and another crewmember were successful in rescuing West. But Brown sank before they could reach him and was never seen again.

A few days earlier, those two young men had walked from their homes in Garnish to Grand Bank, a distance of twenty miles, through blustery weather and waist-deep snow. They had made that difficult trek so as Captain Follett would not have to sail one dorycrew short.

The spare dory carried by Banks fishing vessels during the second World War was commonly referred to as the submarine dory. The reason for so naming her was, if all the other dories were away from the vessel, setting or underrunning trawls and an enemy submarine surfaced nearby with her commander ordering the banker's skipper to abandon ship as he intended to sink her, that spare dory would mean the difference between life and death for the schooner's captain, cook, engineer and others who happened to be onboard. Otherwise, some enemy submarine commanders were not too particular when they did not want to waste the time to take on prisoners, who could not row over to the raider, for theirs was a hit and run game.

In August, 1938, the Gloucester banker, *Adventure* under the command of Captain Frank Mitchell ran down one of her own dories off Shelburne. The dory was crewed by Theodore Babine and Raymond Hubbard. Hubbard was rescued, Babine drowned.

On December 9, 1904, Isaac Olsen and Carl Danielson were drowned when their dory was rammed by their own schooner, *Niagara,* commanded by Captain Gus Swinson, of the Gloucester Fleet. The *Niagara's* dories were all out tending trawls. The vessel was jogging about when a sudden snow squal came on, which cut visibility to nil. While this was in progress, the vessel crashed into the dory capsizing it, spilling both men into the water. Greatly encumbered by the heavy clothing underneath their oilskins, they were unable to grasp the schooner's bobstay, a stay which leads from a vessel's stempost to near the tip of her bowsprit. They soon sank from sight. The unfortunate men were natives of Finland.

These are but three examples of the many times that fishermen were drowned under similar circumstances.

One young man was saved from a watery grave, indirectly, by the activity of a rat, that despicable rodent which so often was such a pest to fishermen. During the winter months, particularly, he would gnaw his way into buildings where fishing gear and dried salt cod were stored. He seemed to select cod-traps especially as a target for malicious damage; while he would eat some of the salt fish, he certainly destroyed and made unfit for human consumption a much greater quantity than he consumed. Consequently, he was exterminated at every opportunity that presented itself. However, after the following incident occured, one fisherman, Skipper John Cousens of Lamaline, not only refused to kill rats himself but he strove to his utmost to prevent others from doing so. It was known also that he entertained such a kindly regard for the rodents that he actually fed them, depositing the food near places where he knew them to be hiding out.

Just before the turn of the present century, Skipper Cousens was the owner and operator of a small western boat type fishing craft. Only sixteen tons, she carried one double dory. Taking on a herring baiting Cousens sailed to the fishing ground known as the Offer Shoal which is situated between Lamaline and the islands of Saint Pierre et Miquelon. His two dorymen were his son

Robert and a young man named Denis Haley. The skipper anchored his little craft on the shoal shortly before noon on the second day of April, 1899.

He sent the two youths out in the dory to set their trawl, while he stayed onboard to cook the midday meal. The two dorymen doused their first anchor and buoy a hundred fathoms from the little schooner, running out the trawl, they dropped the second anchor. Which meant that they were approximately two miles away from the parent craft. Before they had completed the task, the wind which was blowing from the northwest, had freshened considerably and whitecaps were appearing all around. Coming up from the hot fo'castle where he had been busy with his cooking, the skipper noticed that the two men were returning to the vessel. He instantly became very concerned for their safety, for he observed that they were running the dory under full sail. If they had been coming along under a goose wing, he would not have felt so worried for he knew that the wind was blowing too strongly for the dory to be carrying full sail.

Then when the little craft had reached a point a quarter of a mile from the vessel, that which he had been dreading occurred with dramatic suddenness. The dory capsized, turning completely bottom up. Both her crewmen disappeared from Cousen's sight into the chill April water. Directly he saw the mishap occur, the skipper sprang into action. Seizing an axe that was normally used for chopping firewood, which was stuck in a chopping block near the fo'castle companionway, he severed the anchor cable with a single blow. Then by superhuman strength he contrived to hoist the foresail and jib on the schooner. Running aft, he grabbed the tiller, brought the craft about and bore away towards the overturned dory. It was then that he saw to his dismay that there was only one man clinging to her bottom. When he got closer, he could recognize the lone figure as that of his son. The skipper also noticed that the young fellow appeared to be hanging onto the slippery bottom with one hand. Puzzled as to how he could be maintaining his hold on such a surface, as the dory was not equipped with either a plug or bottom strips, but thankful that his son was managing what should have been impossible, the skipper shouted out to him to stretch out his free hand towards the approaching vessel. Effecting the rescue would be an extremely hazardous feat, demanding split second timing on the part of Skipper Cousens.

When the western boat neared the dory, Cousens luffed her up in order to bring her broadside on to the overturned craft. This manoeuvre also had the effect of spilling the wind out of the vessel's sails, which slowed her up considerably. When she was almost touching the dory, the skipper made his move: letting go his hold on the tiller stick, he reached out a powerful hand and grasping his son's outstretched wrist, he yanked him off the bottom of the dory and in on the deck of the bigger boat. When the young doryman had changed his wet clothing and had partaken of warm food and drink, he was none the worse for his harrowing experience. Skipper Cousens did not bother to attempt to recover his dory. Instead he cruised about for nearly two hours in the hope that by some miracle Haley had survived and that he would sight him and pick him up. It was a vain hope, however, his son's dorymate was never seen again. The following afternoon, Cousen's dory was picked up by a coal laden schooner, homeward bound from North Sydney. The craft was returned to Captain Cousens.

Young Cousens satisfied his father's curiosity as to how he had managed to cling to the capsized dory for such a long time. He explained that as the little boat was overturned, he was thrown into the water and went under. As he came back to the surface he made a desperate attempt to secure a hand hold on the slippery bottom, but all that he had accomplished was to peel the skin off his fingernails down to the quick. Then as he was lifted high on the crest of a wave, he noticed a saucer-like depression in the dory's bottom on the side nearest to him. He had only time enough to make but a flashing survey of the hollow when he went back into the trough of the sea. But he could tell that the board it was in must be wafer thin at that point. As he rose up on the top of the next wave, he, with the frenzied strength of a man about to die, drove his clenched fish downward with all the power he could muster. His luck was in, for his fist crashed completely through the weakened board. This enabled him to clutch the inside of the bottom and hang on. But for that, his father could not possibly have arrived there in time to save him.

Upon making an examination of the hole in the dory's bottom board, Captain Cousens and others had very little difficulty in deciding how it happened to be there.

With the conclusion of the fishing season the previous fall, Cousens had housed his dory in a shed on the beach. That boat remained there until he was ready to resume fishing in the spring. Stored in that shed also was a quantity of dried salt codfish and caplin, Evidently, on scenting the fish a hungry rat, in attempting to gain access to it, had gnawed through the floor boards right underneath the spot where the dory was resting. When he came to the boat's bottom, he must have kept on gnawing. Then when he had chewed to within an eighth of an inch of a breakthrough, he may have been scared away by the approach of some human or an animal. In either case, it was extremely fortunate for Robert Cousens that the rodent had failed to complete the job. If such had been the case, the hole would have been discovered when the dory was launched, resulting in the damaged board being replaced, which in turn would have caused the doryman's death.

Following the incident which nearly claimed his life, Robert Cousens was always referred to as the man who was saved by a rat. Looking at it from a father's point of view, one can hardly condemn Captain Cousens for feeding as well as providing protection to the pesky rodents.

Many daring rescues embodying acts of heroism took place on the fishing Banks, the rescuers often saving a shipmate when wind and sea conditions were most unfavourable, but always they performed those outstandingly brave deeds without thought of personal safety. In February, 1930, the schooner *Lenora Silveria* out of Gloucester, commanded by Captain John McInnis, was anchored on Green Bank during a raging gale, when a giant sea came over the vessel's rail sweeping Jimmy Dober, one of the crew, overboard. Tom Cove, a shipmate, immediately jumped into the sea with a buoyline tied to his waist. Two hundred and fifty fathoms of line ran out before Cove reached Dober, who fortunately was kept afloat by the air in his oilskins. He had been unable to help himself as he was knocked unconscious when he went over the side. Despite the heavy seas, the chilling wind and the bitterly cold water, Cove managed to hold on to Dober until they were hauled back to the schooner. Cove was almost cut in two by the line during the process. Great difficulty was experienced in getting them in over the vessel's rail.

Old time Gloucester still talk of that brave deed and of the remarkable fact that Cove was a small man, yet in that very agitated water he had contrived to hang on to Dober who was over six feet tall and heavy.

Another incident displaying outstanding courage and a total disregard for personal safety occurred when the Gloucester schooner, *Ingomar* was fishing in Quero Bank on April 23, 1923. While Christopher Neilson and Augustus Johnson were being lowered in their dory into the sea, a big comber struck the dory hurling Neilson overboard into the icy water. Weighted down by his rubber boots, heavy clothing and oilskins, the water-sogged man was helpless. The vessel's skipper, Captain Carl Olsen, was near the wheel when he observed what had occurred. Without an instant's hesitation he dove in after Neilson. Captain Olsen was a powerful swimmer. He managed to grab one of the floating dory oars and shove it within the grasp of Neilson. Then with the captain holding one end of the oar and Neilson trailing behind him on the other end, the hardy skipper swam back to the schooner where both were quickly pulled onboard.

Captain Olsen was awarded the William Harding medal for bravery by the Massachusetts Humane Society. He died in Gloucester in May, 1965. The man who he had so courageously saved from drowning outlived his skipper by seven years. He passed away in Gloucester in July, 1972, at the very wonderful age of one hundred and six.

The port of Gloucester was built entirely from the proceeds of its fisheries. The schooners were commanded and crewed by men of iron constitutions and dauntless courage. Actually the justifiably, much lauded Gloucester fishermen, with very few exceptions were not native born Gloucestermen at all, for during the early nineteen century they were immigrants from Newfoundland and Nova Scotia with a sprinkling of them coming from other New England states. Further along in the 1800s, newcomers arrived from Ireland, Scotland and Scandinavia, with an occasional Englishman turning up also. Portuguese immigrants joined the ranks of Gloucester fishermen. Then, in the 1900s they were followed by numerous Italians. A few Finns and Russians also put in an appearance.

But regardless of where they first saw the light, Gloucester welcomed them warmly, with open arms, she sheltered them, employed them, encouraged them, outfitted them and when the time was ripe, she promoted those who had the desire for promotion and the ability to assume command, from doryman to captain. They became good reliable citizens in the land of their adoption. Gloucester depended upon their hardihood, courage and resourcefulness and they never let her down. For as long as they had a single breath left to issue a command on the ice-covered, heaving, plunging deck with sails slatting and cracking, after being rent to tatters by vicious winds, or to go in a tiny wave-harassed dory through sleet and snow whipped along by winter gales or groping their way blindly through the foggy breezes of summer; they carried on. In the truest sense of the word, they became Gloucester fishermen and proud they were indeed to be honored with that title, for the fame of Gloucester fishermen spread far and wide.

From Newfoundland came such noted fishing skippers as Captain Benjamin Pine, Captain Joseph Cusick, Captain Wallace Parsons, Captain Felix Hogan, Captain Joquim Murray, Captain Jack Carroll and the most famous of them all, Captain Solomon Jacobs, uncrowned king of the Gloucester mackerel fleet, whose name and exploits were known around the globe. He was always referred to by Newfoundlanders as the 'Great Sol'. That by the way is only naming a few of our great captains.

Then we should not overlook Captain Leo Hynes, a smart and capable skipper fishing out of Boston, who was one of the many and the last captain to command the able, handsome schooner, *Adventure*. In this great vessel, Captain Hynes broke all previous landing records in the fisheries. During the month of January, 1938, he landed seven trips and stocked $13,000. Each of the crew shared $308.00. His total stock for 1940 was $132,000, with a share of $2,900 per man. The total stock for 1943, which proved to be his greatest, was $364,000. Captain Hynes stated that his poorest stock after taking command of the *Adventure* was $96,000. His total stock for the nineteen years that he skippered this schooner was 3.5 million dollars, which amount is believed to be the most money made by any type of vessel along the entire Atlantic coast.

The career of the *Adventure* as a dory trawler came to an end in 1954. She was the very last vessel of a glorious era. It must have been a sad day indeed for Captain Leo Hynes when he was forced to order the trawls taken in and coiled into their tubs for the last time and to watch as his twelve dories were being nested for the final run to port. The *Adventure* had held more than her own against modern fishing vessels and the more sophisticated methods of fishing. The schooner, herself, could have carried on, but her crew were aging and wearing out and no young men could be found to take their places. To Captain Leo Hynes of Newfoundland goes the honour of being the last dory trawling skipper to sail out of an American port.

Captain Jeffrey Thomas, renowned Gloucester skipper is shown in 1910. Twenty-four years later Thomas died at the wheel of his schooner off Gloucester — (Courtesy Gordon Thomas).

From Nova Scotia came such great Gloucester fishing skippers as Captain Jeffery Thomas; his brothers, Captains William, John and Peter, Captain Lewis Wharton; his brother, Captain Bob, Captains Alden Geele, Bob Porper and Elroy Prior. There were many others, of course, whose birthplace was in Nova Scotia. In addition to the skippers, thousands of men from Newfoundland and Nova Scotia, down through the years served on Gloucester fishing vessels as mates, cooks and dorymen. A large number of those sailed out never to return and their bones lie scattered along the ocean's floor from the Grand Bank to Georges Bank.

The skippers of Banks fishing schooners were saddled with a heavy responsibility. The vessels' owners expected them to bring in fish regardless of whatever unfavourable conditions they may encounter. In the meantime, depending on the size of the schooner, the captains were responsible for the lives of from twelve to twenty-six men. A skipper owned the concrete authority while on outward and inward bound trips to keep his craft under full sail during great wind pressure until her spars may snap off, like frozen carrots or her top hamper came tumbling down to sweep men overboard to drown or to kill them on deck. He had the power to order men aloft to stow gaff topsails while storm devils strove to tear them loose from the ratlines and crosstrees. He could order them out on plunging bowsprits during a whistling gale to take in and stow jibs. On the Banks, he alone could make the final decision as to whether the dories went overboard or remained nested, when ugly looking storm clouds were hovering on the horizon. His mate or second hand could offer him advice, but he was not obliged to accept it. In short, the fate of his crew rested on his judgement from the time his banker left port until she returned.

Years ago a story was going the rounds concerning one Newfoundland skipper, to the effect that when his second hand suggested to him that it was too windy to send the dories out, he would order the men to hoist over one dory, he would instruct them to tie the end of a hundred and twenty fathom coil of rope to the nose strap of the boat. Then getting onboard the little craft he ordered the men to slack him back astern of the vessel until the whole length of rope was out. After which, he would ship his oars and attempt to row back to the schooner. If he made it the dories were sent out, on the other hand, if he was unable to row against the wind and had to be pulled back to the vessel by the crew hauling on the long rope, the dories remained nested. That captain was a tall, powerfully built man, noted for his great strength and powers of endurance. On the days that he reached the schooner without aid, he would remark, "Surely, if I could row back cross-handed against that little breeze, two men should not find it too difficult. Toss 'em (dories) overboard mate."

During the days of the salt banker, most skippers questing for cod drove both their schooners and their dorymen hard, many of them embodied in their orders a raw brand of language that would scarcely qualify them to be sent amongst heathens as missionaries. I had often listened with rapt attention as old dorymen told of certain captains they had sailed with, who after they had taken on bait and their vessels lay becalmed would rage and fume at the delay, then would throw money overboard, using the vilest language at their command to call upon the Almighty to send them the worth of that money in wind so as they could get under weight again.

I have heard them telling of young men who had been raised in strict

Christian homes, after making their first trip to the Banks with such skippers, absolutely refusing to voyage with them again, for fear that certain disaster would overtake them because of their captain's wickedness. On the other hand, I personally knew skippers who were religious enough to insist on grace being said in the fo'castle before each meal. They would also frown upon and chastise crewmen who they heard using obscene and profane language onboard their vessels, because they did not indulge in using such language themselves.

Then there was that delightful, old Newfoundland skipper, who after his vessel ceased fishing operations and was tied up for the winter, would live it up going around drinking and carousing. But when spring rolled around again, and his banker was being made ready for sea, he promptly went to the Salvation Army Citadel, knelt before the mercy seat and got saved. All through the summer he would remain an object of piety and reform. Woe betide the doryman he found drinking or heard swearing onboard his schooner. However, when the old man's craft was snugly moored for the winter once more, he would backslide from the Salvation Army, uncork his bottle and go on a winter's binge. Then with the advent of spring, he would smash the remaining bottles, polish up his halo and rejoin the Army. That old guy was certainly taking no chances in offending the good Lord whilst he was out on the briny deep.

To come back to the tough acting skippers, despite their rough exteriors, I have never heard of one who was not soft-hearted on certain occasions, which makes you suspect that the tough attitude which they frequently displayed did not go too deeply under the skin, but was simply an act to impress people. For there were times when those so-called hard hearted captains would pace the heaving deck like expectant fathers outside a maternity ward. Their countenance visibly portraying concern, when their dorymen were away and bad weather put in an appearance. On such occasions, they would worry themselves to a frazzle until all the dorymen were safely back onboard again.

An example of the agony of mind dory trawling skippers went through and the end result is told in the story of Captain Joseph Rose, master of the banker, *Autauga,* out of Jersey Harbour. Newfoundland.

In March, 1936, Captain Rose anchored on Burgeo Bank. He carried twelve double dories, which means that he also had twenty-four dorymen. Shortly after his arrival on the fishing grounds, one morning broke fine and clear, with a gentle breeze blowing from the southwest. All twelve dories were dispatched out to set trawls. While the task was in progress, the wind veered around from the southwest to the northeast and the sky clouded over. The crew returned to the ship for a mug-up.

But as there was no increase in wind pressure, when the men were ready and as the barometer gave no indication a storm was approaching, Captain Rose instructed them to go out and underrun the gear. They had only been gone long enough to take in a few lines when it came on to blow harder. In a short space of a few minutes, the wind increased to half a gale, worst of all it was accompanied by heavy snow. In addition, the weather turned frosty. Then quickly, an ugly sea commenced to build up. Cut off from sight of his dories by the driving snow, worry descended upon Captain Rose as the storm increased to violence and the waves reached a greater height. With each passing moment, the skipper's worry developed into deep concern, causing him to pace the deck and peer futilely into the thick wall of snow. By the time darkness had descended and not a solitary dory had returned he was gone past the point where he could scrounge up a comforting thought. With the wind tearing at his oilskins and nearly whipping the sou'wester off his head, he kept pacing and peering all through that long, weary storm-ripped night.

His cook brought him up warm drinks and food, urging the skipper to take a rest, but Rose waved him away.

"Dear God, Cooky," he groaned, "with twenty-four men gone, how can I bring myself to rest and eat."

To make matters tougher for the skipper, his own son, who was his second hand, was amongst the missing crewmen. Apart from that, all the others came from Captain Rose's home in Jersey Harbour or from the neighbouring village of Little Bay. Furthermore, they were all related to the skipper as well as to each other. Some of them were married with children.

For twenty-four men to be wiped out in a single night, all residents of two little fishing settlements and all related would constitute a major disaster, because it would affect to a greater or lesser degree, every man, woman and child in both places.

With the coming of dawn the snow ceased falling and the wind power slackened, while the seas had dropped down considerably. By the time the sun came up it would have been safe to go out in a dory. But, the improving weather conditions brought no ease to Captain Rose's mind. He was a former doryman and an experienced Banks fisherman. He knew exactly how much punishment a dory could take. He was convinced that all his men had been drowned, for he was confident that no dory could have lived through the storm of the previous afternoon and night. When the morning became fully clear he could make out four schooners lying to anchor in the distance and to the leeward of him. He then decided to slip his cable and with the aid of the cook, get enough sail on the vessel which would enable him to reach the other craft to enquire as to whether their crews had seen any of his men.

It was a vain hope, but he felt that he just had to do something. Then as he was about to call up the cook to assist him in putting the idea into effect his keen eyes detected dark spots in close proximity to the four schooners. He remained staring at them for a few minutes. They were moving towards him, alright. Racing down to his cabin and seizing a pair of binoculars, he came back upon deck and trained them on the specks. By the aid of the glasses, he could easily make out that they were dories, rowing straight toward his vessel. Hope, which somehow he felt he had no right to expect surged through him. Slowly, carefully, he counted the oncoming dories and was overjoyed to discover they numbered exactly twelve, with two men to a dory.

Nearer and nearer they came, twenty-four stalwarts, rowing hard, bucking against the head wind which was still blowing in husky gusts. A few minutes later, Captain Rose knew that his worries of the past twenty-four hours were over. He could identify the rowers as his own men. At that point Captain Rose did not need anyone to tell him why his dorymen had survived. For he realized then that when the storm had struck down so suddenly, catching the crew in the act of underrunning trawls, they had very wisely decided to run before the wind down to the vessels anchored to the leeward of the *Autauga*, rather than attempt to row back to their own schooner right in the teeth of such a raging blizzard.

With his identification of the oncoming dorymen satisfactorily completed, Captain Rose was beside himself with joy. He ran to the fo'castle companionway and shouted down to the cook, "Come up here, Cooky! The boys are safe, they are coming along close by!"

On hearing the good news, the cook came bounding up, taking the steps in long strides. For a moment or two he gazed at his approaching shipmates, then he turned and was walking aft towards the captain, who was standing by the main rigging twirling his sou'wester in his hand. Suddenly, the cook halted in mid stride and stared at the old man in open-mouthed astonishment, he could scarcely recognize his skipper, who in a short space of twenty-four hours had aged twenty years. For his hair which had been dark brown the day before was now snow white!

During the days of dory trawling on the Banks, fifty or sixty years ago, there was no radio to send out weather forecasts. A fishing skipper could only cast anxious and fearful glances at the barometer hanging on his cabin wall. That instrument commonly called 'the glass' was fairly reliable, yet there were occasions when it forecast a storm which did not materialize and often it did not forecast a storm which appeared, as had happened in the case of Captain Joseph Rose. The weather on the Banks has been proven as very unpredictable. It could change with startling suddenness. That dreaded chop of wind changing rapidly from one point to another would transform the ocean from a smiling nymph into a hideous, sour-visaged witch, turning the sea from a near calm to a raging hell. Those howling winds and mountainous waves quickly developed the power to snap a schooner's nine-inch cable, often rolling dories over and over like blankets on a camping ground, spilling their crews into the water from which there was no hope of rescue.

Even when a storm did not reach disastrous proportions and dories remained right side up, there were many times when severe winds blowing up suddenly, caught some dorymen far to the looward (leeward) of their schooner, making it impossible for them to reach the parent craft under oar power.

Captain Clar Williams, veteran of the Newfoundland Banks fishing fleet, recalled a day during the summer of 1936, when he was fishing on Grand Bank in the schooner, *Freda M.* He carried ten dories with twenty dorymen. One fine, clear morning all his men set out to underrun their trawls. What wind there was came from a southerly direction. His barometer gave no indication that a storm was in the offing. While the fishermen were busy tending their gear, the gentle breeze died out to nearly a flat calm. Then, it chopped around to blow violently from the northwest. In a very short time it developed to near gale proportions that whipped up angry waves.

Captain Williams said that all the men who had been fishing to the win'ard of the vessel managed to get back onboard without too much difficulty. But the sudden storm had caught one dory with two men to the loo'ard. The skipper could discern that they were rowing hard but did not appear to be making any headway. On observing their plight he knew that he would have to act promptly in order to save them, before they dropped from exhaustion and drifted off to become lost. So he quickly tied the end of a coil of buoy rope to an unmanned dory and paying it out swiftly, he permitted the rapidly moving boat to drift down on the labouring men. Captain Williams stated that before the dory reached them he was forced to slack out twelve coils of rope with one hundred and twenty fathoms to a coil, which covered a distance of approximately two miles. This made Captain Williams realize that from the time he had first spotted the dorymen's plight until the empty dory connected with them, they had actually drifted further away from the banker despite their desperate rowing exertions.

When the unmanned dory arrived to where the weary fishermen were, they caught her and holding on rested for a brief period. After which they hauled their dory along the rope to finally reach the schooner and safety. The other crewmen did not dare to run the risk of assisting them during that strenuous and ticklish operation for fear that by putting out too much pulling power on the long rope they would either swamp the dory or cause her to yaw sharply about which could cause her to capsize and drown the men. After the distressed fishermen were safely back onboard, the empty dory was hauled back to the schooner, hoisted in and nested.

In all his years as a Banks skipper and a foreign-going captain, Clar Williams never lost a man. A record which he was extremely proud of down to the day of his death.

Each morning, according to the number of dories he carried, a Banks skipper when anchored on the fishing grounds, preparatory to setting trawls for underrunning, would set up courses for each dory to take. If, for example, he carried ten dories, he would prepare ten courses from ten separate points of the compass. These courses which had been carved previously on small wooden blocks would be placed into a canvas bag which was fitted with a draw string. When the skipper held out the bag, he would not set the draw string too tight, but would leave the opening at the top of a sufficient size to admit a man's hand. It was not, however, large enough to permit a doryman to be able to see which course he was drawing. A couple of skippers told me that they always used their hats to hold the wooden course tickets. But Captain George Follett said that he was against using his hat for the ticket drawing because, he asserted, keen-eyed dory skippers after a quick glance into the hat would be able to select the course which suited them best. Anyway, whether the drawing took place from a canvas bag or a sou'wester, when the captain was ready the dory skippers would step forward and draw their courses for the day. Then when the ceremony was completed the dories would set out from the schooner like spokes from the hub of a wheel.

In the early days of trawl fishing, vessels that frequented the Banks carried their dories nested on a heavy plank close to the rails or upright on the checkers. These were criss-crossed two by fours which formed a checkerboard pattern. During heavy weather or when on a long passage dories were usually turned bottom up. In the early 1900s, cradles bolted to the deck came into use for nesting dories. The first fishing vessel to carry cradles was the *John Hays Hammond*, Captain Lemuel Spinney of the Gloucester fleet in 1907.

The cradles were equipped with ringbolts at each end and on both port and starboard sides. One end of stout ropes, called gripes, was spliced into the ringbolts on one side while the free end which contained a heart shaped grommet or a ring was thrown over the nested dories to the opposite side, where they were hauled tight and lashed securely to the cradle ringbolts on that side by means of a smaller rope rove back and forth, several times, through ringbolt and grommet, then neatly made fast with hitches. The gripes were placed there, of course, to prevent the dories from becoming denested and smashed or washed overboard during rough weather. Up to the early 1900s, the largest number of double dories a vessel carried was from six to eight. But eight dories was the limit nested by the largest vessel of the fishing fleets in those days, with the exception of the Portuguese and French who conducted operations from much bigger schooners than did the

American, Nova Scotian and Newfoundland fishermen. However, approaching 1920, when bankers on this side of the Atlantic increased in size and eventually became equipped with motor power; nine, ten and eleven dories were carried. Some of our vessels like the *Alberto Wareham* and *Autauga,* even fished with twelve. Many Nova Scotian and American vessels also carried twelve. But Captain Archie McLeod of the Gloucester fleet while he was skippering the schooners *Gertrude L. Thebaud* and the *Dawn,* broke all records in that respect when he nested fourteen dories.

The fact is that the number of dories a vessel carried had to be governed by the number of fishermen who could be accommodated in her fo'castle. In other words, the bigger the schooner, the larger the accommodation and the greater number of men and dories. For example, it would have been an obstructive and useless encumbrance to nest ten or eleven dories onboard a banker that could sleep only sixteen men. Naturally, eight dories would be her complement. The Nova Scotians and Newfoundlanders were at least twenty years behind the Americans in venturing forth to become engaged at the Banks fishery, with Nova Scotia getting the jump on the Newfoundlanders by three years.

For in 1872, a devil-may-care Lunenburg captain, named Ben Anderson, whose reckless courage and utter disregard for the superstitious beliefs of his fellow citizens, placed him in a class by himself, decided to sail his vessel to the Grand Banks. Partly just to have a look-see at what the damn Yankees were doin' out there, but mainly to catch some fish which he had heard were very plentiful in that area. Moreover, reports had been filtering through to the effect that the New Englanders were doing right well for themselves on the Banks.

Accordingly, the Lunenburger took on food supplies, equipped his schooner with trawls, bait and other essentials which included four double dories, then off he went. The people who had been standing around watching Captain Anderson outfit his vessel the *Dielytris,* became doubly shocked when they observed that the daring skipper was taking on supplies from the considered-unlucky eastern side of the wharf, instead of from the western side. In addition, he loaded those supplies on a Friday, which in the estimation of the watchers, no sane schooner skipper would have done. Then to top it off he signed on a crew of thirteen men. Thirteen, the definitely unlucky number. Sadly and sagely the citizens mournfully nodded their heads. Poor Ben, his schooner and his crew, they told one another, will never be seen again.

But Poor Ben was seen again and when he turned up he was not so poor at that, for the *Dielytris* on entering the harbour of Lunenburg some six weeks later, was so deeply laden with the largest size codfish the townfolk had ever seen, that sea water was swishing back and forth from side to side across her deck through the scuppers and floodgates, which are slots or openings through the bulwarks of a vessel at deck level.

Now, on observing that Ben Anderson had at first brazenly defied superstition, then sailed away to come safely home again after reaping a handsome harvest from the Banks water, many of the other Lunenburg captains soon copied the precedent he had set, which eventually resulted in their building up one of the finest fleets of deep sea fishing schooners in the world. Meanwhile, they developed some of the most capable fishermen ever to sail on the Banks.

It was the practise of some Lunenburgers to carry their superstitions along when they named their new fishing schooners; names embodying three A's were considered to be extremely lucky. For example, *Delawana, Mahaska, Partanna, Mahala.* Unfortunately, the three A's did not work in favour of the two latter named vessels, for they were lost with all hands.

I do not know if the Lunenburg fishing skippers who came after Ben Anderson loaded supplies from the lucky western side of the wharf or whether they performed such work on a Friday, but several of Newfoundland's Banks fishermen have told men in all seriousness that once the Lunenburgers had food supplies, salt, etc., stored onboard their vessels, on reaching the fishing grounds they would not part with a single item for love nor money. For instance, if a Newfoundland or an American fishermen was completing his load and needed a few hogsheads of salt to cure his last few doryloads, or if he was in need of a sack of potatoes or a bag of flour to furnish his crew with a meal or two during the run to port and he requested an adequately supplied Lunenburger to loan or sell him those items, he would be simply wasting his time. For the Bluenoses just would not loan or sell anything. Was it possible that they could be so mean and miserable that they would refuse assistance to a brother fisherman so far from home? Not at all. Under most circumstances Lunenburgers were kindly, generous and co-operative. But not while they were at sea. For then a deeply ingrained superstition took control, forbidding them to dispense any goods belonging to their vessels. They firmly believed that if they did dish out, ill luck for sure would be their portion before the voyage ended.

In times past, Banks dorymen and shore fishing dorymen as well, were the helpless victims of a dominating influence. They were slaves to hard task-masters, namely, the Banks schooner owners and the merchants who outfitted shore fishermen.

It was the day of the vicious credit system when our fishermen were exploited to the fullest by greedy, overbearing businessmen, who were the lords, the supreme rulers of the little kingdoms they had created in our outport settlements. It was a system which shackled most fishermen to an everlasting

A full-sized Banks dory built by the Lowells of Amesbury, Massachusetts. This
one is in the Peabody Museum, Salem, Massachusetts.

debt. Then when they grew old and eventually died, their close relatives such
as sons and grandsons, in a great number of cases, would be called upon to
pay the debts which their deceased fathers and grandfathers had incurred.
Now if one or more of his descendents were living on the old man's estate and
had been paying certain amounts towards the old debts, the merchants could
by process of law force the descendents to continue the payments. On the
other hand, if no installments had been paid for a period of six years, the debt
was automatically cancelled.

During the 1930s while I was on loan from the Newfoundland Constabulary
to the then Department of Public Health and Welfare for the purpose of
conducting special investigations relative to the issuance of able-bodied relief
orders, I came across cases where merchants were demanding and receiving
payments from grandsons to eliminate debts incurred by grandfathers they
had never even seen, for the old gentlemen had passed away before the
grandsons had been born. These grandsons were not then residing, nor had
they ever resided on the so-called estates of their long departed grandfathers.
Moreover, they certainly had never paid any installments towards the debts
all the while they were growing up and not earning money, which was considerably longer than the six years prescribed by law.

In one place I discovered that the relieving officer (now called Welfare
Officer) was paying off his desceased grandfather's debt. The merchant had

been deducting regular amounts from his unhandsome salary of $25.00 per month which an ungenerous Commission of Government was paying him. No, he did not really know if his grandfather had owed all the money the merchant said he did.

"The merchant told me I was supposed to pay it off. I paid without question. After all, that merchant got me the appointment as relieving officer. No, he had never called upon me to pay any installments on the debt previous to the time he had secured the job for me."

I want to give assurances that the fishermen who had been paying off their grandfather's debts were not stupid. If they were not, why did they not seek legal advice in order to ascertain if they could be compelled to pay the debts in question? Or why did they not simply tell their tormentors to go to hell? Well, I am afraid it was not that easy. First of all, there were no lawyers living in the outports back in those days, which meant that people who needed legal advice would have to journey to St. John's. In most cases the absence of roads to isolated communities, at that time, required making a trip to the capital either by train or by coastal steamer, and the passage either way would cost money. Board and lodging in St. John's cost more money, paying a lawyer for advice, still more money. The fact is that the vast majority of fishermen did not possess that kind of money.

After they shipped their season's catch, they knew exactly what the merchant was going to tell them.

"Well, me b'y, that was a nice batch of fish you brought in. You still owe me quite a bit of money, but I suppose I will have to supply you with a winter's grub."

The question is, did they owe the merchant any money at all after they had turned in their catch to him? Many of them did not and they were aware that the merchant actually owed them money, but they refrained from questioning him on that point, for the same reason that they held back from giving the merchant a tongue-lashing, or from seeking a lawyer's advice respecting debts which they had never incurred. They feared the big man too greatly. Believe me, they did not fear him in a pugilistic sense, for those men who had rolled the dice with death every day of their lives while out on the stormy deep did not fear a physical encounter with any man. They were of the same breed of men who so distinguished themselves in battle in World War One. The British Field Marshall, Sir Douglas Haig, when addressing the Newfoundland Regiment, following the conflict said:

"Newfoundlanders, I salute you, you are better than the best." The Newfoundlanders' concern for the welfare of their wives and children came above everything else. Their love for home and family went very deep, so they could not afford to run the risk of offending the merchant, particularly in the more isolated communities where he was the only source of supply. The fishermen feared him because they knew that if he cut off from them the vital necessities of life, their wives and children would suffer as a result. So they thought it much wiser to grin and bear it.

There were more ways than one whereby a fisherman could arouse the ire of a merchant to whom he was in debt. A hardy fisherman named Sam tried to put a fast one over on a merchant back in 1912, only to end up the loser. That was the time when indepedent traders, men who owned their own schooners would pay frequent visits to harbours around the Burin Peninsula. Those vessels could be classed as floating shops for they carried many varieties of goods to sell. The skipper-owners usually anchored their craft in the stream and would buy dried or salt bulk codfish from any person who brought it onboard.

The land based merchants hated those traders, like mosquitos hate cans of killer spray. For not only were the traders paying a higher price for fish than the local lords, they were selling goods a few cents cheaper than those which were on display in the stores ashore.

Now there were a number of fishermen who had contrived to remain independent of the regular merchants. Those were single men and childless married men. They, not having a flock of children to support were debt free, so they joyfully sold their catch to the traders. If they needed an article of clothing, some household utensils or an item of fishing gear they bought them from the traders who paid them the balance owed in hard cash.

Such goings-on really burnt the shore based merchants to a cinder. For were not those he-whores of traders making independent fishermen still more independent? For fish that was being sold to the floating shops would have ended up on the harbour merchants premises, while the goods being purchased from them should have come from their shelves, 'if those bastards of traders did not put in an appearance with such disturbing regularity'.

But, a number of fishermen who were in debt to the merchants surveyed those trading schooners with longing eyes. They were fully aware, however, that if they took the chance and smuggled a doryload of fish out to the traders and the regular merchant learned about it, he would immediately cut off their food supplies; with a long winter in the offing, men with families dependent on them could not afford to take such a chance.

But the young fisherman, Sam, who lived in our harbour, risked the fury of the merchant to whim he was rather heavily in debt, when he sold a doryload of dried salt codfish to a trader.

That young man whose father had died a couple of years before his fish selling incident, was the sole support of his mother and sisters. He knew that the merchant, after taking his summer's catch, which could only partly pay off the debt he owed, would advance him barely enough foodstuffs to tide him over the winter. He was aware, also that the merchant would not let him have even a small amount of cash and cash was someting he needed to enable him to take his girlfriend to concerts, dances and soup suppers, which were social events that always took place during the winter months.

Back in those days it was the common practice in the outports for everyone to retire early each night, so that by 10:00 o'clock not a light would be showing in any of the houses. Consequently, that young fisherman, very artfully according to his own way of reasoning, loaded his dory with ten quintels of prime fish. The hour was midnight. He felt certain that nobody would be around at that graveyard hour to notice his actions. In any case, he rowed out to the trader and disposed of his fish for ready cash. Then he happily rowed ashore and promptly went to bed.

But young Sam had reckoned without taking the merchant's perceptive powers into consideration. For anticipating that some fishermen who owed him money would be tempted to sell fish to the trader, the merchant had posted two spies in such a position that they would be able to observe actions and detect telltale sounds coming from anyone who moved.

It transpired that the two nighthawks on hearing suspicious noises coming from the direction of Sam's premises, had crept over and were quite close to the young fisherman when he loaded his dory. Then they watched while he rowed off and disappeared in the darkness. Of course, they were also on hand when Sam returned in an empty dory, which proved to them that he had made a sale to the trader. So the undercover men reported Sam's nocturnal activities to their master accordingly.

Two days later, the fisherman walked into the merchant's store. The place was crowded with customers. Sam was standing by the counter when the merchant on coming out of his office, eyed him. The sight of Sam sent the merchant into a towering rage for he rushed over and seized the young man by the throat.

"You damned traitor!" he howled. "You went and sold a doryload of fish to that bastard of a trader. Thought I wouldn't larn about your sneaky moves, didn't you? But I found you out alright, hah! That was my fish you sold to that son of a bitch, b'y and now you will suffer for it. Not one item of grub, nor any fishin' gear will you ever get from me again!"

Sam was a powerfully built man, locally famous for the great feats of strength he had often performed. He could have easily taken that merchant by the scruff of the neck and held him out with a straight arm, until the enraged man died of starvation or he could have mopped the floor with him. But to the disappointment of many of those present, Sam did not react violently. He simply reached up a big hand, removed the merchant's fingers from his windpipe, shoved him backwards a couple of feet, then walked out of the store.

I want to emphasize here, that all of our merchants were not grasping, greedy or dishonest. There were many fine, upright men doing business around our shores. I had often heard fishermen speak with open admiration when referring to such merchants. It was common knowledge also, that not too many strictly honest merchants ever acquired any great amount of wealth.

I have to admit that for a few pages I did not deal exactly with the Banks fishery, but I thought it would be alright to drift in nearer the land for a while to acquaint you with some of the troubles which plagued our shore fishermen.

The slavery for Newfoundland's Banks dorymen would commence around the middle of February, that is of course, apart from those who were engaged at the winter fishery on such grounds as Rose Blanche Bank, off Newfoundland's south coast. Yes, the middle of February each year was the time the dorymen left their homes in the various settlements in Placentia and Fortune Bays, as well as other places right up to Port aux Basques and boarded schooners which had been moored with two anchors down in safe harbours during the early winter months.

As those vessels had been swinging around with every change of wind and tide while they were lying up unmanned,very often their anchor chains would be miserably crossed and twisted up. To free those chains in order to unmoor a schooner required a deal of ingenuity coupled with a tremendous amount of hard work. Then all her running gear had to be completely overhauled and replaced when necessary. The standing rigging also, had to be checked over, with broken or frayed ratlines (small ropes fastened across a ship's shrouds to form ladders) replaced with new ones. The sails which had been unbent, tied up and lowered down into the hold after the schooner had ceased fishing operations the fall before, would be hoisted up, laid out and bent onto spars and booms. In large vessels the sail area measured from eight thousand to ten thousand square feet, depending on the size of the craft. Bending on the heavy mainsail alone, was a major operation. That sail, again on the larger vessels, extended from the mast along the main boom for distances of from seventy to seventy-six feet, and upwards of fifty feet along the gaff. Then the leach (outer edge) of such a sail often measured up to one hundred feet. That huge sheet of canvas which was encompassed by rope nearly as large in circumference as a man's wrist, weighed approximately six hundred pounds. The remaining sails: foresail, fore gaff topsail, main fagg topsail, balloon jib, standing jib, jumbo and topmast staysail (called fisherman's staysail by Lunenburgers and windbags by northern Newfoundlanders) were not exactly light weights either. Hoisting that great mass of heavy canvas out of the hold and dragging it around in the proper position for bending on was a muscle rending, gut tearing job.

If a ship had wintered in a harbour apart from her home port when her sails were bent on and everything else was in order or ship-shape, she was sailed to the headquarters of the firm who owned her. Then the crew would really get down to work. Dories were hauled out of storage sheds, each man and his dorymate would be responsible to see that the dory they had drawn or had been assigned to for the coming fishing season was properly equipped, new nose straps, stern straps and painters had to be spliced and knotted in place. Oars had to be served or marled at the sections where they moved at those points of stress. Thwarts and bulkheads had to be checked over and replaced if occasion demanded it. Other items previously described had to be placed onboard Banks dories before they were ready for sea.

Then other heavy equipment had to be lugged aboard, such as chocks for the liver butts to rest in; those liver butts were large puncheons, usually six of them on a big schooner. They were set up in their chocks just forward of the after cabin. Next were four large fish crates in which fish were cut, throated and headed on the Banks. During that process the livers were preserved and placed in the butts. Later the skipper would place a fryer down through the square hole in the top of the butts in order to render out or melt the livers to produce the valuable codliver oil. Those fryers were stove-like contrivances equipped with a grate and a fan shaped funnel. The captain would light a fire inside it by first using dry kindling with soft coal. When the soft coal had become bright embers, he would then use a quantity of anthracite or hard coal. After the hard coal had burned up sufficiently he placed the fryer down in one of the butts amongst the livers, where its heat would render out the oil fairly quickly. When, in the skipper's estimation, the fryer had completed its work, he would remove it and place it in the next butt. While it was merrily sizzling away in the second butt, the captain would dip off the oil from the first butt and pour it into casks. So skipper and fryer would continue the rendering out process until each butt had been attended to and the oil dipped off. The casks containing the oil were stowed on the vessel's quarter deck.

Two large tubs were placed onboard, those were made by sawing an extra large puncheon in two. They were usually called fish tubs because they were used to wash dressed fish in before it was sent down to the holds to be salted.

Then there were four splitting tables on which the upper portion of the fishes' back bones (commonly called sound bones) were dexterously removed with square topped knives — the blades of which were curved — held in the hands of experts at the trade of splitting fish. The curved blade enabled the splitter, when he severed the back bone, to raise it easily and lessened the danger of slicing off portions of the fleshy part which could spoil the fish for marketing purposes. A straight bladed knife would have been next to useless for performing that type of work.

Gurry kids, which were large wooden boxes or pounds, had to be built on deck. Those were used primarily to stow fish offal (gurry) so it could be carried away and dumped far from the fishing grounds to prevent those areas from becoming contaminated. The gurry kids were also used to store spare gear in, such as trawl tubs, bait jacks, dory scoops, tholepins, etc. On American schooners that were engaged at fresh fishing, a large portion of their freshwater ice supply would be stored in the gurry kids as, previous to the days of refrigerated vessels, the catch had to be iced down to preserve it and the schooners would have to make a mad race for market before the ice melted or the whole cargo would become spoiled.

Skipper Tommy Bohlin of the Gloucester fleet took no less than five sets of spars out of his schooner, the *Nanie C. Bohlin*, while racing in for the fresh fish market in Boston.

It follows that salt bankers required large quantities of salt. At least two hundred and fifty hopsheads had to be loaded on large ships. In order to achieve this, the vessel's crew were divided into three groups. The first group shovelled the salt into wheelbarrows in the storage shed. The second group wheeled it onboard the banker via a bridge of planks which connected the craft to the pier. The wheelers then dumped their loads down into the hold where it was shovelled into pounds by the third group.

The dorymen were compelled to work from 5:00 a.m. to 6:00 p.m. every day, with the exception of Sunday, until the vessel was ready to set out on her first trip for the year. The spring trip as it was called. The thirteen gruelling hours which took place between five and six were known as the merchants' time. But the dory slaves' work did not terminate at 6:00 o'clock, for six tubs of trawl had to be gotten ready for each dory, four tubs would be carried in the dories on the Banks, the remaining two tubs were carried along as spares. New trawl gear had to be completely outfitted. A trawl tub usually contained ten fifty fathom lines. It took fifty-eight hooks to outfit a single line, which meant that the entire tub of gear was equipped with five hundred and eighty hooks. Used gear had to be overhauled and refitted, hopelessly rusted and broken hooks were replaced. The main trawl had to be taken out of the tubs, then stretched to take out the kinks. After which they were carefully coiled back into the tubs. The vessel owners would not permit dorymen to perform this very tedious, monotonous work during the daytime, so they were forced to return after supper and work until midnight, sometimes even longer in order that the schooner's sailing time would not be delayed. The period from suppertime onwards was the doryman's time, his very own time, when he should have been resting after having performed thirteen hours of heavy daytime work.

From the day when the crew unmoored the vessel until she had reached the Banks and commenced fishing they were not paid one solitary cent in return for the tremendous amount of labour they had performed over a period of between three to four weeks. Modern Banks fishermen may find that statement hard to believe, but there are many old dorymen still around who have good reason to assert to the truth of it. For they remember all too vividly those days, weeks and years when they were engaged at work which can only be classed as abject slavery.

Somebody once remarked that even a well paid slave is a slave just the same. If that brand of philosophy be true, I wonder how the person who coined the phrase would class our fishermen who for such long periods of hard work received no pay at all.

Then there were times when the crew of bankers were compelled to do all over again the work they had completed the previous day, in getting their vessel ready for sea, as it happed in the case of the crew of the schooner, *Mabel Dorothy,* sailing out of Grand Bank in command of Captain Reuben Thornhill. The craft had been fully equipped to go out on her first trip of the year. As darkness had descended before all the details of outfitting had been finalized and it was very foggy, Captain Thornhill decided to delay sailing until daybreak. That night, however, a heavy gale glew in from the northeast which caused the *Mabel Dorothy* to part her mooring lines. She drifted up Grand Bank Gut and grounded on a shoal. The tide was top high at the time and Captain Thornhill knew it would be useless to wait for another high tide which would give him the same depth of water. The only alternative was to lighten the vessel by removing the two hundred and fifty hogsheads of salt. So the crew began the extremely tiresome job of hoisting the salt up out of the hold and freighting it ashore in dories, then it was unloaded from the dories and wheeled back into the shed that they had taken it from such a short while before. The salt could not be piled up out in the open for the reason that should it come on to rain some of the stuff would melt while the remaining particles would unite to form a solid mass making it absolutely useless.

The entire job of removing the salt from the *Mabel Dorothy* and replacing it again when the vessel refloated occupied two full days of back-breaking labour, for which the slaves again received no pay.

When her banking career was over, the *Mabel Dorothy* was used in the coastal trade. While on a voyage from Roddickton, Canada Bay, Newfoundland, to her home port in Grand Bank, under the command of Captain Jack Ralph, the vessel was lost with all hands.

I mentioned earlier that Banks fishermen usually underran their trawls three times a day, but if the weather conditions and other factors were favourable they often made a fourth trip. I have to explain here that those conditions applied to salt banking American and Nova Scotian vessels, but not to Newfoundland schooner crews who usually made only three trips. The reason why American and Nova Scotian crews were in a better position to make a fourth trip was because of the fact that their schooners carried dressing crews. Those men did not go out in dories but remained aboard and were on hand to cutthroat, head, gut, split and salt the fish as soon as the dories were unloaded on their return to the banker, thereby leaving the dorymen free to get a mug-up, row back to their trawl and haul it again. If fish happened to be plentiful the men stood a good chance of securing a full doryload on each trip.

American and Canadian fishermen did not partake of a full breakfast before setting out on their first trip for the day, which as a rule was 4:00 a.m., just a cup of coffee or tea with maybe a bun or a slice of bread. They did, however, enjoy a full breakfast after they had returned from the first trip and had forked the fish up on deck. The only time that those dorymen worked at dressing and salting fish was after they had made the final trip for the day, when they would join the dressing crews to help stow it away.

The Newfoundland bankers did not carry dressing crews. They also operated quite the reverse of their American and Canadian brethren in that they were supplied with a full breakfast before rowing off in the early morning. Then when they returned to the vessel with the first load they became the dressing and salting crews. Here again, weather conditions had to be taken into consideration, as well as the prospects for good catches. If fish were plentiful and the weather tended to be fair, the men would unload their dories, grab a quick cup of tea and a bun. Newfoundland dorymen used to call that type of lunch a 'savage mug-up' as, with the skipper pacing the deck over their heads, anxious for them to be off again, they literally had to gobble the food and gulp the tea, before he started hurling invective down in the fo'castle strong enough to blister the paint on the bunk boards.

When decks became overrun with fish, usually after the second trip, it was the common practise aboard Newfoundland bankers for the captain to hold one dory crew back. Then the catchee, whose ordinary duty was to catch painters as dories came alongside, would cut fish throats, one of the doryman would gut, head and pull out livers. The captain took over the job of splitter, while the second doryman did the salting down in the hold. After the dories returned from their last trip for the day, Newfoundland dorymen, like their American and Canadian counterparts, pitched in to dress the fish and salt it away. Of course, systems governing working conditions varied on different schooners, depending on what each captain may have considered to be the more favourable and efficient.

The highliner count system called the high and low count by some fishermen, which was in effect for many years, was the cause of numerous drowning accidents on the Banks, as while that system was in effect there was a great tendency to overload dories, for the fish brought aboard by each dory was counted. Consequently, the men who brought in the largest number of fish received the most money. They became highliners. It was quite natural, therefore, for the men to load their dories so deeply that in many cases water was actually lapping the edges of the gunnels. If the sea was absolutely smooth and with careful dory handling they would reach the schooner without mishap, but a sudden puff of wind to raise a lop causing water to flow in over the dory's gunnels, then the boat quickly filled and sank. For men to survive such a sinking would be nothing short of a miracle.

The highliner dorymen received the magnificent sum of $2.00 per thousand fish for every thousand they caught more than their shipmates. So that if the highliners brought onboard ten thousand more fish than the other fellows they were paid $20.00. A paltry sum indeed, considering that they were risking their lives every time that they overloaded a dory whilst they were striving to make a high count. It should be remembered, I suppose that a person was able to buy a fairly hefty package of goods for a twenty dollar bill back in those days and with poor fishermen every dollar counted.

Not only was the high and low system potentially dangerous, it was also a very unfair method to be foisted on a group of dedicated, hard working seamen. For example, say that the men in number two dory when hauling their trawl happened to strike a run of fish that were of a large size, while the men in number eight dory at the same time caught fish that were much smaller, whereas both dories would be carrying the same weight, number eight, owing to the smaller fish would have the highest count.

One former doryman told me that while he was fishing on the Grand Bank, one day when he and his dorymate underran their trawl every fish they gaffed aboard was of an exceptionally large size. They returned to the schooner with a full doryload. When the count was taken they discovered that it had required only seventy-two fish to load the dory. If those two men had continued catching extra large fish there was no way they could have reached the coveted highliners position.

In the latter days of Banks dory trawling, the highliner count system was abolished. But the wily schooner owner who had inaugurated it in the early days had really discovered the right incentive to encourage dorymen to catch fish, for under its influence all hands strove to become highliners, which had the effect of filling a vessel's holds more quickly.

When a Banks fishing schooner arrived back in port after a long, hard trip, it was quite natural for her crewmen to request time off so as they could go home for a visit with their families. They had slaved tending trawls, endured hardships, suffered agonies from infected cuts and inflamed pus-filled water pups (boil type sores brought on mainly from constant chafing of oil jacket wrist hems against fishermen's lower arms). Three or four days of well-earned rest would have been greatly welcomed. But such respites did not take place, for the salted fish in the vessel's holds had to be unloaded, washed and placed on beaches or flakes in bulks called waterhorses in readiness for the fish makers to spread out heads and tails to dry in the sun. The work of unloading, washing and lugging fish up to beaches had to be performed by the schooner's crew.

There was, however, one way in which a doryman who desired a visit with his family could be granted time off. That was if he hired a lumper to take his place. Lumpers were young boys or youths who, glad of the opportunity to make a few cents, would hire themselves out to any doryman who took shore leave.

For working thirteen hours or more, the lumper was paid eighty cents per day with the doryman who had engaged his services footing the bill. But meagre as that amount was there were many dorymen who could ill afford to pay it. If the doryman was absent for three days the lumper realized the sum of $2.40. Not bad pay for a younger slave, according to the reasoning of a schooner owner merchant, but which was a bloody disgrace even in those days of cheap labour.

Frederick Tessier of Grand Bank, Newfoundland. He recalls the ays of his boy hood when he worked as a lumper on Banks fishing vessels —(Jerry Kelland Photo).

My good friend, Fred Tessier, who is at present serving as mayor of the town of Grand Bank, can easily recall the days of his boyhood and youth when he worked as a lumper on fishing vessels. The lumpers apparently, were not misnamed for dictionaries define them as labourers employed in (un)loading

157

cargoes.

Many shore fishermen washed salt bulk fish in puncheons (tubs). Others pulled the bottom plugs out of floating dories to permit them to fill with water. After which they replaced the plugs, when the falling tide left the dory high and dry the fish washed out in the doryload of water. When the washing job had been completed the plug was pulled out again to let the soiled water drain away, but was replaced once more before the tide rose around the boat.

Banks fishermen operated differently during their fish washing activities. They washed their catch in large crates called pounds. These measured twelve feet by twelve feet by two and one half feet deep. They were constructed of two by fours which were nailed on lath style with spaces of about one inch between laths. One pound was placed in the water opposite the schooner's fore hatch, another opposite the after hatch. The sides of the pounds nearest the vessel were fastened securely with ropes to the ships while the off or outer sides were held up by the vessel's dory burtons or gaff throat tackles.

The pounds were let down deeply enough so as they filled with water, which poured into them through the spaces between laths. Using open lath pounds in the process of washing out fish from a banker was an excellent idea, as while the soiled water kept escaping through the lath openings, a supply of clean water was continuously pouring in via the same route. As many of the larger vessels could bring in cargoes which ranged from eighteen hundred to twenty-five hundred quintals of fish, the automatic changing of water was a great time as well as labour saver.

To start things off, the fish was pitch-forked up out of the holds to the tops of the slaughter houses, from there it was forked to the vessel's deck. Then it was forked over the side into the pounds. The slaughter houses can be classed as box-like structures built up from the bottoms of the holds to the height of five feet. They ran underneath the centers of both fore and after hatches and were mainly used for stowing away ballast and water barrels. There were also four bait lockers in the after hold, two on each side of the slaughter houses.

After the pounds had been filled with cod, two crews, numbering six men to each pound, would board them. So while four men swabbed the fish with long handled mops, the remaining eight men would wash each individual fish with ordinary scrubbing brushes. Taking one large specimen at a time or two and even three smaller ones which were held firmly by their tails with one hand and scrubbed clean with the other.

As the fish were washed they were loaded onboard dories which were tied broadside on to the pounds. When the dories had been fully loaded they were rowed across to the beaches or flakes and placed on barrows, then were lugged up over the crop of the beach and bulked in waterhorses. Weather permitting the fish would be spread out to dry the following day by the fish makers. Incidentally, the drying or curing of codfish was always called 'making fish'.

Of course, the fish washing dorymen, like the lumpers, started work at 5:00 a.m. and were supposed to quit at 6:00 p.m. But for the dory slaves things did not always work out that way. For example, if some of the dories were partly or fully loaded when the clock chimed six, they would have to return after supper, unload the dories, barrow the fish then lug it up over the beach and pack it on the waterhorse bulk. Consequently, you could say that a fish washing doryman knew what time his day's work was going to start but he could never judge the hour it might end. Moreover, those men did not receive any pay for all that fish washing, barrow lugging labour which, depending on the size of the catch, could extend over a period of several days.

In the Banks fishing trade, the schooner owner merchant claimed half the catch while the other half was divided into equal shares amongst the crew. The fish makers' pay also, was deducted from the dorymen's share. But there was another angle which worked in the merchant's favour. He bought his schooner's crew's shares at what was supposed to be the best price available. But get a load of this: A former doryman told me that the merchant he had fished for back in 1931, paid him $2.50 per quintal for his share, with the merchant giving the fisherman to understand that that was the very best price he was able to pay, as prospects in the foreign salt fish markets were anything but bright. However, when the captain of the vessel who had freighted the fish to Oporto returned, he informed the fisherman confidentially that the fish had fetched $22.00 per quintal in that market.

Speaking of the same merchant, another former doryman told me that he had slaved from March to October on one of the man's bankers. They had done well with fish that season. After they had returned from the final trip, he said he was in a pound busily washing fish, when his father who had skippered the schooner he was on came along and informed him that they would not be permitted to collect any of their earnings in cash, for the merchant had issued an order to the effect that all monies earned had to be taken up in trade goods in his store. The ex-doryman said that his premium $24.00 on his life insurance policy was due. He went to the merchant's office and requested that he be given at least enough cash to pay the premium in order to prevent his policy from being cancelled. His request was denied. At that, the fisherman lost his temper and told the merchant very forcibly, "If you do not pay me what you owe me in cash, I will go to the magistrate and have you summoned before the court. For I intend to collect what is due me!"

At the outburst from the fisherman a look of shocked surprise came over the merchant's face, for nothing like that had ever happened before. But the man had not been in business for so many years without having acquired the ability to see a long distance into the future. For a few seconds later he changed his tune.

"Oh, alright, b'y," he said. "Let's not have too much fuss over this little matter." Then turning to his accountant, he shouted, "Pay him! Pay him!"

The merchant paid him because he was shrewd enough to foresee that a court case would reveal, to his snug, little world, the fact that one fisherman had bearded him in his den, then had had the audacity to threaten to seek assistance from the law to collect his wages. That was a type of publicity the merchant wanted no part of, for he knew it would result in many other fishermen endeavoring to bring him to the prong also.

When that merchant died, he left an estate of eight hundred and twenty-five thousand dollars in cash, his headquarters, business premises and several branch stores, all debt free.

Many years have passed by since the final curtain was rung down on the dory slaves. Men no longer have to venture on the Banks in little dories to set, haul and underrun trawls. The fishermen of today still live dangerously for no man who engages in a daily battle with the sea can be expected to live otherwise. But the modern fisherman does not have to shuffle into the vessel owner's office with his cap held respectfully in his hands to beg for some favour which he had already earned, like his father and grandfather were forced to do.

If there is any fear in evidence today, it eminates from the big man sitting behind the desk, not from the fisherman standing in front of it. For the unionized fishermen of the present time are in a powerful position to bargain and fight for their rights, which is exactly the way it should be.

A rew remnants of the old dory slaves still remain, men in their sixties, seventies, eighties and nineties whose hands still bear the livid scars from the infected cuts and whose wrists remain pitted from the painful effects of water pups. Their conversations respecting their battles for survival against former bosses contain very little bitterness. Rather, they seem to reminisce more in a nostalgic vein than in tones which depict deeply buried malice.

One seventy-six year old ex-doryman told me, "It was late in October, the weather was shockin' bad, severe winds with seas rollin' that looked like the South Side Hills of St. John's. It was impossible to put dories overboard, so our skipper decided to come in and clew up the voyage for that year. But the merchant who owned the vessel was furious. He told the skipper that he should have stayed out until he'd caught more fish. The merchant then penalized the entire crew by refusing to pay them the balance of the money he owed them. I appealed to him three or four times to give me my money as I had a large family dependent on me. Each time he refused.

"Well do you know somethin'?" grinned the oldtimer, "That merchant did not live to collect his old age pension, but I did and I'm still around and goin' strong."

In his 'History of Newfoundland', second edition, published in 1896, Judge D.W. Prowse, after commenting on the great potential wealth relative to our mineral resources, wrote: 'Mines and minerals may peter out. The gold, tin and coal will vanish away, but the fish around our shores is an everlasting harvest in which the results are sure, the success certain, ever ready for the benefit of man. The free gift of the Almighty Ruler of the sea.' How wrong was the Judge's prediction regarding the everlasting fishery harvest.

In 1906, the Reverend William Pilot made this observation: 'Not withstanding that for four centuries these Banks have been fished, they show today no decrease in productiveness.'

Neither Judge Prowse, nor the Reverend Pilot, nor any other person in those days could possibly foresee that a resource which had remained steadfastly prolific for four hundred years would be almost wiped out in less than a quarter of a century by the voracious ravages of European and Scandinavian fishing fleets.

The following is an extract from one of my poems, taken from my book of poems, 'Anchor Watch'. I offer it as a salute to our great sailors who fished various Banks, always under perilous circumstances, also to the beautiful schooners they manned and to the reliable little dory.

> They're gone now, those grand old ships and crews
> Yet we should make them live in model, song and story
> In the sagas of great schooners, men of mighty thews
> And ice-glazed straying dory.

CHAPTER TEN

A Wild Day in Saint Pierre

At the time France entered World War One against Germany, most of the young men who were crew members of French bankers were also reservists in various units of their country's armed forces. With the result that when the war got into high gear, French warships paid visits to their fishing vessels both on the Banks and in port during September 1914 and took those men away to project them into action on the war fronts, therefore leaving the fishing skippers with skeleton crews or enough men to enable them to sail their vessels home to France. Those were middle-aged and elderly men who had somewhat lost the vigour of youth and who were considered to be too old for war services.

With all their active, young seamen gone and with the vessels in those days being under sail power alone, the skippers were aware that the nested dories piled up high on both port and starboard sides of their decks would prove to be a great encumbrance to their aging crewmen, whose joints had become a little stiffened from attacks of rheumatism and who would be required to scuttle back and forth repeatedly, both alow and aloft, to work sails coincidental with the moods of wind and wave. Consequently, after leaving the Banks on the homeward voyage, they all came into Saint Pierre Harbour and put their dories ashore, retaining only a sufficient number to serve as lifeboats in case they should be compelled to abandon ship due to some urgency.

The French bankers carried anywhere from ten to twenty double dories depending of course on the size of the ship. Therefore, approximately two hundred dories were landed. These were left in charge of Saint Pierre merchants who acted as agents for vessel owners in Saint Malo, Dieppe and other seaports of France.

As it was impossible to find indoor storage space for such a large number of boats, they were nested together and stashed away in every nook and cranny along the waterfront.

The captains of the French fishing vessels, like so many other persons, were

162

confident that the war would be over in six months. Come spring, they told the merchants, the Allies will be victorious, peace will be restored and our young men will be with us again; then we shall return here, pick up our dories and resume fishing.

Both fishing skippers and merchants were in a jocular mood as they drank toasts to the glory of France, the Tri-colour, the President, the Premier, Field Marshall Foch and General Joffre. They were confident that those two old soldiers would quickly teach the German Kaiser a lesson he would never forget. Then, with much planting of the traditional double kiss on the cheeks of their hosts, which caused the dapper, smooth-shaven merchants to shudder and wince when the captains' rather odorous, bristly mustaches connected over-enthusiastically with their facial structures, the old salts set sail for their home ports in France.

Unfortunately and very tragically, those hardy French skippers, as well as thousands of other wishful thinkers were dead wrong in their forecast concerning the war's ending. For, by the spring of 1915 the situation overseas was far from promising for the Allies. By the spring of 1916, war conditions for our side even worsened, so that Allied people generally viewed with dismay the gloomy prospects of having to endure several more years of conflict.

The French bankers did not put in an appearance at Saint Pierre in the spring of 1915, nor did they show up in the spring of 1916, with the result that their abandoned dories remained nested on dry land. Sad too, was the fact that many of the spry,young dorymen whom the French captains had hoped would be there to crew their schooners lay dead on the field of battle or on the bottom of the sea.

The non-return of the fishing fleet in the spring of 1916 created quite a problem for the caretakers of the dories. For apart from cluttering up much needed waterfront space, exposed as they had been to sun and all sorts of weather conditions for eighteen months, the merchants knew that if the little boats were to spend another summer ashore they would be rendered unseaworthy and in all probability be gone beyond repair.

As every man who has been familiar with dories is aware, when these boats remain resting on dry land for an extended period without the protection of some sort of covering, their side boards which are only 11/16 of an inch in thickness have a tendency to split wide open from end to end; bottom seams, too, will shrink apart.

The Saint Pierre merchants were fully aware of what dry land exposure could do to the dories. Apparently they did not intend to go to the expense of purchasing yards and yards of canvas to make covers for them, an expense for which they stood a slim chance of getting recompense. Those men knew also, that by the fall of 1916, the dories would be good for nothing but firewood.

'Mon Dieu, what can we do with all that firewood', they asked each other. Yes, what to do about the unwanted craft before they deteriorated to the firewood stage was the important question. After considerable discussion on the vexing problem, the merchants figured that they had found the answer. Sell them to Newfoundland fishermen, a little cheaper, perhaps, than usual.

Far better to sell them cheaply than to let them fall apart to become an obstructional nuisance to the activities of themselves and their employees for many years.

After reaching the decision to sell, no time was lost in posting the information that the sale would commence at a certain hour on a specific day. News of the sale spread quickly around the nearby Newfoundland coast, with result that on the day designated, our fishermen by the dozens converged on Saint Pierre. Now there were two gatherings which Newfoundlanders in general dearly loved to attend in years gone by. Those were sales and political meetings. I had always enjoyed making trips to Saint Pierre, for you left an English speaking community and if your engine was working well, two hours later you landed on a little piece of France, fourteen miles away, where with the exception of visitors of vessels anchored in the harbour, everyone spoke French. It did not matter that their language made no sense to you, you enjoyed listening to them jabbering just the same. Strangely enough, despite our close proximity to the French islands and our daily dealings with the residents there, very few of our people could speak or understand the French language. I would not want anyone to get the impression that Newfoundlanders found French too difficult to learn, quite the contrary, they had the ability to adapt themselves to speaking French very quickly when it became necessary for them to do so. When any of our young men or women went to Saint Pierre and secured employment, in a remarkably short space of time they could speak French as fluently as a native. The main reason why our citizens did not go to the trouble of learning to speak the language was that all the people with whom they had dealings in the Isles of Gaul could speak English. So they experienced no language problems when they visited the stores to make purchases. Meanwhile, of course, there were thousands of French residents who could not speak English. Therefore, as far as the majority of people from both races learning each others' language was concerned, you might say that they ended up as a pair of sixes. In short, those who needed to learn learned and those who did not, simply let it be.

My father was in need of a spare dory, so early on the day of the French dory sale he, together with three members of his trap crew went to Saint Pierre for the purpose of trying to purchase one. I managed to persuade him to take me along. It was the first day of June. The fog which usually arrived with the caplin between the 15th and the 20th of that month had been kind enough not to come in ahead of schedule. It was a beautiful morning, with brilliant sunshine and a gentle southwest breeze

As there had been no violent wind storms for three or four weeks, the waters of the Atlantic were as level as the floor of a bowling alley. With our six horse power Acadia engine working perfectly, we arrived in Saint Pierre without incident an hour before the sale was due to start and tied up our boat opposite the store of J.B. LaGasse. Anchored in the harbour at the time of our arrival were one banker from the American fleet, two from the Nova Scotian fleet and two from the Newfoundland fleet.

It appeared that nearly all the crew members from those vessels had been ashore for a considerable time as the majority of them were reeling about in various stages of intoxication. The fishing schooners carried anywhere from sixteen to twenty dorymen each, which meant that upwards of one hundred men from the deep sea fleets were roaming around the town. Added to those were the shore fishermen who had arrived to attend the dory sale. The two groups increased the population of Saint Pierre by approximately three hundred men.

Many of the shore fishermen like their Banks fishing brothers took advantage of their Saint Pierre visit to liquor up, as rum was cheap and plentiful. Then the town crier put in an appearance and in a loud tone of voice, made an announcement in rapid French. At first everyhone thought he was declaring the commencement of the dory sale. But one of our men who could speak and understand enough French to carry on a half-ass conversation with a Frenchman, said, "He's talkin' a bit too fast for me to get all he's sayin', but I'd say he's tellin' us that someone is after losin' a purse with money in it."

Our man was right, for a few minutes later a very agitated policeman came up to Uncle John Hann and managed to tell him that he had lost his purse containing much, much money. Although his English was very poor, he got the point across that their crier was unable to speak our language and would Monsieur Hann be gracious enough to announce his loss in English, in case that some English-speaking man, who did not understand the words of the French crier, who picked up the purse.

"Oui, oui," agreed Uncle John, who was quite proud of the fact that he could say yes, yes in French. Here I would point out that those old time Newfoundlanders referred to the French police, the gendarmes, as john-of-arms.

John Hann was a born rhymster. He possessed the ability to produce, off the cuff, a rhymed verse on any incident that happened to occur. He always maintained a state of good humour and was ever ready to lend a helping hand whenever it was needed. A jolly, giant of a man, he was liked by everyone. He never permitted reverses in his fishery operations, nor losses by storm and tide to get him down. Meanwhile, he was as mischevious as any imp.

Uncle John complied with the gendarme's request by using a verse which had instantly formed itself in his agile brain. Shouting the words quickly in the loudest voice he could command, he announced:

"A john-of-arms have lost his purse, money in it that's worse, he who lost it let him seek it, and he who finds it, let him keep it!"

The old fisherman risked his neck by repeating that verse three or four times. Fortunately for him, neither the policeman not any other Frenchman in the vicinity apparently understood the true meaning of the words. Of course, John uttered them very rapidly. That is probably what saved him. Although the gendarme appeared greatly surprised and annoyed at the great roar of laughter which went up from the Newfoundlanders present when Uncle John reeled off his verse, he showed his appreciation to the old rhymster by shaking his hand and patting him vigorously on the back, saying, "Good man, good man, tank you, tank you."

"Say, Uncle John," enquired a friend, "do that john-of-arms know you? Cause I heard 'im call you by name."

Sure he knows me and I knows him," replied Uncle John, grinning from ear to ear. "The son of a bitch locked me up one night last year because he figured that I took a couple of drinks too many. Well, me son, that little pome (poem) of mine have settled that score a little bit."

The moment we landed in Saint Pierre, our three lads had darted away to enjoy a few rums, my father went over to inspect the dories, he would have a few snorts later on, no doubt. As for me, I sneaked off to buy some bananas, a fruit that was not available in the stores back home.

A large number of the discarded dories were practically new, as they had been used for only three or four months. The remainder varied in age from one to three years. All of them were in good condition and ready for the ocean.

A new dory right out of the factory in Saint Pierre, back in those days cost $35.00, while the American and Shelburne types, sold for $40.00. A price of thirty-five or forty dollars per dory compared to present day costs, could be considered an absolute steal. However, the price tag on the second hand dories from the French bankers was $8.00 each, regardless of their age. That proved to be a mistake. For when the sale got underway all the prospective buyers who had recognized the newer dories previously, naturally tried to get their hands on the number one dories. If the merchants had had the foresight to divide them into two categories, then have them nested accordingly, with the older dories being priced a little lower than the newer ones, things might not have gone too badly. Now with a mob of half-drunken men striving to get at the newer dories, all hell broke loose. The older craft were lifted out of their nests by powerful hands and cast to one side, so as the buyers could gain access to the newer dories stacked beneath them. Fights broke out, eyes were blackened, lips were battered and noses flattened, as blows from iron hard fists connected. Men were sent rolling over and over in all directions. Some of them bounced right up to enter the fray once more, others did not rise so quickly. Shortly after the melee started, I had climbed to the roof of a small shed and from that ringside vantage point, at one time, I counted five men who had been knocked out cold.

After a while, I arrived back to where my father and our three men were standing. It was obvious that the boys had indulged in a few shots of liquor and were in the mood for men, women or war. I found them urging my father to move in and pick up a good dory before they were all gone.

"Not yet," he told them, "do you see that dory at the bottom of the second nest? The red and white one. Well, that is the boat we're goin' to take. You will notice that her paint is scaled off quite a bit, which gives her a shabby appearance. So, apparently everyone is under the impression that she is one of the older craft, as nobody has tried to get down to her. But I looked her over when we arrived here and discovered that she is nearly brand new. When she is finally cleared, we will move in quickly, turn her bottom up, lift her on our shoulders and take her along to our trap boat. I have already paid for her."

At this juncture, half a dozen gendarmes arrived on the scene and by exerting superhuman efforts managed to bring about some semblance of order, which made things go more smoothly. When there was only one dory left into the craft my father selected, he said to me, "You start off now, go down to our skiff, get onboard and stay there until we arrive."

So I took my departure.

I had been seated in our boat for about fifteen minutes when I saw my father and the three other men approaching at a dog trot. They had secured the red and white dory and were toting her along bottom up with the gunnels resting on their shoulders. Incidentally, that is the easiest way in which four men may carry a dory, as it is less strenuous than lugging her mouth up by holding on to her risers or gunnels, as then the boat will chafe against and impose distressing pressure on the legs of her carriers. As the men drew near, I wondered why they were running, for there was nobody pursuing them, in fact no person was anywhere near them.

I had already heard my father say that the dory was paid for, so evidently they were not trying to sneak her away free gratis. In any case, I sensed that something was amiss, so I stood upon the skiff's fore cuddy and commenced to untie her painter from the ringbolt of the pierhead. Then Bert Hooper, who was nearest to me yelled.

"Don't take the time to untie it, b'y, grab that sheath knife stuck in the timber and slash it. We gotta get outa here fast."

Well in those days a kid did not ask questions when he was given an order by a grown man. So as the men laid down the dory and yanked her onboard the skiff to lay her fore and aft along the larger boat's thwarts, I severed the painter with a single cut of that razor sharp, Green River knife.

Gasping with the exertion of lugging the heavy dory and running, the men scattered. My father darted aft and seized the tiller stick, Len Pitman raced to the engine and bent over it, while Bert Hooper and Tom Haley pushed the skiff's head away from the wharf with a boathook and a dory oar, The engine started the first time that Len threw the flywheel. Very reliable engines, those old Acadia's. A moment later we were heading for home.

Bert Hooper went aft to sit beside my father, who was steering, Len Pitman stayed with the engine, giving it all his attention, while I sat on the bow thwart with Tom Haley. As we sped down the harbour, I noticed that my father and the other men kept looking back over their shoulders, as if they were expecting someone to give chase after them. Most of the Newfoundland trapskiff owners and trawlmen were commencing to move out with their newly acquired dories. But apart from that activity no other boats were in sight, French boats that is. I imagined that those were the type our men would be worried about. That they were edgy about something was very obvious. When we had reached outside the northeast exit from the harbour, Tom Haley turned to me and remarked, "Ya know, it's a peculiar thing that them john-of-arms don't come out in the *Saint Pierre* (small French steamer) and try to capture us."

When Tom uttered that statement I could contain my curiosity no longer.

"Tom," I queried, rather apprehensively, "what happened back there?"

The genial Tom reached into a hip pocket, produced a fresh plug of French chewing tobacco, studied it quizzically for a moment, then he bit off a generous chew. It is funny how a man will remember a little thing after a lapse of more than half a century. Yet, there are times today when he cannot even remember his own telephone number. For I have always remembered the trade name of that tobacco. I read it on the label while Tom was holding it up. The name was 'Ladanza'.

Tom rolled his cud over a few times, then said, "Well, me son, I might as well tell you the truth. The fact is, yer father flattened one of them john-of-arms. Knocked 'im a cold junk. You remembers," he continued, "that when the dory sale was on, there was six john-of-armses around, well, when the crowd thinned out and things quieted down they all went away. Now," said Tom, "just as we was goin' to pick up our dory, up comes this brave warrior of a john-of-arms, I knows 'im, Freyleau is his name. He is sportin' a black eye. Anyways, he grabbed yer father be the arm, then pointin' to his sore eye, he shouts out, 'You done that! You the man! You are under arrest! You come

168

along now! One day in the night last week, you strike me, bang, bang, wit your fist. You run away then, but me know you and now me got you!' "

It was clearly a case of mistaken identity, for my father had not visited Saint Pierre for more than six months prior to the day of the dory sale.

According to Tom Haley, the skipper did everything in his power to try and convince Freyleau that he was attempting to arrest the wrong man. But the gendarme with stubborn detachment insisted that he had the right man. Then Freyleau made a bad mistake, for he let go his hold on my father's arm and seized him by the throat raging as he did so, "You, the man, you come!"

Getting nipped by the throat apparently, was the last straw as far as dad was concerned. The gendarme's grip was tightening on his windpipe and was hurting as well as choking him. So he tore Freyleau's squeezing fingers away from his throat with his left hand, then according to the way Tom Haley described it, he hit the officer a dazzler, square on the snout with his right fist.

"Freyleau," continued Tom, "went down and out with blood pourin' from both nostrils. We left Freyleau lyin' flat on his back, we picked up the dory and runned and here we is."

It was several months later before we learned why there was no pursuit by the French police on the day of our escape. The painter of the skiff which I had severed was they key to the puzzle. For that piece of Manilla rope was the slim thread which had spelled the difference betwen incarceration and freedom. We learned also that a squad of gendarmes had arrived on the wharf searching for my father shortly after we had taken our departure. According to the French law of that day, had our boat been still tied to the wharf when the gendarmes arrived there, she would have been considered a part of France, thus giving the police the right to board her and arrest my father. But, when her painter was severed freeing her from the wharf she had to be classed as a British vessel on the high seas, with the result that neither the boat nor any member of her crew could be seized, detained or arrested without the French Authorities first going through usually long drawn out extraditional procedures. That piece of intelligence had been imparted to my father by the French Administrator when he met him at the conclusion of the Freyleau affair.

Meanwhile, word had gotten around Saint Pierre that Freyleau had been assaulted by a former Anglais soldat (English soldier). My father had never been a soldier, English or otherwise. As I have stated in another chapter, he was an ex-policeman. Apparently that fact had in some way become confused with the soldier business.

At this point I will have to go back one year from the day of the Freyleau incident in order to prove that one man at least adhered to the old adage, 'One good turn deserves another.'

169

At 9:00 a.m. on a fine day in June, 1915, the little French steamer, *Saint Pierre*, came into our harbour and landed the Honourable Ernest Phillippe Lachap, the Administrator of Saint Pierre et Miquelon, his wife and six of their friends. The official and party intended to enjoy a day's fishing in a chain of ponds situated a mile west of the settlement. Lugging picnic baskets, fishing rods and other paraphernalia, they proceeded to the ponds on foot. After landing the Administrator, the steamer returned to Saint Pierre. It had been arranged for her to return to pick up the group at 6:00 p.m.

Monsieur Lachap, although not a full-fledged governor, was always called the Governor by both Saint Pierre and Newfoundland residents and was addressed as Your Excellency. So from now on I will use those terms when referring to Monsieur Lachap.

After the French visitors had been at the ponds for about two yours, the sky became overcast, the wind started to blow pretty strongly from the southeast. Then it commenced to rain, lightly at first, but it quickly developed into a real downpour. Under those unsavory conditions, the Governor and his friends quickly deserted their fishing and headed for the settlement as fast as they could walk. But before they even reached the first houses they were drenched to the skin.

Going down to the waterfront, they huddled in shivering misery under the lee of an old fish store, which afforded them only cold comfort at best. Many hours would pass before the steamer called back for them. So, ordinarily they would have been in for an extremely miserable time.

My father, on observing their plight went down and invited them to come up to the house. The half-drowned couples gratefully accepted his invitation. My mother bustled around serving them hot tea and food. Then she lit a fire in the parlour grate. Ushering the ladies into that room, she made them divest themselves of their wet clothing. Then she wrapped them in blankets while she dried their garments in front of the fire. With my father in attendance, the men followed the same procedure out in the kitchen.

When the *Saint Pierre* returned at the appointed time, there was no rain falling and the wind had just about died away. The Governor, his wife and their friends boarded the steamer warm, well fed and dry. But before he took his departure the emotional Frenchman with tears of gratitude streaming down his cheeks, thanked my parents most profusely.

"My good friends," he told them, "if at any time I am in the position to return the wonderful favour you have done us today, then you will not find me indifferent. I assure you both, that should you ever make a request of me whether it be great or small, then consider me as your servant, for I shall grant it immediately if it is in my power to do so."

Now one year after the visit of his Excellency, my father set out for Saint

Pierre to purchase a dory, a venture which ended up with his becoming a wanted man on the French island, with a price on his head.

That a reward was being offered for his capture was attested to by several men from our place, when when they visited the French town had been advised by the gendarmes that if they could entice my father to come to Saint Pierre so as they could arrest him, the reward would be a great many francs. For my father, a man who was gaining his livelihood mainly from the fisheries to be unable to visit the French island was a decided inconvenience, that hampered him greatly. For at times it was necessary to visit Saint Pierre in order to obtain items pertaining to fishing operations, which were not available in the stores at home. My father reflected on the promises made to him by the French Governor when he had befriended that official a year before. He wondered if his Excellency would keep his word respecting returning favours and granting requests.

Accordingly, he wrote the Governor explaining how Freyleau had evidently mistaken him for some other man and how when the gendarme had violently assaulted him, he had felt compelled to defend himself. For after all, he pointed out, he was innocent of any wrongdoing and had been wrongly accused. He then asked the Governor if he was endowed with the power to have the charges made against him withdrawn. His Excellency promptly replied. Here in part, is his answer:

'Of course, my friend, I have the power to clear you of all charges which I will do, as I have not by any means forgotten the kind hospitality you showed us on that terribly stormy day last year, but it is with extreme regret that I have to advise you, I am unable to clear you of charges by letter alone. For according to our laws, you must appear before me in person, on French soil to make your plea or request. But, here, my friend, will be your greatest handicap, for if and when you land in Saint Pierre and are making your way to my office should the police manage to apprehend you enroute, then I will be powerless to aid you, for then the charges against you will have to run the full course.

'If you are convicted, I do not have the power to interfere with the decision of the presiding judge. Any decision made in that regard would have to come before a higher authority in France. On the other hand, if you reach me before the police manage to arrest you, all will be well. On that you may rest assured. Once again I have to express regret at what must appear to you to be a peculiar law. But, unfortunately for you my friend, it is the law and I have no choice but to abide by it.

'For your peace of mind, I am delighted to be able to inform you that the gendarme, Freyleau, whom you were forced to defend yourself against, is now well and has returned to duty.'

For my father to seek an audience with the Governor at that time was manifestly impossible. As he had been informed by the men from Lamaline, who were visiting Saint Pierre from time to time, all boats arriving there from Newfoundland were thoroughly searched by a squad of gendarmes. While both day and night a guard of officers kept up a steady patrol along the waterfront. Apparently the police were obsessed with the mistaken idea that Freyleau had been bested and humiliated by the same man on two separate occasions. Evidently, they were determined that this man was going to pay the penalty, which in all probability would mean serving a long term in some prison in France. For assaults on their policemen were viewed with much greater concern by French judges and the penalty for such an offence was far more severe than would be the case in Newfoundland, if a member of our Constabulary were the victim of an assault.

The gendarmes continued their waterfront patrols and the searching of boats for three months. Then suddenly their activities in that capacity ceased. Visitors returning from Saint Pierre reported that no longer were they being harassed by the police. They reported also that the steady waterfront patrols by members of the gendarmerie had been discontinued. My father, thinking with the mind of a former policeman, was suspicious of that turn of events. Could it be, he wondered, that the gendarmes had removed their patrols and discontinued the searching of boats in order to lull him into a false sense of security? ... with the hope that he would throw discretion to the winds and return to Saint Pierre. Anyway, after three weeks had gone by without police activity being renewed as far as his case was concerned, he decided to take his chances and return to the French island.

Accordingly, he left Lamaline in his trapskiff at 3:00 o'clock on a Sunday morning, hoping that if the engine kept working he would search Saint Pierre by 5:00 a.m. He was accompanied by my brother Ron and Bert Hooper. He was aware that at that early hour on Sunday there would be no police or citizens moving about. In those days even the fishermen who were always on the go long before dawn, did not go fishing on the Sabbath.

The wind and sea, when he left home, were reasonably calm. But when he had gotten halfway to his destination, or 'half bay' as the oldtimers termed it, a stiff breeze sprang up, blowing southwest or dead ahead of his boat. This caused a nasty windlop which slowed him up so greatly that he did not arrive in Saint Pierre until 6:00 a.m. which meant that when he pulled into the wharf that he had vacated so hastily three months before, he was one hour behind his planned time of arrival.

He instructed Ron and Bert to stay in the boat, then peering cautiously up over the pierhead he could observe that not a living soul was in sight. Then he decided it had to be now or never. So he sprang up over the wharf and made for the Governor's residence as fast as he could walk. He was tempted to make a run for it, but feared that if he did so he might attract the attention of some early riser who happened to be looking through a window and might decide to let the police worry as to why a man was running around that early in the morning.

As he neared the Governor's home, he suddenly experienced quite a chill, for church bells started to ring, causing the unhappy thought to come to him that Excellency at that moment may be on his way to attend an early mass. The skipper admitted later that his hand was trembling when he pressed a finger against the doorbell. But he was in luck, for seconds later the door was opened by the Governor himself, who greeted him warmly and invited him to come in. When they were seated in the office of his Excellency, my father's first words were, "I must apologize sir, for disturbing you at this ungodly hour. Then when I heard the church bells ringing I must confess I feared that you had gone to mass."

"You did not disturb my slumbers," replied the Governor, "for I always rise at an early hour." He added, "My wife, daughters and the maid have gone to attend mass, but this morning I decided to stay at home and I am very glad now that I did. For I do not know what you would have done had I not been here. Now," continued the Governor, "first we will have one drink, then I shall prepare and sign the document which will declare you free from arrest."

When the paper was ready, the Governor conducted my father over to the gendarmerie headquarters where his Excellency instructed the officer in charge to call his men on parade. When they were lined up (Freyleau was included in the group) the Governor read the contents of the document to them, patting my father on the shoulder occasionally, as he proceeded.

When the reading was completed he instructed the C.O. to dismiss the parade, he also instructed him to post the document on the wall of the genarmerie parade room. Then turning to my father, he shook hands with him and told him, "You are now free to go. You may walk the streets of Saint Pierre at any hour without fear of being arrested or of being harassed by the police."

The man who had first assaulted gendarme Freyleau, blackening his eye, and who obviously was identical to my father in appearance, was never located. There was a strong rumour floating around to the effect that the mystery man was a crewmember of an American Banks fishing schooner, but no fact concerning the rumour could be substantiated.

Needless to say, my father's thanks to the Governor for intervening on his behalf were most profound. When he took his departure from the gendarmerie headquarters, he, in all probability, was the happiest man on the island of Saint Pierre.

CHAPTER ELEVEN

The Dory and The Trawl

Captain Angus Walters, skipper of the famous fishing/racing Canadian schooner, *Bluenose,* once affirmed: 'The dory is the finest small row boat that was ever invented.' I am confident that you would not find a single Banks dory or shore fisherman who will disagree with the internationally known captain on that point. For Captain Walters was a man who certainly knew all about dories. He first went to the Banks at the age of fifteen, as a doryman in his father's vessel. Later he rose to command, in addition to the *Bluenose,* many other fine vessels sailing out of his home port of Lunenburg, Nova Scotia.

Newfoundland's Captain Arch Thornhill, a veteran of forty-two years of Banks fishing, told me that whilst he was fishing on the Grand Bank in the schooner, *Florence,* during World War Two, one of his dories broke loose from the ship and drifted away. He could not risk sending men out to try and recover her as the wind was blowing too strongly and the water was rough. Some months later, a brother of one of Captain Thornhill's crewmen, serving in the Royal Navy, noticed a dory hauled up on a pier in a seaport town in England. When he observed the name *Florence* painted on the dory's quarter, he conjured up fears that the banker had been torpedoed and her crew, which included his brother, had either been taken prisoner by the Germans or in some manner had lost their lives. He instantly made enquiries along the waterfront with a view to ascertaining how the dory came to be there.

He learned that she had been picked up by a British destroyer two miles off the English coast a few days before. The naval men who had discovered the craft informed him that they were unable to enlighten him as to where she came from, nor why she happened to be in that locality. The young New-foundlander then dispatched a cablegram to the vessel's owners telling about his finding the dory and enquiring as to the safety or otherwise of the schooner and her crew. A reply from them assuring him that the banker was in her home port and that all her crewmen were safe and well. The message added

Captain Archibald Thornhill, a Newfoundland Banks fishing skipper for 42 years —(Courtesy of Captain Thornhill).

that Captain Thornhill had reported the loss of one of his dories when he had returned from one of his Banks fishing trips a couple of months before.

That little boat had drifted clear across the Atlantic Ocean, a distance of more than two thousand miles. The amazing part related to her long journey was that when found, she was right side up, she contained no water and all her equipment, including her oars and sail, were in place. Just how many storms she encountered enroute may never be known, but she commenced her unmanned voyage during a wild wind storm that was accompanied by high running seas.

Captain Thornhill concluded his story by adding, "I am sure that no other sail boat could have gone over that great expanse of ocean and yet have remained unwaterlogged and so perfectly seaworthy. Of course," he concluded, "apart from that incident I have known the dory to prove her superior qualities on numerous occasions."

After Simeon Lowell built his first dories in 1793, it was not too long before shore fishermen who had been using keel boats known to Newfoundlanders as punts and rodneys, but to Americans and Nova Scotians as skiffs, quickly recognized their capabilities as excellent sea boats. They noted also, that for their size, dories were remarkable carriers, for they could bear up more than a ton of homely, banjo-eyed codfish and still have enough freeboard left over to keep them seaworthy even in rough water. In addition, they were easier to manipulate than keel boats and could be operated in shallower water. Being

175

flat bottomed also, they could be launched out and hauled up with far less labour.

Contrary to what most people believe today, the dory was not specifically designed nor developed for the Banks fisheries. Actually, according to tradition, the reason for her being used on the Banks at all came about as the result of the incidental invention. In brief here is that story.

One day in the late 1840s, a young fisherman on the deck of an American schooner which was anchored on the Banks (probably Georges) during a rest period, idly tied a half dozen baited hooks to a half dozen small lines and attached them a few feet apart along a larger single line. He weighted one end of the main line, then holding the other end fast, he threw it off from the vessel's side. Minutes later he hauled it back onboard and discovered, to his delight, that he had caught a half dozen fish. Right then and there the idea for that wonderful piece of equipment, the trawl, sometimes call 'bultow', was born.

For many years both before and after Simeon Lowell invented the dory, the fishermen of all nations who frequented the great fishing Banks handlined their take from the decks of their vessels using single, baited hooks. So for a considerable period of time or until the trawl was invented, the dory remained strictly a shore fisherman's boat.

One American writer gives a Frenchman from Dieppe the credit for inventing the trawl, however, in his article he does not produce proof to substantiate his assertion or belief, nor does he divulge the source of his information. Neither do I have any proof that the trawl was invented by an American fisherman in the manner I have described, I simply used the words, 'according to tradition'. What is tradition anyway? Well, I have always been led to believe that it is an opinion, a belief or a custom handed down from ancestor to prosterity, or from father to son. Whereas, the citizens of Dieppe may be rejoicing in the belief that one of their ancestors was responsible for inventing the trawl, the old time fishermen of Saint Pierre et Miquelon, apparently, never entertained that idea. Sixty years ago, at any rate, they always gave the credit for the innovation to the same people to whom Newfoundlanders gave the credit. I presume that they must have gotten their information from the same source that we did. It was simply handed down.

Regardless of who invented the trawl there is one fact that cannot be denied which is, the Americans were the first fishermen to use dories at trawl fishing on the Banks. For the first dories used by Frenchmen were purchased from the Lowell factory in Salisbury Point. A resident of Amesbury who visited a French city several years ago, informed Ralph Lowell that on entering a museum there he was extremely pleased to see a full-sized American dory on display with the builders name, 'Hiram Lowell and Sons, Salisbury Point,

Massachusetts, U.S.A.' plainly visible on the boat's stern. The fact that this dory carried the name Salisbury Point, means that she must have been built there before that village was incorporated into the town of Amesbury, which event took place in 1886. After the amalgamation of Salisbury and Amesbury, dories built in the Lowell shop were stencilled with the latter name.

Vessel owners and ship captains took to the trawl as avidly as a codfish takes a caplin, for they were quick to realize its great potential as a fish killer. But, they reasoned also that in order to make trawl fishing successful, their schooners would need to carry a number of small row boats to the Banks, which could enable fishermen to depart from the parent ship for the purpose of setting and tending that type of gear. They realized also, that the traditional keel boats which they carried previously, to serve mainly as lifeboats would be entirely unsuitable owing to their style of construction; for the required number could not be stowed away neatly enough on a vessel's deck to permit the area of space needed to carry other equipment vitally necessary to the operation of trawl fishing.

To tow a string of six or seven keel boats along behind a schooner all the way to the Banks, like chicks after a mother hen, was unthinkable, for a variety of reasons. Here are two of them: Firstly, the boats would undoubtedly break adrift and become lost during any severe blow that happened along. Secondly, the tremendous drag which they would impose upon a vessel that was dependent on sail power alone could make her most difficult to keep on course, particularly during adverse weather and more especially if she was strenuously clawing her way off from a dangerous lee shore. Then, somebody remembered the dory which had been invented by Simeon Lowell several years before. The little flat bottomed boat with the 'V' shaped stern which up to that time had been completely ignored by Banks fishermen, although over the intervening years she had become a great favorite with shore fishermen.

It was already known that dories built from a single plan or pattern may be fitted into one another and nested as snugly and neatly as soup plates in a kitchen cabinet. Consequently, it was felt that dories would be the boats most suitable for vessels to carry when they became engaged in the new venture of trawl fishing. For dories so nested would occupy the space, beamwise and lenghwise of only a single boat. Furthermore, being flat bottomed they would not heel over like the keel boat with the result that more badly needed deck space would be reserved to accommodate other equipment. In addition, dories were by far cheaper and quicker to mass produce than the more frequently timbered keeled types.

The exact date when American fishermen first carried dories to the Banks cannot now be determined, but it was probably in the early 1850s. French and Portuguese fishing skippers who had witnessed the dory's excellent performance while being handled by Americans during their trawling activities on the very often turbulent Banks waters became so impressed with the lively little craft that they lost no time in outfitting their vessels with dories also.

According to an article which appeared in the 'Daily Colonist', in 1875, Henry J. Stabb, who at one time was a customs collector, made a tour of the southern shore of the Avalon Peninsula in September of that year. At Cape Broyle, he spoke to a Captain McGrath, a native of St. John's, who was in command of an American banker sailing out of Gloucester.

Captain McGrath was unhappy because Newfoundland shore fishermen were idle while American, French and Portuguese vessels were getting plenty of fish, one hundred miles or so at sea. McGrath also referred to the methods of fishing on the Banks, namely the use of bultow, a long line from which hung numerous hooks baited regularly with supplies of caplin and herring, kept fresh in ice pounds on deck. The boats used were termed dories. Mr. Stabb remarked that there was an increasing interest in the industry and he expected to see some participation before long, perhaps by the spring of 1876. If one were to judge from the foregoing it appears that Newfoundlanders had not been involved in Banks fishing until after 1875.

However, I located a short item in the 'Evening Mercury', another St. John's newspaper of that period, which disputes that fact; for according to the 'Mercury', 1875 was the year our countrymen actually commenced to prosecute that branch of the fisheries.

'In the spring of 1875,' says the paper, 'the Government issued a bounty to encourage men to fish on the Banks. The bounty was discontinued in 1881, because after six years of trial, the business of deep sea fishing was not self sustaining. They simply could not make it pay.' The article does not state the number of vessels or men who were engaged nor does it say who owned the bankers or who outfitted them, apart from the Government bounty which it must be assumed was but a mere subsidy.

Then on April 10, 1883, the 'Evening Mercury' came back with the following announcement: 'The banking schooner *Betsy*, Captain Nickerson, has been fitting out for the Banks fishery and will be ready for sea this evening. It is hoped that the *Betsy* will be followed by many more under the stimulus of the bounty.' This means, very obviously, that the Government bounty which had been discontinued in 1881 must have been restored in 1883.

Later the 'Mercury' proclaimed that the Newfoundland Banking fleet grew from three vessels in 1883 to thirty-five a short time later and had made excellent progress. 'It surely behooves us,' continued the 'Mercury', 'not to lose our growing supremacy on the Banks of Newfoundland, nor allow it to lapse into the possession of foreigners, for our Banks fisheries have developed in importance equalling half a dozen factories employing one hundred hands each and created a return of its own to the venue prosecuted by our own hardy fishermen instead of them sailing out of American ports on American vessels. In addition, it adds strength and productiveness to our country.'

Well, according to the 'Evening Mercury' our people were worried about encroaching foreigners away back in 1883, when foreigners to Newfoundlanders meant, mostly, Americans and Canadians. For strange as it may seem, although a number of French vessels were operating on the Banks at that time, our people, particularly those of the southwest coast, did not consider Frenchmen to be such dyed-in-the-wool foreigners as the men who came from the United States and Canada.

To begin with, Newfoundlanders were far more inclined to enter into friendly relations with the polite, orderly French than they were with the swaggering, swashbuckling Americans and the bitingly sarcastic Canadians. Then there was our close proximity to the French possession of Saint Pierre et Miquelon. Where on the shore fishing grounds, which could be classed as a communal area, pleasantries and favours were exchanged daily between the fishermen of the two races. But I am confident that one of the most important factors which cemented the spirit of friendliness and co-operation the strong nuptial ties that existed. For down through the years numerous marriages took place between French and Newfoundland residents. There was a time then, when young Frenchmen had fathers and mothers-in-law in the villages along that strip of Newfoundland coast which extends from St. Lawrence to Point May. Therefore, it was not likely that Newfoundland parents would look upon their in-laws as foreigners.

The newspaper editors and fishermen who were so concerned over encroaching foreigners taking possession of our fishing grounds back in 1883, would really know what foreign encroachment is all about if they were around today. If they are aware of it, gazing down from some other realm, they are probably dancing in futile rage on some fleecy cloud high up over our heads.

Research has disclosed that Samuel Harris, of Grand Bank, founder of the firm Samuel Harris and Company Limited, commenced at the Banks fishing industry in 1887, and George Buffett, founder of the firm of G. and A. Buffett of the same town set out on a likewise venture in 1888. Later other firms in Grand Bank and Fortune, Burin, Belleoram, Harbour Breton and Gaultois, to mention some of the places, became active in prosecuting the deep sea fishery. So that by the outbreak of World War One, Newfoundland had a sizable fleet of large ships and a host of smaller craft plying that trade.

The trawl which had such a tiny beginning developed and expanded rapidly so that within a comparatively short space of time it became the golden string from which several schooner owners amassed fortunes. It was also the medium through which many fishing skippers attained such a wealthy status that they could afford to abandon their humble cottages and build towering, impressive looking mansions, that in truly salty style, usually commanded a view of the sea. But too many thousands of ordinary fishermen it caused to be set adrift in tiny dories, it became the means through which their life expectancy became considerably shortened. For it took them from the relative safety of a vessel's deck out amongst towering seas, fog, ice floes and storms with one and one-eighth inch of a dory's bottom between them and the great beyond.

The double or two-man dory usually carried four tubs of trawl, the tubs being approximately the size of three quarters of a flour barrel. The trawl was made up by fastening small lines, which were three feet or so in length, at six foot intervals along a larger line. Hooks were attached to the smaller lines by passing the loops which had been tied previously in the free ends, through the eyes of the hooks, then they were slipped up over the barbed sections and drawn tight. The hooks were baited with herring in the spring, caplin in the summer and squid in the fall.

Coiling the trawls neatly into each individual tub was a paramount necessity, for every section of the main line was at least fifty fathoms in length and there were ten of them to a tub. So that when these were all joined together with the mooring ropes added, it meant that the entire trawl from the four tubs covered a distance of two and one half miles. Then along that great length dangled two thousand hooks. Consequently, dorymen had to be extremely careful when they were setting out or retrieving gear, for should the hooks become entangled on the choppy sea, with the dory bobbing up and down violently, there would be one hell of a grandma's wool snarl of a mess to straighten out. Of course, grandma did not have those pesky hooks on her ball of wool, but there must have been times after her pet cat had created a tangle that she experienced rough going when she was trying to bring her little sphere back to normal again. In that respect she had one advantage over the dorymen, for she was not seated in a bobbing dory far out on the broad Atlantic, so she could do her cussin' in comfort.

In addition to the four tubs of trawl, each dory was required to carry two anchors, one to be dropped at either end of the gear, a bait jack (tub to hold bait), two keg buoys, one of these also was attached to each end of the trawl. The buoys carried flags, usually circular in shape, which were commonly called black balls, as in most cases they were painted black with a white oversized dot in the center, on those white centers were painted numbers which corresponded with the numbers on the bows of the dories that carried them. This was done so that each dory crew could identify their own equipment. The trawl tubs and bait jacks were marked in a similar manner. One of the trawl buoys had its flag staff fastened on the end of the keg and when the dorymen went out to set their trawl, that one was dropped first or nearest the schooner. The other buoy's flag staff was set through the center of the keg and that was put over at the end of the trawl farthest from the mother ship. The reason for the two buoys being rigged differently was when they sighted a buoy, the position of its flag staff would tell them which end of the gear they had located, while the number painted on the flag informed them as to whether they had come upon their own trawl or one belonging to some other doryman.

Each dory also carried five oars and in Newfoundland, Nova Scotian and American dories, a boom and gaff rigged sail, which when the peak was hoisted and the sail set, resembled a schooner's mainsail in miniature. French dorymen used a square sail that was bent on to a gaff with the halyard tied or spliced on at the center so that it was hoisted in a transverse position. The sail was not rigged with a boom but was outfitted with two sheets, one on the lower port side corner, the other on the starboard corner. This rig which Newfoundland fishermen called a lug sail was of the same style as carried on the long ships of Viking rovers. Portuguese Banks dories were (and still are) equipped with Arab dhow or lateen type sails. These are so cut and fashioned that when the gaff is hoisted it serves the dual purpose of forming sail peak and jib.

In addition, the dories carried a conche shell (shell of a mollusk which produced a loud booming sound when a fisherman blew into it), a scoop or water bailer, a hand gaff for hooking fish and pulling them onboard, a compass, a mallet to pound ice off dories which formed during winter fishing. In dories fishing for halibut, the mallet was used to stun or kill the big fish when they were flopping around causing the dorymen trouble. Dories carried two sealed metal containers which were filled: one with water, the other with hard tack. These were emergency rations and were to be used only if dorymen had been astray from their vessels for an unusual period of time.

In connection with emergency food and water rations being carried in Banks dories, I will quote from an article on dory building in Newfoundland which appeared in the newspaper 'Daily Columnist' dated October 23, 1886:

'Before leaving this subject (dory building) it will be remembered that the 'Colonist' referred last summer to the necessity of placing a watertight box in each dory, in which food and water should be placed for use in case of a dory straying from her vessel on the Banks. At this point when dory building is likely to become a permanent local industry, it would be well that something was done in the matter. The size of the box, its position in the boat, the quantity of food necessary, should be regulated by experienced men, from whom any information on the details of the subject will be thankfully received.'

After noting the very fine suggestion made by the 'Daily Colonist' in 1885 and which the paper repeated in 1886, I decided to interview former Banks fishing skippers and dorymen with the hope of ascertaining the exact time that dories on the Newfoundland bankers became outfitted with emergency food and water rations. As a result, I learned that approximately thirty-five years were to pass by before those vital necessities were added to a dory's equipment. None of the skippers and dorymen I talked with could remember the specific year in which that very important innovation took place, but they all were unanimous in declaring it was some time between 1917 and 1920. Had the suggestion, made by that concerned newspaper, been carried out and maintained over the years, it goes without saying that miseries from hunger and thirst suffered by dorymen astray from vessels would have been greatly alleviated. Despite the extensive enquiries I failed to discover where any law or regulation had been implemented which compelled the owners of bankers to have their dories equipped with food and water rations. None of the old fishermen I interviewed in that connection can recall any such law. They are simply under the impression that dories were so outfitted only after the owners had received urgent requests from skippers and dorymen to have it done. The food and water containers were usually made by local tinsmiths from light weight galvanized tin, and when they had been filled with hard tack and water the covers were clapped on, then sealed with solder.

Apparently there was no regular inspection of those containers by any responsible officials from the firm who sent the bankers out, or from the Government, so that when they were sealed they probably remained unopened for years or until some unfortunate dorymen who had gone astray, suffering from hunger and thirst, upon opening the seals and removing the covers, discovering to their dismay that both food and water were unfit for human consumption, as had happened in the case of dorymen William Dodge and George Bishop.

Two other items most indispensable to Banks fishermen were the roller and the runner. The roller, a circular shaped block of lignum vitae wood of an exceptionally hard nature, has a hole bored in the center of its flat surface, which enables it to be suspended from an iron rod between the ears of a galvanized iron frame. The two merge below the roller to form a single staff which is inserted into a hole in the dory's gunnel a short distance aft of the stemhead. The roller which revolved freely on its shaft is deeply grooved completely around the center of its edge. The main trawl line is placed in this groove when fishermen are hauling or underrunning a fleet of gear. The roller then adequately shows the reason why it is so named, for it rolls when the trawl is being pulled inboard thereby making that arduous task much easier to accomplish than if the lines were hauled in over a dory's somewhat resistant gunnel.

The trawl runner or running stick may be classed as a roller also, although in design it is entirely different from the gunnel roller. It is made up of a section of plank, five feet long, four inches wide and two and one half inches thick. A foot and a half back from each end of this piece of wood the center is sawn out to the depth of one and a quarter inches which forms a square edged niche two feet long. A hole is bored in an up and down position in each end of the niche, then a rounded stick, two feet long and one inch in diameter is inserted into the holes, which permits it to roll or revolve without jamming. Both ends of the stick holder are tapered wedge shape. This is done so that the contrivance may be stuck down firmly between the dory's gunnel and her riser, which places the running stick facing inboard in a perpendicular position. In the days of dory fishing, underrunning a trawl and hauling a trawl were two different operations.

In setting a trawl preparatory to underrunning it, an anchor with the main trawl line, keg buoy, buoyline (called a haul-up line), moorings and slablines were dropped. The entire fleet of gear was then run out and a second anchor equipped with the same accessories as the first was put over, mooring the trawl. The mooring ropes were of six or nine thread manila being usually sixty fathoms in length. The slablines which were eighteen pound lines, reached a length of approximately fifty fathoms. One end of those lines was fastened to the ends of the mooring ropes, the other to the ends of the trawl. Where mooring ropes and slablines joined, the buoylines were attached. The length of the buoylines were governed by the depth of the water being fished. The reason for the mooring ropes and the slablines having such a great length was that while the trawl was being hauled up there was far less danger of the anchor jumping out of its holding ground and tripping over to leave its flukes lying flat. With a strong tide running such an incident could prove extremely troublesome, as it was possible for the anchor to drag one hundred fathoms or more before it turned upright again and got another grip on the bottom. Meanwhile, the trawl could have doubled up and become hopelessly tangled. In an underrunning operation also, the trawl remained moored with the men hauling along, taking off fish and rebaiting hooks.

In the Banks fishing industry, weather, of course, was the key factor. It was the banker's captain's responsibility not only to locate a good fishing area but it was incumbent upon him to use his judgement as to how weather may affect the coming and going of his dorymen. Normally each dory carried four tubs of trawl, when all those lines were set it meant that dories were more than two miles from the parent ship. So previous to his men starting out, if the skipper on reading his barometer and gazing anxiously at the sky, reasoned that bad weather might show up fairly quickly, he would not permit his dory crews to take a full complement of gear, but would often limit them to two, sometimes three tubs, so as they would not be such a great distance away if a storm broke. It was while a trawl was being underrun that the running stick played an important role. It was jammed down in the dory's riser a little aft of midships; when the lines were hauled in over the bow roller they also ran along on the roller in the running stick. This stick not only had the effect of keeping the dory broadside to the trawl, it assisted the man hauling to keep his grip on the lines when the winds and tides were working against him. The direction in which tides were moving was an important consideration. Former dorymen have told me that sometimes they would find it handier to haul in the same direction it was running. But for example, if ten dories set out to underrun trawls, they went in ten different directions, therefore, some of the men would be obliged to operated with the tide running at right angles to the trawl and the dory or to use a dorymen's expression, they would be hauling across the tide. On such an occasion the main trawl line was stretched bar tight. Add some wind pressure blowing in the same direction which the tide was running and there was every possibility of the man hauling the trawl losing his grip on it. Then if it should snap overboard as the second man was in the act of rebaiting, the chances were that the barbed hook would enter one or both of his hands and then be torn out again as the trawl twanged away, inflicting injuries that could prove serious. The use of the running stick greatly eliminated that danger. Even if no injuries resulted when the gear was disappearing, the men would have to row back to the haul-up lines and start all over again, which would be a distressing and tiresome chore.

Banks fishermen usually underran their trawls three times a day, before breakfast, after breakfast and during the afternoon. But if weather conditions and other factors were favourable, they often made a fourth trip.

Like I stated previously, the underrunning of the trawl gear and hauling of it were two distinct operations. For while the gear being underrun remained moored, in the hauling process it did not, but was taken back onboard the dory and coiled into the tubs as the fishermen proceeded. Then again in preparing to set trawls for underrunning, the dories were rowed out from the parent ship which remained anchored. However, in making ready to set trawls which were to be hauled, the opposite was the case. The vessel did not remain at anchor but kept moving ahead putting over her dories as she advanced. This method was called flying setting. Later when the dorymen had recovered their trawls the schooner which had remained in the vicinity cruised around and picked them up.

Two systems could be employed in making a flying set. One was to tow the dories in two groups. To effect this strong lines called dory ropes were put over the vessel's stern through the rouse chocks on her taffrail, one on the starboard side, the other on the port. All along the dory ropes, loops or bights were tied or spliced in at regular intervals and of a sufficient distance apart so that the dories would not bump into each other as they were being towed along. A schooner which carried ten dories would have five trailing from the starboard side and five from the port.

As the dory ropes were being payed out, the painter of each dory, as it was dropped into the water, was rove through the loops, the end was then brought back onboard the dory, passed down through her riser aft of the fo'ard thwart where it was nipped and held by the bow doryman. By passing the painter down through the riser and niping it against the thwart, it could be held with very little effort. On the other hand, if that method were not employed and the man was holding the end of the painter that had been passed through the loop in the dory rope only, it would be most difficult to hang on to it, more especially so if the vessel was forging ahead over a turbulent ocean. At such a time there was every possibility of the doryman losing his grip on the painter. If that should occur in one of the dories at the head of or center of the tow, the painter would slip out of the loop in the dory rope, the craft would go adrift and turn broadside, then the dories coming from behind would collide violently with her, capsize her and be towed right over her as she went bottom up. Unless they were exceptionally fortunate two more fishermen would have been sent to watery graves.

When Banks fishermen were engaged in making a flying set, towing dories, usually it was the skipper himself who steered the ship. He would tow his dories along until he reached an area where, according to his judgement, fish were plentiful. Then on a prearranged signal from him, the men in the dory on the end of the tow rope on the port side would put over a keg buoy, when the buoyline was all out or nearly so, they would release their dory from the tow rope, drop anchor and run out their trawl. The vessel would then be moved ahead a trawl berth and the men in the dory at the end of the tow rope on the starboard side, also acting on a signal, would throw over their keg buoy and release their dory. The process of dropping a dory from the port side and another from the starboard side would be repeated until all dories were out.

The second method used when making a flying set was as follows: First all the dories were not towed, but instead the top dories on both port and starboard sides were hoisted out of their nests and put over the schooner's sides. They were not dropped into the water immediately, however, but would remain suspended, held up by their burtons or hoisting tackle on the ends of which were four foot long iron hooks, called dory jigs (or as the dorymen used to say, they would be kept in slings).

The men assigned to those dories boarded them, with one man going for'ard, the other aft. A line which had one end made fast onboard the vessel and the other end held by the bow doryman was called a safety rope. The end of this rope, which was held by the bow man, had first been passed through the dories' nose straps then down through the risers and nipped in the same process of handling which had taken place during the towing operation. The main function of the safety ropes was to keep the dories running parallel or broadside with the schooner once they were dropped into the water and the jibs released from their nose and stern straps. If there were no safety ropes and the man in the bow should unhook his jig before the man aft had released his, the dory would swing across the seas and there was every possibility of her being capsized. Such an incident could very well end in tragedy.

The dories would remain in slings until the men in the one hanging over the port side received a signal from the captain to throw over their keg buoy. Then when the buoyline had run out the dory would be dropped into the water, the jigs unhooked and the safety rope let go releasing her from the vessel. The skipper, carrying on, would drop dories from the port and starboard sides alternately, until they were all out. When making flying sets preparatory to hauling trawls, the long mooring ropes and slablines used during an underrunning operation were dispensed with, those were replaced by a short mooring rope only, for when hauling trawl, following a flying set, it was a business fraught with danger, that called for perfect timing and co-operation between skipper and dorymen.

Before the advent of the large motor dory, there were three sizes recognized in Newfopundland as far as regular fishing dories were concerned. Those were the fifteen foot, the fourteen foot and the thirteen foot. By these measurements I am setting forth bottom lengths only, for some types had considerably more fore and aft rake (at the ends) than others, resulting in their being longer on the top sides. Any sizes in between or larger or smaller than the three mentioned above were referred to as bastard sizes.

In the early days of salt banking, after various sizes had been tested, the fifteen foot was finally settled on as being the most suitable to accommodate two men. Consequently, they wee known as the double or two-man dories. The fourteen foot in some instances was used by one or two men engaged at the shore fishery when dory trawling. But the thirteen foot became more popular with the shore fishermen, who desired to fish cross-handed or alone, as many of them did. For that handy little boat was light to row and not too difficult to launch out or haul up by a lone fisherman.

Just how tough is a dory and what is her life span? Well, despite her rather flimsy, sparsely timbered appearance, she is deceivingly strong, as indeed she needed to be, particularly when caught out in heavy weather, to withstand the mighty punches of vicious Atlantic seas.

Alfred Johnson, a Gloucester fisherman, personally proved the strength and seaworthiness of his dory when he voyaged alone from Barrington, Nova Scotia to Liverpool, England in 1875. Johnson encountered many storms enroute and rough seas that would have drowned him if he had been in a boat of different design. By rowing and sailing, he completed the voyage in sixty-seven days. It is believed that Johnson's epic journey inspired Rudyard Kipling to write his famous novel, 'Captains Courageous', which was eventually made into a movie depicting a dory fisherman's life on the Banks.

The Banks fishing dory's life span could be anywhere between three and five years, depending, of course, on the usage she had received. The daily pounding against a schooner's side whilst fish was being unloaded from her, coupled with the great strain imposed when she was hoisted outboard and inboard so frequently quickly took their toll of the Banks dory. The shore fishing, trawling dory in the majority of cases lasted much longer, as she was not subjected to the rough treatment which conditions forced the Banks dory to undergo. Moreover, she was usually anchored in a safe harbour each night or was resting upon a beach or slipway. I have known some shore fishing dories to keep in shape and remain seaworthy as long as fifteen years under the care of the gnarled, but loving hands of their owners.

With regard to dories which were in use as secondary boats to codtrap skiffs, however, a different picture is presented. They wore out quicker and usually received damages more frequently than did the trawling dories. Heavy trap anchors would be taken onboard them to be set out, then later when the occasion demanded it, they would be hauled up from the dories and placed onboard them again to be transferred to the skiff. I have known cases where fishermen were in the act of placing one of these anchors in a dory when they slipped and dropped the weighty hook causing the sharp pointed fluke to descend and punch a hole in the bottom or a side board of a boat. Then when loaded down to the rubbers with fish, she would be towed by the trapskiff which often occurred twice or three times daily. At such times with a heavy following scend in the water or there was a towering wind lop racing up from behind, a tremendous strain was placed on the dory, particularly when the larger boat jerked the slack of the towline tight. On one occasion, under those conditions, I saw Skipper Tom Tuff's trapskiff pluck the stempost completely out of his loaded dory towing behind.

A new or nearly new dory purchased in Saint Pierre would have a sheer as crooked as a rainbow. But after a couple of years accompanying a trapskiff, her upper lengthwise profile would appear as almost straight. If a codtrap owner managed to get a dory to last out for four or five years, then he was extremely lucky.

During the days of the great salt bankers, seamen and landlubbers alike took plenty of time out to view and voice praises towards the graceful beauty of those fine vessels. Their yacht-appearing lines drew expressions of admiration from young and old, male and female.. But scarcely anyone wasted a second glance on the little yellow painted dories nested on their decks, which from a distance reminded one of lemon slices stacked on a platter. Yet the great schooners, beautiful though they were, would have been useless as the boobs on the Statue of Liberty without their accompanying dories. For when all is said and done the dories were the real, the super fish catchers.

Reliable wooden dories are used today as lifeboats on draggers and longiners — (Robert Kelland Photo).

The secret of the dory's outstanding seaworthy qualities lies in her flat bottom, sharp ends and outward flaring sides. Her wedge-like shape causes her to be forced up on top of murderous seas that roar down on her, which would swamp and destroy a boat of wall sided design with comparable dimensions.

By the time the United States had entered the second World War, the dory output of Hiram Lowell had shrunk to a mere handful, for another revolution hit the Banks fisheries, replacing the once revolutionary trawl and the handsome able schooners were forced off the seas by the diesel powered draggers which drew tough fibered nets along the ocean's floor, bringing up everything that swam or crawled. Meanwhile, wreaking destruction, irreparable on the spawning beds of various species.

Today, powerful, refrigerated vessels set out from Newfoundland, Nova Scotia and New England, make speedy trips to the Banks, then if they are lucky, return with cargo spaces filled with fresh fish. So, today's fisherman has landed right back where his great-grandfather started. He is pulling in the fish from the deck of a vessel.

CHAPTER TWELVE

Oars

As a Banks fishing schooner would have been useless without dories, it follows that dories would have been useless without oars. I am referring, of course, to the days of 'the absolute row dory'.

Meanwhile in the present day of motor dories, no sensible motor doryman would go to sea without taking along one pair of old reliable oars. For in case of an engine breakdown he would stand a good chance of rowing back to land. Without oars, well, he would just be obliged to drift to wherever wind and tide fancied to take him.

When I was a youngster, I had quite a fascination for dory oars; they were so cleanly and beautifully shaped and very smooth. To use the words of one fisherman who gazed upon his new set of oars with admiration, 'they are as smooth as a glass bottle'.

Our fishermen made their own trapskiff oars. Fifteen foot sweeps manufactured by hand from spruce logs which were purchased onboard schooners arriving in our harbour from Bay d'Espoir, loaded with various types of timber to sell. They did not make dory oars, however. These were usually shipped in from St. John's or bought in Saint Pierre et Miquelon.

Those which arrived from St. John's were imported from Massachusetts, by St. John's merchants who, when they received orders, consigned them to the merchants of our town, who sold them to fishermen as they were required. An entry in the account book of Richard Hackett, Salisbury, oar maker, states that the firm exported large numbers of whaleboat oars to Nantucket for the Wherry. So it is quite possible that this firm, in later years, also manufactured the dory oars used by our fishermen. The entry is dated 1753, forty years before the dory was invented. The oars acquired in Saint Pierre were purchased by our fishermen themselves when they had occasion to visit the French town and had happened to be in need of them. The codtrap men made their own skiff oars for the very good reason that none of this type were imported to Newfoundland. The American whaleboat and seine boat oars would have been ideally suited to use in our trapskiffs, but they just were not available.

Certain types of Newfoundland spruce would make good dory oars, but that wood did not grow in our section of the country. In any case, the fishermen who possessed the skill to make dory oars would have to use up so much valuable time during the operation that it was far cheaper in the long run to buy the imported, factory-made variety. Prior to World War One, a pair of dory oars cost $1.50 and even after the war got into high gear and prices escalated in all commodities, the price of dory oars did not go beyond $3.00 a pair.

There was a noticeable difference in the style of the oars that came from Saint Pierre and the American oar which arrived in St. John's. The French oar was narrower in the wash or blade than the American type and the lum or handle was of a different design. In the French oar, the handle was smaller at the tip, then it gradually increased in size to the center where it decreased in size again until it reached the base, which left it somewhat barrel shaped. The larger center of this type handle fitted the palm very well and was not too difficult to get a grip on. But in my opinion, and I have used the two types, the American style oar handle was the better of the two. The handle of the New England oar was larger out at the tip, then it gradually slimmed away to the base, which made the gripping of it more comfortable and consequently, was not so tiring on the rower. I have always considered the lowly dory oar to be a very fine piece of art, expertly fashioned from a shapeless log of wood into an object of symetrical beauty.

The exact number of men which reliable dory oars were responsible for keeping alive, for example shore fishermen from drifting over rocks and shoal where hungry breaking waves were waiting to destroy them, and the Banks fishermen enabling them to force their craft against high winds and towering seas in order to reach their distant vessel or make land when astray from the parent ship, will never be known, but over the one hundred and eighty years that men were engaged at Banks and shore fishing, there were many thousands of cases.

The dory oar manufacturer, therefore, like the dory builder, was burdened with a heavy responsibility. It was vitally important for him to select from his stock only the strongest, toughest wood, material that contained no cross grains, burls or knots that would make an oar tender, for those deficiencies would naturally weaken them at points of stress, causing them to snap off easily when under heavy pressure.

So in addition to being expert craftsmen, the oar maker was obliged to be a conscientious, honest individual; for in those days of the row dory the lives of a far greater number of men depended upon him than on the manufacturer of any other item connected with the fisheries.

In recent years the dory oars used by Newfoundland fishermen have been imported from Nova Scotia, as both the American and the French products have disappeared from the scene long since.

On first glancing over the Nova Scotian made oars, I imagined that they were fashioned from soft white pine, as the wood is very light in colour and its appearance generally, closely resembles that delightful aromatic lumber, but soft pine for the manufacture of oars of any type is out of the question as they would break into two halves at the first pull, even when rowing a boat in fairly light airs. No, these Bluenose oars, I decided, were definitely not made of ash either, that fact I could easily determine as I had been familiar with ash.

Enquiries disclosed the information that the Canadian oars are manufactured from spruce, which is straight grained and of slow growth and is native to Nova Scotia. The fact that it does not resemble any member of the spruce family which grows in Newfoundland made it impossible for me to identify it as that type of wood.

When I visited Nova Scotia in June, 1973, I learned that the oars were turned out in the tiny village of Blockhouse, situated between Mahone Bay and Bridgewater. I easily located the oar factory, which is sitting just a few yards from the side of the main road leading past the village.

David Boston, one of the new owners of the oar making factory in Blockhouse, Nova Scotia displays a newly-completed dory oar —(Jerry Kelland Photo).

On entering the builting I met the manager and one of the present owners, David Boston, who together with his father and brother, purchased the factory from Nathan S. Joudrey in the spring of 1973. The business is now

191

trading under the name of Dafron, Limited.

David told me that when they bought the factory, they retained all the skilled oar makers who had been hired and trained by Mr. Joudrey, seventeen men in all. My arrival found the factory going full blast. The whole staff was busy at lathes and other machines. Sawdust pyramided while chips flew about as oars and paddles were being skillfully and rapidly turned out. Personally, I found the sight especially pleasing to behold. For as a youngster, I had often wondered where and how dory oars were made and wished that I would one day locate that mysterious place. Now more than half a century later, my childhood dream was being fulfilled. Furthermore, I was realizing considerably more than a childhood dream, I was witnessing the carrying on of a great tradition.

The factory turns out every type of oar and paddle used today by men who sometimes prefer to desert their outboard and inboard motor craft to engage in the healthy and muscle-toning exercise of rowing.

Dafron, Limited produces dory oars of all sizes from those which measure six feet in length used in rowing the tiny eight-foot dory to the ten-footer carried onboard the huge twenty- and twenty-two foot motor dories as emergency equipment. Here also is manufactured race boat oars, straight paddles and double-ended kayak paddles. They even make a retriever paddle that is fitted with a brass hook which enables sports fishermen to clear lines which have become tangled in some underwater snag. When David Boston informed me that they had bought the business from Nathan Joudrey, I inquired from him if Mr. Joudrey was still in the vicinity.

"Why yes," he replied. "Nathan lives just a short distance up the road, in fact he has only recently finished building a new house."

A few minutes later I met both Mr. and Mrs. Joudrey who kindly invited me into their home. While his wife went about her kitchen duties, I interviewed Nathan. Mr. Joudrey told me that in 1914 his father, the late Simeon Joudrey got the idea of turning out dory oars and he put the idea into effect.

Setting up his workshop in a section of his barn at Middle New Cornwall, he began sawing the rough timber in the general shape of the dory oar, using handsaw and ripsaw. He then turned the oars out on a foot driven lathe which he improvised himself, using sprocket wheels and chains from a bicycle. Later on, he moved to the larger center of Mahone Bay where he built a small workshop, meanwhile acquiring a band saw and a turning lathe powered by a stationary engine. During his lifetime, Simeon Joudrey made dory oars only, catering mostly to the Lunenburg Banks and shore fishing trades. He must have been kept very busy at that, for in his day there was a time when a thousand dories sailed for the Banks nested on the decks of Lunenburg schooners. With five oars to a dory, in addition several spares were carried onboard the vessels to replace those that had been broken or lost. Nathan Joudrey learned the art of making dory oars from his father at an early age and was his only helper up to the time of his death in 1940. Nathan told me that his father died on Nathan's nineteenth birthday, so he said he was left alone with the Mahone Bay workshop.

In 1941 he moved the shop to Blockhouse where he built a small mill to which he has joined on four additions. Joudrey must be a mechanical genius for he designed and hand-built all the machines that are in use in the factory today, which include the rough and fine sanders and the oar turning lathes. He had made great strides in expansion following the death of his father. He also departed from the single line product of making dory oars, designing and perfecting the various types of oars and paddles mentioned earlier. As more and more orders continued to pour in and the fame of his masterpieces continued to spread, Nathan shipped oars and paddles to England, South Africa, and to various points in Newfoundland, Nova Scotia, the United States and Saint Pierre et Miquelon.

When his only son came of age, Mr. Joudrey entertained hopes that the young man would follow in the footsteps of his father and grandfather. But like many a son, he possessed such a spirit of independence, he let it be known that he preferred to branch out on his own. He is at present a senior draftsman with a Halifax utility firm. With the departure of his son, Nathan's ambition to further expand the industry was considerably dampened. With orders for his product coming in faster than he could take care of them, he realized that he had to either expand or sell the business.

So in 1970 he began casting an eye around for a possible buyer. He emphasized that just any buyer would not do. It was essential to his way of thinking, that it should be a person who maintained the same high quality in oars which he had taken such pains to perfect. He finally decided that the father and son team of Bostons were the right people.

Said Mr. Joudrey, "I always selected the wood that went into the making of all oars, with great care. They just had to be without flaw and weakness, for the lives of many men depended upon them."

Having departed from the business of oar manufacturing, he is not the type to sit around doing nothing. Now in his fifties, he has started out on a brand new venture. During the time of my visit he had a gang of men busily building a structure measuring one hundred and twelve feet by sixty feet. This building will be a museum. He has acquired fifteen antique motor cars which, by his skill and dedicated labour, a genuine labour of love, he has put into working order.

Meanwhile, the Blockhouse oar factory has progressed and expanded under the genial, capable management of David Boston and the skilled hands of the seventeen men who were trained by Nathan Joudrey. For not only do men need oars and paddles in this modern day of motor propelled boats, more orders are being placed for them now than ever before.

Skilled oar maker Clarence Fancy is shown at work in the Blockhouse, Nova Scotia factory —(Jerry Kelland Photo).

CHAPTER THIRTEEN

Cooks on the Banks

ARTHUR RIDEOUT OF NEWFOUNDLAND

I guess you have heard it said that an army travels on its stomach. So I presume it would be in order to surmise that Banks dorymen rowed and fished on their stomachs.

If an adequately fed, well-nourished army marched better and fought harder, then it is reasonable to assume that adequately fed, well-nourished dorymen rowed stronger and fished more zealously than those who were ill-fed and under-nourished. The Banks cook, therefore, was an extremely important individual. Of the culinary skills of their cooks or the lack of them I have heard feelings expressed by dorymen as follows: "Yeah, we did real well with the fish and we were lucky enough to have the best damn cook on the Banks!" Or, "Oh, we did alright with the fish, made a very good voyage, but we sure had a lousy cook, I never seen that man's equal for spoilin' grub."

The mate or second hand on the banker ranked next to the captain from the nautical point of view, but in the minds of hungry dorymen, the mate had to take second place to the cook.

The cook was required to furnish meals for any number from sixteen to twenty-eight men, depending on the size of the schooner, for the bigger the schooner, the bigger the crew. The clean, pure air of the Banks coupled with hard toil caused dorymen to work up prodigious appetites.

It was a known fact that the crews on some vessels were heartier eaters than those which were on other vessels. It seems that by some quirk of fate, the Samuel Harris Export Company of Grand Bank, owners of the banker *Nina Lee*, must have unwittingly signed on a complete crew of gormandizers. For the business partners Patten and Forsey of Grand Bank, who also owned fishing schooners, publicly expressed amazement at the voracious manner in which the *Nina Lee's* dorymen could stow away grub, which caused some person who had overheard the partners talking, to remark, "Patten and Forsey cannot see how Sam Harris feeds the crew of the *Nina Lee*.'

Then another fishing skipper who was forced to knock off fishing frequently so as he could make trips to land to replenish food supplies in order to keep his lusty crew well fed and happy, told the owner of the vessel, when that individual bitterly complained that his men were making away with an awful lot of grub, "Sir, that crew of mine got such big appetites they can eat the Virgin Rocks then wolf down the sins of the world for dessert." The cooks on both those bankers must have had more than their hands full to cook, bake and dish out food to such hearty crews.

The Banks cook did not spend all his time juggling pots and pans in his heated fo'castle. For hardly a day passed without the cook being called upon the deck to assist in some emergency. I have heard fishing skippers remark, when telling of some gruelling experience, that it was pretty tough, nip and tuck for a while.

"We made out alright, but it took all hands and the cook to do it."

Arthur Rideout of Newfoundland who spent forty years cooking on Banks fishing vessels, Government patrol cutters and naval ships —(Courtesy Arthur Rideout).

Arthur Rideout of Little Harbour, Fortune Bay and St. John's, put it very concisely when he said, "The cook didn't always stay in the galley, any more than the captain stayed in his cabin."

Mr. Rideout easily recalls how he had to be busy at his stove by 4:00 a.m. and was required to work steadily until 8:00 p.m., sixteen hours every day while the vessel was at sea. The flour was carried in barrels in years gone by.

Said Mr. Rideout: "I have opened a full barrel, one hundred and ninety-six pounds in the morning and be scraping the bottom of the barrel that same night." Twelve hours steadily mixing and baking bread, buns and pies, as cooks were required to do all their own baking.

196

Very little praise, if any, was ever directed towards Banks cooks. Yet those faithful, dedicated, hard working men spent most of their time in a potentially dangerous locality while the schooners were at sea, namely the forecastle, for nearly always the cooks were below deck. The skippers spent a lot of time on the deck and each day that the weather was suitable the dorymen were away from the vessel tending trawls or were on deck baiting up gear. There were many times when a steamer rammed a schooner sending her to the bottom, the cook being the only casualty. When the American banker, *Arthur James* was cut down in a dense fog on October 31, 1916, by the big passenger steamer *Campden*, the captain and the sixteen dorymen who were on the deck at the time, jumped into the vessel's seine boat and were saved. The steamer struck the schooner just for'ard of the fore rigging shearing her bow (which included the fo'castle) completely off. The cook, Malaska Hager, who was down below busy with his duties went to his death. The *Arthur James* plunged to the bottom in three minutes.

When the American fishing schooner *Rex* was cut down by the liner *Tuscania*, the vessel's cook, Charles Firth and his ten-year-old son Austin died in the fo'castle. The boy had been enjoying his summer vacation at sea with his father. When Mr. Firth, who was on deck realized that the approaching liner was going to strike the schooner, he instantly jumped down into the fo'castle in a brave but futile attempt to save his son who was asleep in his bunk.

Strangely enough, when vessels were lost with all hands, people rarely mentioned the cooks. Their sympathetic remarks centered around the deceased captains, mates and dorymen. Apparently apart from their own relations, not too many people regretted or mourned the loss of the cooks. Yet those individuals died with the others when the vessels went to the bottom.

During his forty years as a seacook, Arthur Rideout experienced many escapes. One of the closest calls he had came when he was cooking on the Newfoundland banker, *Beatrice and Vivian,* commanded by Captain James Gosling.

"We had set sail from the fishing grounds off Cape North, Cape Breton Island to come in for a fresh supply of bait," said Mr. Rideout. "When the vessel encountered high winds and heavy seas, I had just vacated my bunk when a monstrous wave came over the bow of the *Beatrice and Vivian.* That mighty wave lifted the spare anchor from its resting place, then dropped it. The five hundred pound hook landed with such force that one of its big flukes crashed right through the deck landing squarely into my bunk."

Mr. Rideout still shudders when he reflects on what would have happened to him if he had been lying in that bunk when the anchor fluke crashed down.

It was a mighty close shave, but there was yet another one on the way.

Shortly after the foregoing incident occurred, the *Beatrice and Vivian* ran into heavy fog. Mr. Rideout said he was walking along the deck when he met the captain near the after cabin. The captain told him, "Arthur, I just woke up and I had a funny dream. I dreamt that I saw the masts falling down on the *Beatrice and Vivian*."

"Those words," continued Arthur, "were scarcely out of the skipper's mouth when the towering bow of the *S.S. California* appeared out of the fog. The nineteen thousand, nine hundred ton liner sliced into the schooner on the port side, just for'ard of the nested dories, cutting her nearly in two. When the collision occurred I was thrown flat on my back on the deck. Captain Gosling was knocked down also, he fell right on top of me."

Fortunately neither man received any injuries. On glancing up from their prone position both captain and cook saw the schooner's foremast snap off and go over the side. Then the mainmast snapped off and quickly followed the foremast. On witnessing the destruction of both masts, Captain Gosling calmly remarked to the cook, "Well, Art, look at that, my dream came true after all." Nothing, it seems, could upset the nerves of those old Banks fishermen.

On that particular trip the *Beatrice and Vivian* was carrying eleven dories, five of those nested on the port side and six on the starboard side. When the foremast fell, the jumbo stay which was attached to it over the crosstrees and was also fastened to the ship's stempost, tore loose from the stemhead shackle, then sprang violently to the amidships section of the schooner, where like an angry boa constrictor it coiled itself twice tightly around the six starboard dories with the free end disappearing over the side. Later that heavy steel wire became so securely spooled around one of the liner's propellor shafts that it brought the engine to a stop.

Very fortunately, when the collision occurred all hands were on deck. Miraculously not a man suffered the slightest injury despite falling spars, flailing blocks, springing wire stays and whipping rope ends. As it would have been useless even to attempt to free the six starboard side dories from the entanglement caused by the jumbo stay, the crew seized the five port dories one by one and literally threw them over the vessel's side, as there was no time to hoist them out in the regular way by using the dory burtons. The men were in a hurry doing this, as they had need to be, but, there was no panic. All twenty-seven crewmembers managed to board the five dories and reach the steamer without capsizing one of the little boats or losing a man.

The *Beatrice and Vivian* sank just as her crew reached the steamer's side. After the schoonermen were safely onboard the liner, their five dories were hoisted up and placed on the top deck of the big ship. Both the fishing crew and their dories aroused much interest amongst the steamer's passengers, many of whom had never seen a Banks fisherman or a dory.

When the engines of the *California* were started again and she recommenced her voyage, it was then discovered that the trailing end of the jumbo stay had become wound around one of the liner's propellor shafts, while the other end of the stout wire was still firmly coiled around the six nested dories. As the vessel descended to the bottom the wire became taut and the dories were plucked out of their cradle and were then trailing along behind the steamer. The big ship was brought to a stop three or four times while members of her crew made attempts to sever the annoying stay which had assumed the role of an unwanted towing cable. But all efforts to do this proved futile, as no instrument could be found on the *California* which was capable of severing the heavy steel wire. So the six dories were towed in that most unusual manner, right up to Nova Scotia and into Halifax Harbour. There the captain of the liner contacted parties ashore and a tug was dispatched out to the *California* to take off the schooner's crew.

When the five dories had been hoisted up to the deck of the big steamer they were not nested together as there was plenty of space to let them lay around singly. But when they were lowered down to the deck of the tug they were nested as there was not sufficient deck space to accommodate them otherwise. A passenger on the *California* who was watching interestingly while the dories were being nested on the tug, shouted out, to the amusement of the banker's crew, "Just get a load of that there, those little boats fit into each other the same as saucers."

Mr. Rideout said that after the crew of the *Beatrice and Vivian* were landed in Halifax, they were given accommodation in the Y.M.C.A., where they spent a whole week awaiting a passage home.

Arthur Rideout did not spend the entire forty years cooking on Banks fishing vessels. He served for eight years cooking on the Newfoundland customs patrol cutters, *Shulamite* and *Marvita*. Then with the outbreak of World War Two, he joined the Canadian Navy, once again as a cook. He served all through the War in that capacity.

CLARENCE NAAS OF NOVA SCOTIA

One July day five years ago I was standing on a street corner in Lunenburg, Nova Scotia, talking with a couple of old time dorymen. Suddenly, one of them pointed to a man on the opposite side of the street who was walking along the sidewalk at a pretty fast slip.

"See that man over there? Well he spent fifty-one years cooking on fishing vessels. He's seventy-nine years old now, but you'd never think it to look at him, very active too, see how fast he can walk."

I decided to catch up to that cook and have a chat with him if it was possible. The day was very hot, not a breath of wind stirred. I was aware that when it came to fast walking, I was rather out of condition. Anyway, I lit out after the cook who by this time had quite a head start. In a little while it became very obvious to me that I was going to lose the race. I shouted out to the man, but the noises from the passing traffic evidently prevented him from hearing me. I was about ready to give up when he stopped by a car and started to unlock the door. Putting on a fresh burst of speed, which must have come from some energy source I did not know I possessed, I reached the vehicle, grasping for breath, just as he started the motor.

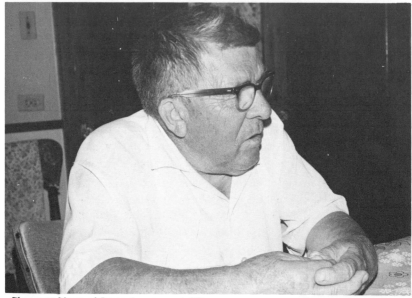

Clarence Naas of Lunenburg spent fifty-one years as a cook on various fishing vessels —(Jerry Kelland Photo).

His name, he told me, was Clarence Naas.

"Yep, I served as a Banks cook for fifty-one years."

Meeting with Mr. Naas was a disappointment in one way for despite his having served as a cook on fishing schooners for more than half a century, he had never gone through any experiences worth relating. At least that is the way he expressed it. But personally I think for a man to follow the sea for fifty-one years in the most hazardous of sea-faring jobs and to survive is a major experience in itself.

"Oh sure," said Mr. Naas. "We ran into many storms, we stuck 'em, or I should say they struck us on the way to the Banks, or while we were anchored on the Banks and on the way home. But I guess that I was more than lucky, because I was never on a vessel that encountered any real hard gales. None of the vessels I served on were in collision with either steamers or schooners. I'd often heard steamers' whistles blowing in the fog, dozens of times. Some of the big ships came close to us, too close for comfort as the saying goes. But they never did come near enough to striks us.

"Never," continued Mr. Naas, "In all the fifty-one years did the crews of the various vessels I served on have to take to their dories to save their lives. Furthermore, I was never on a craft that sprang a leak or that had piled up on the rocks or shoals. An awful lot of poor fishermen met their end in that way," added the old cook, reflectively.

"But I do believe to this day that our captain in his wisdom avoided the one big gale that would have sent us to Davy Jones' Locker. I was cooking on the banker, *Robert Esdale,* commaded by Captain Allan Mosher. That was on August 23, 1927. We were anchored on Sable Island Bank. Four Nova Scotian vessels and the American vessel, *Columbia* were in sight of us. Although the weather looked pretty good, Captain Mosher became restless. He kept glancing at his barometer and sniffing the air win'ard. Evidently he didn't like what he saw or smelled for he never sent the dories out. Instead he ordered the cable warped in and the anchor catted. Then he set sail and returned to port. On the way he told us, 'I predict that a big blow will be coming along shortly, we'll be a lot better off out of it.'

"His prediction proved correct, too, for that night the great-grandfather of all storms struck out of the northeast. A real hurricane. Before it ended the four Canadian schooners and the American schooner went down with all hands."

I asked Mr. Naas if any men had been lost from the schooners he had served on.

"Only once," he replied. "I was cookin' on the banker, *Muriel Isobel,* commanded by Captain Walter Crouse. The incident occurred on a Sunday, between 5:00 and 5:30 p.m. It was on the twenty-first of April, 1940. We were comin' up from the Grand Banks with a load of fish and we ran into a pretty bad storm. By the time we'd reached to thirty miles from the coast of Nova Scotia the seas were running very high. At that time, every Sunday, some radio station in Sydney or Halifax was broadasting a hymn singing program. One of the men, Allan Wentzell, asked me to go back to the captain's cabin to listen to the broadcast, as Wentzell's wife had told him before he sailed she would be requesting the hymn, 'Nearer My God To Thee', on that date. I went back with Wentzell, but left the cabin after a while and returned to the galley. Wentzell was making his way for'ard shortly afterwards when a big sea came over the rail and swept him overboard. I, with other crewmembers glimpsed the unfortunate man on the crest of a huge breaker. We threw everything wooden that was moveable on deck, like trawl tubs and dory oars towards him hoping that he could hang onto something until we could launch a dory to try and rescue him. But he failed to grasp any of the objects thrown. Then he quickly disappeared.

"Sure cooks were called upon many times to perform tasks apart from cookin' and baking," continued Mr. Naas. "That could go from assisting in baiting gear to hoisting dories in and out or lending a hand on the windlass. I was on one vessel when we were forced to sail a doryman short as one of the men had been taken ill suddenly, just as we were about to leave. When we reached the Banks the skipper himself went out in a dory to replace the man he'd left behind.

"On that trip it was the foggiest weather I'd ever witnessed. Day in and day out the vapour continued to roll in. With the skipper and all the other men away tending trawls I was left onboard alone. So, in addition to cooking and baking, I would have to leave my stove every few minutes and rush up on deck to blow the foghorn so as to guide the crew back to the schooner. What with cooking and baking in that hot fo'castle, then rushing up on deck so frequently to blow the foghorn so much perspiration was runnin' off me that I must have looked like a little Niagara Falls.

"I started out cooking on June 24, 1918," continued Mr. Naas, "on the schooner, *Warren G. Winters,* with captain Warren Allen. Yes, I started cookin' in 1918 on a banker and ended up in 1969 cookin' on a sword fisherman. I was seventy-five years of age then. Although I was still strong, healthy and active, I decided that the time had arrived for me to quit. I had been very fortunate over the years, so I did not want to push my fabulous luck beyond fifty-one years at sea."

HARRY EUSTIS OF MASSACHUSETTS

In the great deep sea fishing port of Gloucester, Massachusetts, from whence hundreds of cooks sailed on the able, smart looking bankers over the years, very few members of that excellent race of men survive today.

One of the last of the Gloucester Banks cooks is Harry Eustis. Mr. Eustis was boen in Canso, Nova Scotia. In 1923, ast the age of seventeen, he immigrated to Gloucester, where he signed on as a catchee on the schooner, *Cathrine,* commanded by Captain Archie MacLeod. A short while later he advanced to the more perilous occupation of a doryman. During the short period he was thus engaged he was considered to be one of the best. But it seems that Harry Eustis had a hankering to become a seacook and that is the avocation he finally settled on.

During his thirty years spent as a fishermen's cook, Mr. Eustis served on

Harry Eustis, a Banks fishing cook for thirty years. He sailed out of Gloucester, Massachusetts — (Courtesy Gordon Thomas).

various vessels. The bankers, *Dawn, Ruth and Margaret* and *Elk*, which were exceptionally well-known and are remembered today by elderly Gloucestermen. He was also the cook on the famous fishing/racing schooner, *Gertrude L. Thebaud*, when she raced against the *Bluenose* in 1938. Harry Eustis, like so many of the men who were cooks on bankers went through his share of harrowing experiences. The two close calls which he has good reason to remember most vividly he relates as follows:

"I was cooking on the knockabout (no bowsprit) schooner, *Louise B. Marshall*, with Captain John Marshall. We were bound for home from the Banks with eighty thousand pounds of fresh fish when we ran into a heavy gale off Seal Island, Nova Scotia. The vessel was struck right on the broadside by two giant seas, one following the other in quick succession. Those mighty walls of water threw the *Marshall* right over on her beam ends, or as we used to say, she got hove down. All twelve dories were swept overboard. The foreboom and the main boom were snapped off. Everything that was moveable on deck disappeared, trawl tubs and buoys, fish crates and even the housing over the deck engine was smashed. The fo'castle stove shifted, scalding one of the crew pretty severely.

"The schooner slowly righted herself. It was lucky for us that those fine craft had been designed and built to withstand such rough treatment. When the *Marshall* had returned to more or less even keel, the first thing I noticed was a part of one of the dories dangling from the lower fore rigging.

"After making some necessary repairs we proceeded on to Gloucester under our own power. We arrived without further incident.

"The second close call I had," continued Mr. Eustis, "came when I was cooking on the banker, *Elsie G. Silva*, commanded by Captain Manuel Silva.

203

It was on the night of February 14, 1927, that we ran into big trouble. We were sailing through a blinding northeast snowstorm when the vessel ran ashore on the sand bars of Cape Cod. We were carrying sixteen cross-handed dories. The first three dories we put over the side were smashed to splinters. Then the fifteen of us managed to get away in other dories from the seaward side of the vessel. Captain Silva and five crewmen decided to stay with the ship. On the skipper's orders one dory was left onboard, in case they too should decide to leave the stranded craft.

"We rowed six hours covering fifteen miles," said Mr. Eustis, "when we were picked up by the Wood End Coast Guardsmen. Captain Silva and his five men who had remained onboard the vessel were eventually forced to leave her. They were successful in launching their dory and boarding her. They reached the Pamet River Station safety. It was well," concluded Mr. Eustis, "that all hands managed to get away from the *Elsie Silva* for she was pounded to pieces by the big waves. Within four or five hours there wasn't a piece of her left."

Like Clarence Naas, Harry Eustis commenced his cooking career on a salt banker and finished it cooking on a sword fisherman. Now over seventy years of age and in failing health, Mr. Eustis, like his Newfoundland and Nova Scotian counterparts, Arthur Rideout and Clarence Naas, is a survivor of a great, dedicated uncomplaining race of seamen, who voluntarily adhered themselves to the Banks cooking trade; who, in many years they served on pitching, rolling, often storm harassed ships, must have suffered unmercifully from excessive heat when their craft were battened down, cutting off all sources of fresh air during severe weather conditions.

In my humble opinion, when it comes to erecting monuments which memorialize unselfish devotion to duty and displays of outstanding human courage, then none are more deserving of such an honour than the Banks fishing cooks of yesteryear.

CHAPTER FOURTEEN

Short Stories

MR. HARDING RELATES

Certain areas of the great fishing Banks were criss-crossed by the wakes of mighty ocean liners, plying back and forth between Europe and America.

The big ships caused a great deal of concern to both fishing skippers and their dorymen, who either from necessity or by choice wrested their living from Banks fishing. There is hardly any doubt but what a number of vessels and dories vanished beneath the waves after being run down by those speeding greyhounds of the sea, during periods of dense fog or in thick snowstorms.

The late I.G. Harding of Marystown, used to tell of a day in 1892, when he and his dorymate, Harry Ellis were hauling their trawl on Grand Bank while a peasoup fog completely surrounded them. Suddenly they heard the bellow of an Atlantic liner and not too far off, judging from the sound of her whistle, Harding said his dorymate remarked that he would like to see her as she was undoubtedly a grand, big one.

"'Well," replied Harding, "I for my part don't want to see her. My only wish is that she passes by without hitting us."

Then the ship's whistle sounded close by, too close. Harding frantically started to blow the tiny dory foghorn, hoping that someone onboard the steamer would hear it and that she would swerve to avoid colliding with them. Then he noticed that the white wall of fog ahead appeared to grow darker. Instantly, not thirty feet away, rose the towering black bow of the huge steamer. Harding and Ellis shipped their oars and commenced to pull away with all their might to avoid certain death. While they were so engaged a kindly and very welcome voice sang out from the ship's bridge high above them.

"It's alright, men. We see you."

Then the giant steamer passed on, leaving the little dory and her crew safe but being rocked violently about by her big bow wave and the lop that was kicked up by her wake. Set forth below is a stanza from my poem 'On The Banks'.

> You can hear the liner screaming
> As she bears down on your craft.
> See her bow wave hugely gleaming
> As it rocks you fore and aft.
> You can feel your body lagging
> While you fight to gain your breath,
> And can't keep your knees from sagging
> For you've had a brush with death.

Mr. Harding, while out on the same trip related how he had turned in one night, after a very busy day fishing. While enjoying his hard earned rest he was visited by a most startling dream. He dreamt that he was leaning over the side of the schooner when he saw the corpse of a drowned man floating by, the fact was turned up and the sightless eyes were wide open. So vivid was his dream that Harding easily recognized the face as that of Bill Turner, a member of their crew.

The dream shocked him into wakefulness and he discovered that he was bathed in cold sweat. After a while he turned over and dropped off to sleep once more, whereupon he dreamt the same thing over again, each detail appearing exactly as it had the first time.

Harding stated that Bill Turner was a good friend of his and as he worried considerably over the dream he had no hesitation in telling Turner about it.

"For heaven's sake, Bill," he cautioned his friend, "be careful today, for I believe that dream was sent to me as a warning to you."

Turner laughed a bit at Harding's fears, but at the same time he promised him that he would not take any unnecessary risks.

That afternoon, the vessel's barometer showed every indication of a gale brewing. So the dorymen hurried off to get all their trawls hauled up before the weather got too bad. The wind and sea appeared to rise with every passing moment and Harding's dorymate remarked, "I think that we are in for a bad blow this time."

The two men reached their trawl without mishap and started to haul it aboard. They had gathered in about sixty fathoms when their dory, with a sickening roll, turned completely bottom up, spilling Harding, Ellis, the fish and all the loose gear into the water. Harding said that he went under but he did not go too far down, as he rose again his sou'wester fell down over his eyes, blinding him. He managed to shake it off and get the strap between his teeth. He then swam to the overturned dory and got a trip on the plug line, by the aid of this he contrived to climb up on the bottom of the dory and hang on. Incidentally, the plug line referred to was usually made from a manila rope, one end of which was fastened to the dory's riser, the other end was passed through a hole in the center of the bottom plug where it was tied to form a fairly large loop, large enough for two men to pass an arm through. The plug line was responsible for saving the lives of dorymen on many occasions after their craft had capsized. In fact, it was the only reliable thing a man had to hang onto when a dory overturned, as where the bottom and garboards meet, the surface is completely smooth, for unlike the shore fishing dory, the Banks dory was not equipped with bottom strips. Those strips were usually made of hardwood, such as oak in the United States and Nova Scotia and birth in Newfoundland, were fastened from the stem to the stern around the rim of the dories' bottoms and placed so as they would completely cover the edge of the garboard boards where they joined the bottoms.

In many Newfoundland outports, those strips were very necessary equipment for shore fishing dories that had to be launched out and hauled up frequently over sand and gravel beaches. For without the protective strips, which went from one half inch to five eighths of an inch in thickness and were at least two inches in width, both bottoms and garboards would be worn away in a very short space of time. The Banks dory was not equipped with bottom strips because, first of all she was always operating in deep water and rarely came in contact with sand and gravel beaches. Then again those heavy hardwood strips would add unwanted weight, as not only do they make a dory much harder to row, they would make her far heavier to hoist inboard and outboard, an operation that took place frequently on Banks fishing vessels.

After Mr. Harding had climbed upon the dory's bottom, he looked about for his dorymate and was very delighted to observe that Ellis had reached the bow, but was having great difficulty in securing a hand hold on the slippery bottom. Fearing that Ellis would be swept away at any moment, for the water was very turbulent, Harding edged over to him and seizing his wrist, he managed to haul him over in reach of the plug line, which Ellis gripped firmly and held on. Ellis's fingers were bleeding badly and his fingernails were broken down to the quicks from where he had been attempting to gain a hold on the dory's bow section. Just as the great strain they were undergoing began to become almost unbearable for the distressed dorymen, they saw to their intense joy one of their dories approaching. A few minutes later Harding looked up into the face of Bill Turner, the man he had seen as drowned in his dream and now one of his rescuers.

"Well, boy," said Bill, "there must have been something to your dream after all, even though it turned out in the reverse of the way you dreamt it."

In a short space of time, the water soaked and chilled men had reached onboard their schooner. The following day they were none the worse for their gruelling experience, although Harry Ellis had some difficulty baiting trawls for a couple of days because of his sore hands. Very regretably, when relating stories of their experiences, many old time dorymen omitted to mention the names of the vessels, the names of the captains who had commanded them and the names of the ports from which they sailed. Although such information may be rated as insignificant, to my way of thinking, it would make the reading of those narratives much more interesting.

Shortly after the incident which involved I.C. Harding and Harry Ellis, two other dorymen, namely; Richard Stevens and Robert Wells, who were crewing members of a banker sailing out of Fortune Bay, were hauling their trawl one afternoon on Grand Bank, when a dense fog rolled up causing them to lose sight of their schooner. Late that evening, a gale blew in very strongly and their dory capsized. It was nearly noon the next day before their overturned dory was sighted and picked up. The men in the rescue boat discovered that Richard Stevens had evidently been washed off and drowned during the night. No trace of him was ever found. Robert Wells, his dorymate, was barely alive when he was taken off the dory's bottom. The plug line which he had attached to his wrist, being the only thing that saved him from a watery grave.

No coherent account of their night's suffering could be gotten from Wells. He was in a pitable state and stark naked. Never afterwards was he able to explain why or how he had lost his oilskins and the heavy clothing underneath them. Although the incident occurred during the summer, both wind and water can be very cold even to a man heavily clad, but to Wells in the nude the effect of those elements must have been actually chilling.

When the men from the rescuing dory took him off, he kept repeating feebly, "It's snowing so hard and it's so frosty."

Presumably in his half frozen condition and upset state of mind, he imagined the wintery weather.

The shock of seeing his dorymate being swept to his death, coupled with the rest of his suffering, permanently affected his brain, for during the remainder of his life, he nver returned to normal.

LOSS OF THE COLUMBIA

The American fishing and racing schooner, *Columbia* was proclaimed by all who saw to be the most beautiful vessel ever to glide down the slipways of any shipyard on this side of the Atlantic.

The craft was designed by W. Starling Burgess, one of the greatest designers of ocean-going yachts of the twentieth century and was built in the yard of Arthur D. Story in Essex, Massachusetts during 1923. Owing to *Columbia's* yacht-like appearance when she floated on the Essex River, following her launching, she was promptly dubbed the *Yacht Fisherman* by Gloucestermen. Of all the American contenders for the international honours against the great Canadian schooner, *Bluenose, Columbia* came closer than any other in taking the fishermen's trophy away from her.

Captain Angus Walters, fishing and racing skipper of the mighty *Bluenose*, claimed that it was his undivided opinion, *Columbia* was the greatest of all the American vessels which sailed against him. In their first race, off Halifax on October 29, 1923, *Bluenose* won over *Columbia* by a scant one minute and twenty seconds.

It was during this race that the famous fight for the weather berth took place off the rugged rocks of Chebucto Head, with all sails drawing and the two big schooners racing neck to neck. Captain Ben Pine, a former New-foundlander, skipper of the American vessel, kept edging Captain Walters up to weather. The *Bluenose* skipper gave it everything in his power, but he could not shake off the Gloucesterman.

The schooners kept tearing along with *Bluenose* dangerously close to the *Three Sisters*, one of the most dreaded shoals along the coast. They neared Bell Rock Buoy, which marked another shoal, but Pine's determination remained inflexible and he forced Walters into green water inside the marker whereupon the pilot onboard the *Bluenose* yelled out to the helmsman, Long Albert Himmleman, to bear away.

"Bear away and we strike him," Albert shouted back.

"Then strike him or strike the rocks!" snapped the pilot. *Bluenose* bore away with Pine still holding his course. Then Walters swung his mainsail and foresail wing and wing, which meant that one sail was dragged over to port, the other to starboard. Wung out, as the Lunenburgers called it, and winged out as the Newfoundlanders called it. This move completely blanketed the Gloucesterman. Next the mainboom of the *Bluenose* touched the main shrouds of the *Columbia*, still Pine held his course. Then the Canadian's mainboom swept the forestays of the American, doubling up her sheer rod. Finally, the end of the eighty foot mainboom of the *Bluenose* caught in the downhaul of the *Columbia's* jib and for upwards of a minute, the defender towed the challenger. Then *Bluenose* cleared and raced for the finish line, winning the contest.

In the second race, again sailed off Halifax, on November 1, 1923, *Bluenose* beat *Columbia* by the narrow margin of two minutes.

From 1923 to 1927, *Columbia* was fairly successful as a salt banker and during that period she sailed under the command of various skippers. On July 3, 1927, the vessel left Gloucester for the Banks on a dory handlining trip in charge of Captain Lewis Wharton. On August 23, Captain John Carrancho in the schooner *Herbert Parker*, also out of Gloucester, came up with the *Columbia*, anchored fifty miles off that treacherous graveyard of the Atlantic, Sable Island. Captain Carrancho, who was homeward bound, held a brief conversation with Captain Wharton. Apparently, the *Parker's* crew were the last people to see the *Columbia* as a proud, handsome fishing schooner, for the following day, August 24th, was one of the worst gales in the history of the Atlantic fisheries raged over the Banks.

On September 12, five battered dories marked *Columbia* were washed up on Sable Island. The American cutter *Tampa* was dispatched out to search for the missing craft, but met with no success.

On October 27, the haddocker, *Mary Sears*, picked up *Columbia's* dory number eleven. With the finding of this dory, more than two months after the vessel had disappeared, all hope was abandoned for Captain Wharton and his men.

While Captain Carrancho was speaking to Captain Wharton on August 23, he had observed that four Canadian fishing schooners were anchored in the vicinity. They were the *Uda R. Corkum*, Captain William Andrews; the *Joyce Smith*, Captain Edward Maxner; the *Mahala*, Captain Warren Knickle; and the *Clayton Walters*, Captain Selig. Those four schooners were lost with all hands, in the same storm that had claimed the *Columbia*. All five vessels took with them an awful total of one hundred and seven men to watery graves.

A remarkable incident related to a member of the *Columbia's* crew is worthy of mention here. Vernon Goodick had shipped on the vessel when she was making preparations to sail on her final voyage, but, just as she was about to leave the wharf, he changed his mind, took ashore his gear and shipped on another vessel. This same man away back in 1911, shipped on the banker, *Ella M. Goodwin* for a trip to Newfoundland, but just before she sailed he changed his mind and left her. The *Ella M. Goodwin* too, was lost with all hands on that trip.

It appeared that on both occasions, Vernon Goodick must have been warned of impending disaster by that mysterious something which lies far beyond the range of ordinary human knowledge.

THE LOSS OF THE *YOSEMITE*

In January, 1897, when the Gloucester schooner, *Yosemite* with Captain John McKinnon, was homeward bound from Placentia Bay, with a cargo of herring, she ran ashore on the south end of Ram Island. Ram Island is situated one and a half miles off the Nova Scotian mainland.

Following the vessel's grounding, there occurred incidents of hardships, severe injury, suffering, herosim and death that make up a story seldom equalled in harrowing detail.

The accident occurred at 7:15 a.m. on Thursday, January 21. The schooner at the time had been running in a heavy southeast gale which was accompanied by a blinding blizzard. All hands were on deck and the vessel was scudding before the wind fully twelve knots, when without warning she brought up suddenly, she has struck a reef. In an instant the staunch craft (only six years old) was at the mercy of wind and towering waves.

As the giant seas commenced to break over the schooner, all hands were forced to flee to the rigging for their lives. Not once after the *Yosemite* struck did anybody attempt to go below and after the rigging was gained, no man ever trod and stricken vessel's deck again. For fully an hour, the men clung to the rigging suffering terribly from the biting cold. In the fore rigging were Captain McKinnon, the cook; Joseph Ferry and doryman; Philip Fiander. The remainder of the crew were in the main rigging.

When the *Yosemite* struck nearly the whole bottom was torn out of her and within an hour she broke squarely in two halves. Then without warning the mainmast fell, taking most of the foremast with it.

Then came the desperate struggle for life, a battle with the sea to attempt to gain a foothold on a rock that was close by. While the winds continued to rage the pitiless snow liberally besprinkled with shot-like hailstones drove at them in relentless fury.

The trip to the rock was finally accomplsihed. Then it was discovered that the cook, Joseph Ferry was missing. He had evidently been killed by the falling foremast and his body must have been swept away as he was never seen again. One of Captain McKinnon's legs was badly injured, while Fiander had both legs broken below the knee. His boots and oilskins were gone, apparently he had been caught in the wreckage and literally pulled himself out of them in his struggle to get upon the rock. That he must have been an exceedingly strong man goes without saying, for with both legs broken and useless he had managed to climb upon that rock unaided, by the strength of his hands and arms only. Although he must have been suffering intensely from his broken limbs, he was never heard to voice a complaint. While the men were successful in reaching the rock, they were far from safe as it was high tide and the big seas kept breaking over it, threatening with each wave to sweep them to their doom.

They managed to secure pieces of wood that had washed in from the broken *Yosemite*, these they thrust into crevices. Then, with ropes which fortunately had been thrown ashore also, they lashed themselves to the improvised stakes and held on.

Tough on a rock that was only seventeen feet in circumference, in the midst of a raging gale and a blinding snowstorm, their captain suffering from a badly injured leg and Fiander with both legs broken, coupled with the sad fact that one of their shipmates had been drowned and while hungry waves were striving to tear them from their precarious position, not a single man was heard to bemoan his plight. Those brave, hardy fellows hung on through the long hours of the night, so dark that they could not distinguish each other. When daylight dawned, they discovered that between them and Ram Island was another ledge which was bare at low water. At 10:00 a.m., Philip Fiander who had borne his terrible suffering so courageously, died.

All day the greatly distressed crew watched patiently hoping that the vessel's log time would come within reach. So that with it one of them could swim to the next ledge and haul a heavy rope across with the hope of saving the remaining members of the crew. About the middle of the afternoon, Captain McKinnon called the mate, Pat Rose, to his side and whispered to him that another night here means death. Rose nodded solemnly in agreement. He did not say a word but crawled to the edge of the rock, carefully noting the action of the waves, tide eddies and the possibility of a landing place on the other side of the violently agitated water. Then he arose and stripped himself to his underclothes. He stood straight up shivering from the effects of twenty hours of severe exposure and the divestment of heavy outer clothing and oilskins. His freezing legs scarcely supported him. Then he said, "It's no use, boys, to stay here and die. I'll chance it for you."

Without further comment he leaped into the waves and struck out for the opposite ledge. His companions watched his course with fearful anxiety.

Rose was a very strong man as well as being an expert swimmer. After a hard battle he succeeded in reaching the ledge around 4:00 o'clock. From this ledge he waded to the island and his shipmates could see him running along the shore towards some fish houses. He was looking for a boat or some human being to assist him in rescuing the others. For fully half a mile he ran, clad only in his underclothes, then he came back and walked out to the inside ledge. He shouted the discouraging news to the others that he could find no aid and that their only chance was to swim. Now, as if by an act of Providence, the log line which all day had eluded their graps, came within reach, John Hickey, one of the men on the rock, seized it and made it fast around his own body. He then without hesitation, bravely plunged into the sea. As he neared the other ledge the indefatigable Rose met him and helped him ashore. Rose and Hickey then hauled across a stout rope which the men on the rock had fastened to the log line and made it secure. By means of this rope the men went from ledge to ledge, hand over hand, then wading to Ram Island they made their way to the fish houses for shelter. They placed a coat on a pole to let the people on the mainland know that some men had survived the wreck and would come to their rescue.

The people on shore had observed the signal, but claimed that at that time the water was too rough to launch a boat. Can you imagine that? Too rough to launch a boat, yet Pat Rose and John Hickey swam through the boiling winter surf, fearlessly to save their comrades. For twenty hours they had been soaked to the skin by icy water, battered by gale force winds and lashed by driving snow, that was powdered with stinging sleet, yet they had reached their perilous objective, although they had not partaken of food or drink during all that time. They must have been giants in strength and men of iron constitution to boot.

In one of the huts they found an old stove with a pile of kindling underneath the stove they discovered four matches, only one of these was good. With this they managed to start a fire, but as there were no stove pipes, they were forced to endure added misery from dense smoke all night. Morning found them all smoke blind and unable to see the people who came to rescue them. When they reached the mainland, the American Consul in Shelburne was notified and medical attendance was secured and everything possible was done to make them comfortable. All of them were more or less ill, which in view of what they had gone through is scarcely to be wondered at.

On January 25, all that was mortal of Philip Fiander was taken off the rock where it had lain since the wreck. Much difficulty was experience recovering the body as it was frozen slidly into a crevice. The remains were interred in the Methodist cemetery at Little Harbour, Nova Scotia. Fiander was twenty-seven years old and was a native of St. Jacques, Newfoundland. Only small pieces of the *Yosemite's* bow could be seen on the rock, nothing but broken fragments of her hull came ashore.

Ironically, Captain John McKinnon was saved from the wreck of the *Yosemite* to lose his life four years later when his schooner, *Eliza H. Parkhurst,* was lost with all hands while on a Newfoundland herring voyage.

If ever any men deserved a plush seat in the sailors Valhalla, it should be those dauntless dorymen, Pat Rose and John Hickey, who so bravely risked their lives to save their shipmates.

Finally, I am proud to state, that both Rose and Hickey were Newfoundlanders.

DORYMEN FROM THE WALDO STREAM

The following story is one of the strangest occurrences ever recorded in the annals of the fisheries.

On Wednesday, February 26, 1908, the Gloucester schooner, *Waldo L. Stream,* Captain Frank Stream in command, was anchored on Quero Bank. Her dorymen were out hauling their trawls when a heavy fog shut in. All the dories returned to the vessel except one with crewmen Sven Larsen and Augustus Johnson. The fog remained thick with the mother ship blowing her horn continually all through the night while a torch was kept burning at the masthead.

The next morning the fog was so thick that the bowsprit was scarcely visible from the cabinhouse. There was still no sign from the missing men. The sea remained smooth with a light wind. That afternoon, Thursday, four of the crew, Paul Williams (a big rugged fellow), Alex Campbell, John Tompkins and Sylvine Landry (a small, young man), volunteered to make a search for the missing dorymen. Although it had not been rough enough to endanger them, the thick fog, they believed, was the only reason preventing their comrades from returning to the schooner. In any case, they were confident that they could find them. With the captain's permission, the four men left in a dory taking along a foghorn. After rowing for a few hours, they were successful in locating the missing men. But by now the fog was thicker than ever with the result that they too, could not find their ship.

They decided to anchor for the night but the next morning and into the afternoon, the fog still surrounded them. They then decided to divide the party whereupon Larsen got into the dory with Williams and Landry, with Tompkins and Campbell joining Johnson in the other dory. Waving goodbye to the other men, Larsen, Williams and Landry departed as they made the decision to make a try to locate the schooner. They rowed off into the fog and became another mystery of the sea, for they were never seen again.

The other three men decided to anchor for another night. By this time the captain and the other crewmen of the *Waldo Stream* were thoroughly alarmed. They kept the foghorn sounding with a signal fire at night.

The other three men decided to anchor for another night. By this time the captain and the other crewmen of the *Waldo Stream were thoroughly alarmed. They kept the foghorn sounding with a signal fire at night.*

On Saturday afternoon, the fog lifted and the vessel was sighted by the three men out in the dory. They were picked up, then for two more days, the vessels searched but in vain for the other three men.

Williams and Larsen were fifty-three years old and Landry was only twenty-three. When Williams and Landry had volunteered to set out on a search for their absent shipmates, with no concern for their own safety, they were in effect, setting in motion the circumstances which ultimately caused their own deaths.

The *Waldo L. Stream*, went out of the way of a large number of fine Gloucester fishing vessels, when she was sold to Newfoundland interests in May, 1922, she was put into service as a rum runner.

The end came to this beautiful schooner when she was smashed to pieces off Muskegat Island, off the southern coast of Massachusetts on December 26, 1924. She was bound for Nassau, Bahamas Islands, with two thousand, two hundred and ninety-five cases of liquor. Her twenty-two-year old skipper, Newfoundlander William Cluett, was not acquainted with those treacherous waters.

Incidentally, Captain Cluett was later killed onboard his rum running schooner *Josephine K.*, when a warning shot from a pursuing coast guard cutter crashed through the pilot house where he was standing. The miraculous escape of the Helen G. Wells.

The schooner *Helen G. Wells* was a famous Gloucester fishing vessel. A very handsome craft of clipper bow or fiddle head design, which means she had a straight raking stem and carried a cutwater underneath her bowsprit. This fine schooner was built during the winter and spring of 1893, at Thomas Irving's yard in Gloucester, for her skipper, Captain William Wells. She was successfully launched on April 19, 1983 and slid gracefully into the water at Vincent Cove.

On June 28, 1896, four of her crew went astray on Grand Bank during thick fog. George Upham and Herbert Foley, after being adrift for four days were picked up by the British schooner, *Dorothy* and landed at St. John's, Newfoundland. The other two men, Philip Merchant and John Thomas were never seen again. These men were the first ever lost by Captain Wells during his twenty-four years as skipper.

On February 1, 1897, the *Helen G. Wells* arrived at the 'T' wharf in Boston with her flag flying at half mast. This time it was to report the loss of her skipper, Captain William Wells. It appeared that the vessel had been fishing for one day when she encountered the terrible gale of January 28, 1897, and she was forced to run before it. All that night the storm continued, while the vessel was kept running under the shortest possible sail.

At 1:00 p.m. on January 29, Simon Muise, who was at the wheel was knocked down by a heavy sea, which had surged in over the taffrail. Fortunately he did not go overboard, as he was lashed to the wheel. Captain Wells, noticing his plight, rushed to his assistance. As the skipper arrived by Muise another sea much larger than the first smashed down on the vessel's deck and swept Captain Wells overboard. He quickly disappeared beneath the waves. That giant sea had swept the ship's deck completely, taking all her dories, gurry kids and everything else that was moveable. It also broke off the vessel's big main boom.

Captain Wells, who was forty-eight years old, left a family of eight orphans, his wife having passed away two years previously.

It was the next episode in her life that really made the *Helen G. Wells* famous. After the death of Captain Wells, the ship was taken over by the firm of Gardner and Parsons and Captain Joachim Murray. Captain Murray was a Newfoundlander, one of the many young men from our country who had emigrated to the famous port of Gloucester and who through sheer courage, ability and perseverance had worked their way up from a doryman to skipper in an amazingly short period of time.

The *Helen G. Wells,* under the command of Captain Murray, sailed from Gloucester on October 29, 1897 on a halibut trip. From the very start bad weather was encountered and no fishing was done. On November 10, while the vessel was anchored on Green Bank, a heavy northwest gale descended upon her. The cable parted and she was hove to under a double reefed foresail, shortly after midnight a huge sea broke over the *Wells,* striking her amidships on the port side, it rolled her over until she rested bottom up and she remained in that position for a short period.

Two men were on watch when they observed the big comber approaching and they dived for the cabin to escape being carried overboad. As the second man's head vanished below, the enormous sea boarded the vessel and a torrent of water poured down the open companionway. Seven men were now in the cabin and eleven were in the fo'castle. As the schooner capsized they were tossed out of their bunks and thrown around violently. All of them thought that their time had come, but they battled fiercely to keep their heads above water, that threatened to drown them every moment. The crew could form no idea what had happened, but the position of the cabin and the fo'castle indicated to them that the vessel had turned completely over.

Jack Barnable was the first man out of the cabin. Although the schooner had come back to rest on her beam ends only, he seized the wheel and heaving it hard up he succeeded in righting her and keeping her running before the seas. Captain Murray was washed out of his cabin and back again twice before he could reach a place of safety. In the fo'castle, Axel Johnson was thrown against a bulkhead, he suffered a badly injured hip. Ernest Nickerson was hurled from his bunk and received a cut in his head two inches long. In fact, every man onboard was cut and bruised to a greater or lesser degree.

Nickerson was the first man out of the forecastle. He discovered that the three hundred fathoms of cable which had been ranged on deck had gone through the foresail and was then hanging over the side. He managed to get hold of an axe and cut it away, thereby lightening the vessel considerably.

While the men were engaged in clearing away the wreckage, the schooner was boarded by another big sea that plucked Jim Murphy away from the wheel, sent him high up in the air, then dropped him down on the roof of the cabin.

After some semblance of order had been restored and the vessel was going fairly off before the wind, the crew got the opportunity to look around and take stock of what devestation the storm had wrought. Everything was soaking wet, both clothing and food. The two stoves had been smashed in the upset and when the schooner had turned bottom up all the fresh water ran out of her tanks. Conspicuously stuck up on the fo'castle ceiling was a large lump of butter. For many years afterwards the imprint of a cover of the galley stove could be seen on that same ceiling.

Not a single splinter was left of the eight dories. The foreboom gaff and foresail were gone. The mainsail and the main gaff had also disappeared. The main boom, a spar as thick as the average man's body was broken into six pieces. Halyards, stays, headsils, topmasts and bowsprit were stripped as clean as if the craft had been in the yard of a scrapper. She looked a regular derelict.

The pump gear was carried away and she had to be bailed out by hand of the water which had poured down the open companionway when the first sea boarded her. But despite the awful strain that had been put upon the schooner, she did not leak a single drop.

The secret of the salvation of the *Helen G. Wells* and her crew was owing to the fact that both her ice supply and ballast had been securely stored and did not shift when she capsized. On the 12th. the storm abated and the badly battered schooner under a ragged headsail made for St. John's. Off that port a tug got a line aboard her and towed her in. She was reported to be in the worst condition of any vessel that had entered the harbour of St. John's up to that time.

The *Wells* was repaired in St. John's. She arrived in Gloucester December 6, 1987.

Captain Melvin McClean, a Banks fishing skipper himself, designed the *Helen G. Wells*. When speaking of the vessels being hove down or capsized during violent storms, Captain McClean made this statement: "It makes no difference, shoal or deep, when a monster sea strikes fair, down goes the schooner on her beam ends. If she is well designed, strong built and properly ballasted, up she comes again, if otherwise, sad is her fate."

Exactly how many vessels suffered the sad fate that nearly overtook the *Helen G. Wells* will never be known, but unquestionably the number was very great. For the grim headlines, 'Lost with all hands', after the fishing fleets had been attacked by raging tempests appeared all too frequently in the days of the dory bankers.

Captain Joseph Cusick, another outstanding Gloucester fishing skipper a native of St. Lawrence, Newfoundland, also commanded the *Helen G. Wells* on several occasions.

In December, 1915, this fine schooner was sold to parties in Havana, Cuba. Nothing was heard of her after that. Captian Joachim Murray, her skipper when she capsized, died in Europe on October 26, 1917. He was serving as boatswain's mate in the United States naval reserve. He was fifty years old at the time of his death.

BELATED WEDDING BELLS,
THE SUPERNATURAL AND A TALL TALE

On February 15, 1905, the Boston owned fishing schooner, *Manhasset*, Captain George Roberts, arrived at Boston and reported the loss of two of her crew, John Barry and James Lambert, who had gone astray on Georges Bank on February 6. A sad feature connected with the loss of the two men, was that one of them, John Barry, was to have been married on February 18.

On Hearing of John's supposed death, his bride-to-be adorned herself in appropriate black and wept. On February 23, the schooner *Monitor*, in command of Captain Foreman Spinney, arrived at Boston with Barry and Lambert onboard. Captain Spinney reported that he had picked them up twenty-eight hours after they had gone astray.

The men had suffered terribly from exposure in zero weather. But thanks to Captain Spinney and the schooner, *Monitor*, Barry, although a few days late, had come home for his wedding after all.

In what was a very remarkable case that crossed the border of the supernatural, the *Monitor* again made the news headlines On March 4, 1908, this vessel in command of Captain Jack McKay, sailed from Gloucester to the southern edge of Grand Bank on a halibut trip.

Soon after leaving port, Captain McKay was beset by a presentiment that something out of the ordinary was going to occur, but he was at a loss to account for this feeling. Some mighty inner force seemed to be urging him to get to his destination with all possible speed. So he set every stitch of canvas the *Monitor* could carry, then drove the vessel for all she was worth.

On reaching the bank, the Gloucester schooner, *Cavalier*, was sighted. All the *Cavalier's* dories were out underrunning trawls. Billy McKay, brother of Captain McKay was a member of the *Cavalier's* crew. So when that vessel was sighted, Captain McKay ran the *Monitor* down through her line of dories with the hope of seeing his brother and having a chat with him.

The uneasy feeling which had haunted Captain McKay all along now surged up more strongly than ever. Suddenly, one of the *Monitor's* crewmen spotted an overturned dory with two men clinging desperately to its bottom. On being informed of this the skipper altered course and crowded on all possible speed in order to reach the little craft. When he arrived on the scene, imagine Captain McKay's surprise when he discovered that one of the men clinging to the capsized dory was his brother Billy, who with his dorymate, Milton Aiken, were just about to the point of letting go their hold on the slippery bottom. As they were chilled from their immersion in the icy water and their strength was all but gone.

It appears that not only had Captain Jack McKay been urged onward by some mighty unseen power, he had seemingly also been guided over one thousand miles of ocean to the exact spot and at the right moment to snatch his brother from the brink of a watery grave.

As I had lived in Lamaline at a time when the all-sail Banks fishing schooners had reached their heyday, I had often enjoyed the privilege of being onboard many of those vessels. The enjoyment was double fold when I was allowed to rub shoulders with the dorymen, sitting enthralled in the forecastle listening intently as each weaved a yarn of their sea adventures. On looking back today, I know that many of the stories which they related were true, but in other cases the narrators would have been elected to the top position in any liar's club. For example, a grey-haired, white-bearded, saintly looking old doryman named Ed, used to tell us a story that had such an effect on us that it would send us scurrying homewards at top speed, if we vacated the forecastle after darkness had descended.

Ed recounted that one winter he was a hand on a schooner out of Gloucester. They set sail, he said, in February, finally anchoring on Georges Bank. One particular day dawned with the weather very windy and cold, with heavy seas running. Their skipper decided that it was too rough to put over the dories. So, continued Ed, all hands with himself being the exception, returned to their bunks. He had been detailed to remain on deck as a lookout – an anchor watch – whose duty it would be to warn his captain and shipmates should he observe danger approaching.

He related that he had been pacing the deck for about fifteen minutes, meanwhile casting a sharp eye alow and aloft as well as out over the boisterous waters, when suddenly he noticed a large bird winging its way towards the vessel from the port side. Ed said he was tickled pink when the bird pitched on the ball of the main topmast. Although he thought he knew the name of every bird that flew over the Atlantic, the old doryman could not identify that feathered creature. He was a big, a fine heavy specimint (specimen) a lot larger than a goose or a loo (loon), plenty big to make a good meal for all hands.

"So, I raced down into the fo'cle and grabbed up the double barrelled shotgun that we always kept there just in case we had the need to shoot a feed of seabirds. When I got back on deck, I was delighted to discern that the big bird was still perched on the top-mast ball. Then taking aim I let go with both barrels and instantly the bird came tumbling down, ass over breakfast. But then a most horrifyin' terrible thing happened, for when the big bird's carcass reached to a point halfway between the topmast ball and the deck, it suddenly turned into a large black coffin, which plunked down right against me feet."

In reply to a question from one of us, Ed said, "Of course, I was terrified, for tis not every day that a poor fisherman sees a bird change hisself from a bird to a coffin."

It appeared that Ed, though terrified as he was supposed to be, calmly went to the coffin and raised the lid, whereupon, he said, he got the surpirse of his life for there laying deader than a haddock under salt, was none other than the schooner's mate, Mr. Perkins.

"Now," continued Ed, "I didn't have the nerve to go down to the after cabin and wake up the mate to tell him that besides being asleep in his cabin bunk, he was also layin' dead in a coffin up on deck. So, instead," he said, "I went down in the fo'cle and aroused me dorymate, Tom. After I'd got Tom really awake, I told him what had happened and asked him for advice. Well, first Tom said he would go up on deck to take a peek into that coffin. But when we arrived topside, I got an awful shock, for we discovered that the coffin had entirely disappeared, even the body of our mate was gone, too. T'was than I was sure that Tom was goin' to call me a liar, but he never did. A great dorymate that Tom, and right smart, too. For he soon had the answer. He turned to me and said, "Ed, what you seen was a token, a sign that some member of this schooner's crew is goin' to be called to his last home before many more hours has passed by.' Sure enough, Tom was right, for the next morning the wind and sea had calmed down. The crew were sent out to set their trawls and our mate was drowned when he capsized his dory."

On the early morning of New Year's Day, 1928, the Canadian beam trawler, *Venosta*, in command of Captain G.M. Myrhe, was engaged in dragging operations forty miles west-south-west of Sable Island. Suddenly the vessel's big steel net became fouled in some underwater object, which brought her to a standstill. Captain Myrhe ordered full speed ahead on the engines. As the trawler commenced to move, it appeared that a phantom ship was rising from the bottom of the sea, for a schooner's mastheads broke surface slowly and evenly, when the masts had fully emerged, they were followed by the hull. The vessel was without booms and sails, her nameplate, too, was missing, but the astounded trawler's crew had very little difficulty in recognizing the smooth, beautiful lines of the *Columbia*, lost in the great gale of August 24, 1927.

The powerful floodlights of the *Venosta* were thrown on the ghostly derelict. In the 2:00 a.m. glare of the bright lights, she presented an eerie sight to the gaping watchers. The vessel seemed to be in good condition, the major portion of her standing rigging was intact and it was festooned with seaweed of every variety which slatted about in the stiff wind.

The water was very turbulent at the time, the rough seas preventing any attempt at boarding her to ascertain if there were any bodies in the cabin or forecastle. Then the schooner commenced to advance on the trawler, this created a potentially dangerous situation, but just as Captain Myrhe was beginning to fear that she would contact and batter in the sides of his ship, the steel cables holding her up, parted and she slowly sank once more to the bottom. The gem of the ocean had taken her final plunge.

As the *Columbia* was disappearing, the *Venosta's* crew to a man, whipped off their sou'westers and bowed their heads, for suddenly the realization dawned on them that they were standing over the graves of Captain Wharton, his cook, his youthful catchee and his twenty brave dorymen.

CHAPTER FIFTEEN

Captain Solomon Jacobs

Captain Solomon Jacobs was born in Twillingate, Notre Dame Bay, New-foundland in 1847, the son of Simon and Mary (Roberts) Jacobs.

He started his career as a fisherman with his father, operating on the grounds near Twillingate. But Sol Jacobs was not content to spend his days as a shore fisherman. At the age of seventeen, with very little education, he went to sea in a square rigger. His ability as a seaman was quickly recognized. For shortly he was promoted to second mate of the ship *J.S. Winslow* of Portland, Maine.

Captain Jacobs arrived in Gloucester, Massachusetts in 1872, after hearing about the port and the money to be made there. He was then twenty-six years old. Now began his amazing career that was to take him to many ports of the world, earn him sizable fortunes and an enviable reputation. Little did Gloucester realize what a dynamic individual had entered its midst.

His first trip out of Gloucester was in the schooner *Navada* on a Georges Bank trip. He soon switched over to mackerel seining with Captain Ben Wonson, where he learned the ropes. The following year, 1873, he went master of the schooner, *Sabine* to Georges. His next command was the fine schooner, *S.R. Lane,* from the Samuel Lane Co. fleet. In 1875 in the *S.R. Lane,* he landed 124,000 pounds of cod, one of the largest trips ever brought from Georges. He followed with fares of 105,000 pounds and 197,000 pounds.

Captain Jacobs later took command of the Samuel Lane Company's best vessel, the *Moses Adams.* His average stock in this vessel each year was $14,000, which was big money back in the 1879s. By this time skipper Sol had become an American citizen.

In January, 1878, Captain Jacobs, in the *Moses Adams,* was a participant in the famous or infamous Fortune Bay riots. Two American vessels sailed into Fortune Bay, Newfoundland, to seine or purchase herring. The Washington Treaty between the U.S.A. and Great Britain allowed those vessels to carry out such operations, but the Newfoundland fishermen felt that

Captain Solomon Jacobs —
(Courtesy Gordon Thomas).

their livelihood was being undermined and they, it seemed, made a determined effort to ignore the clauses contained in the Treaty, which affected them most.

A crowd of two hundred men came out in boats seized the American seines and emptied them. They tried to seize the seine of the *Moses Adams*, but Captain Jacobs had evidently foreseen such a move by the fishermen and had armed his men with pistols. By the threat of using those weapons, Jacobs' crew held the crowd at bay while they secured a partial cargo. Next day the herring struck off shore and the Americans set sail for home.

Later on, trouble flared up again in Newfoundland. Sol was not permitted to fill his vessel up. He decided to sail for home with a partial cargo of two hundred and twenty-five barrels. A Government Fisheries Officer came onboard and told the Captain that he was not allowed to sail. But Sol did sail and along with a reluctant Government Officer. The man's unwanted cruise ended when Skipper Sol dropped him off at Saint Pierre. When Sol decided to sail, he sailed. He did not have too much love for Fisheries Officers.

Captain Jacobs commanded some of the finest schooners to sail from

Gloucester. Apart from the three already mentioned, there was the *Sarah M. Jacobs* (named after his wife) 1878; the *Edward Webster*, 1881 to 1891; the *Ethel B. Jacobs* (named after his eldest daughter), 1891 to 1899; the auxiliary schooner *Helen Miller Gould*, (first motor powered schooner to fish the Banks), 1900 to 1901; the *Alice M. Jacobs* (first large steamer to become engaged in fishing operations), 1902 to 1903, named after his youngest daughter; the auxiliary schooner, *Victor*, 1904; auxiliary schooner, *Veda M. McKown*, 1905; schooner *A.M. Nicolson*, 1906 to 1908; auxiliary schooner *Benjamin A. Smith* 1909; schooner *Georgia* and schooner *Elmer E. Gray*, 1910; gas boat *Quartette*, 1911; schooner *Killick* 1912; schooner *Romance*, 1913; schooner *Pythian* 1914; steamer *Bethulia* 1915.

It can be seen from that long list of fishing vessels that Sol Jacobs could handle them whether they were driven by sails, steam or gasoline.

Captain Jacobs was a pioneer in the fisheries. Away back in the 1880s he sent his two fine schooners, *Molly Adams* and *Edward Webster* around Cape Horn to the Pacific coast to fish for halibut and seals. Then in 1899, he took his crack schooner, *Ethel B. Jacobs* along the Irish coast on a cruise for mackerel. At that time the *Ethel B. Jacobs,* Sol's pride and joy, was probably the fastest schooner in the Gloucester fleet.

His success in the mackerel fishery was uncanny. Not one man could top him in that field of endeavor. Somebody named Sol the Mackerel King, and the title stuck. It has been said that Captain Sol would never set a seine until he took the temperature of the water (a practice well in advance of his time). If it was 44 degrees Fahrenheit, or higher, over would go the seine. Captain Jacobs' voyages to distant seas spread the name and fame of Gloucester more than did the exploits of any other man.

My good friend, Gordon W. Thomas of Gloucester and Ipswich, Massachusetts, able writer of the life stories of Gloucester fishing vessels, when writing of Captain Solomon Jacobs said, 'Captain Sol Jacobs, the Mackerel King was one of the greatest mariners ever to take the wheel of a Gloucester fisherman. The fame of this son of Twillingate, Newfoundland, was known all over the globe. Tall, raw-boned and strong, he possessed outstanding courage, determination, judgement, great vision and ability.Captain Sol made and lost several fortunes, but he always had the courage to go on. A number of books could be written about the daring exploits of this great man.'

Many stories have been told about Sol Jacobs. One of the most popular went as follows:

Sol liked doughnuts and had the peculiar habit of cutting or peeling off little pieces with his jacknife before eating them. One day while Sol was in a tavern, a practical joker came in and thought he would have some fun. He slapped Captain Jacobs on the back and said, "Hi, Sol, peeling any doughnuts lately?"

Sol turned around and smiled, pulled a big wad of bills out of his pocket, threw them on the bar and replied, "Yup, and there's the peelin's."

Death claimed this great Newfoundlander and superb Gloucester fishing captain on February 7, 1922, when he suffered a stroke. He was seventy-four years of age.

A Window on the harbour — the Captain Solomon Jacobs Memorial Park in Gloucester, Massachusetts —(Courtesy Gordon Thomas).

A new park was opened in the city of Gloucester. It instantly became known as a window on the harbour, as it fronts on the harbour shore. The name of this marine park is: Captain Solomon Jacobs Memorial Park. It is situated quite near the wharf from which Captain Jacobs sailed so often.

The fact that the name of Captain Jacobs was selected over all the other names of master mariners who sailed from Gloucester gives one a clear conception of the high esteem in which he is held today, by the people of Gloucester, fifty-nine years after his death.

Gordon Thomas in his comments on the park, wrote: 'The Gloucester Fisheries Commission and the City Council are to be congratulated for selecting Captain Solomon Jacobs' name for the park on the harbour. This man had no superior, he was a pioneer, an adventurer, sail carrier and highline fisherman. He was smart, capable and he had guts.' That compliment comes from a man whose father, Captain Jeffrey Thomas, was also a famous Glucester fishing skipper.

CHAPTER SIXTEEN

Sea Mysteries

When a fishing schooner was approaching her home port with her flag flying at half mast from the main rigging, it was a sight that filled watchers on shore with dismay, particularly, of course, did it affect viewers who had relatives onboard the vessel. For a flag at half mast was the dreaded sign or signal that some member or members of the crew had been lost.

On April 8, 1905, the handsome American schooner, *Moween,* sailed into the harbour of Gloucester, Massachusetts, with her flag fluttering from half mast. The vessel was commanded by Captain Daniel (Little Dan) McDonald. After the *Moween* had been tied up, Captain McDonald came ashore and reported that six of his men in three dories had gone astray on St. Pierre Bank, on the morning of April 5, during dense fog. The captain who was so affected by the loss that he could scarcely talk, stated that apart from the fog, it was the finest kind of day for fishing.

The day passed, he said, and the three dories failed to put in an appearance. The captain then set out in a dory, accompanied by another crew member, to conduct a search for the missing men. They were gone so long that those onboard the schooner feared that they too, had been lost. But as darkness closed in, Captain McDonald and his companion returned without having sighted the absent dories.

Shortly after their arrival, it commenced to blow a pretty stiff breeze which continued throughout the night, but the wind was not so hard that dories would be unable to live through it, particularly if they had drogues (sea anchors) out, at least that was the opinion of Captain McDonald and his remaining crewmen.

His search by dory, having proved fruitless, the skipper hove up his anchor and set his sails. He cruised all over the fishing grounds for two days, covering many miles, but he failed to find any trace of his straying dorymen. From that day to the present time, nothing was ever learned of their ultimate fate.

It fluttered there that awful sign,
Which chilled the hearts on shore,
While wharf dogs howled as if they knew,
The dreaded news it bore.

Slowly the schooner came to dock,
Her flag was half mast high,
When counting her nested dories there,
Each woman breathed a sign.

For three were missing from the nest,
Which meant six men were lost.
Six husbands, fathers, brothers, sons,
Had paid the priceless cost.

Sadly the Captain stepped ashore,
His features lined from strain,
Then women swooned when he named the men,
Whom they ne'er would greet again.

At the time those six men went astray from their schooner, April, 1905, that area of the Atlantic must have been virtually covered with fishing vessels, with dozens of men in dories scattered all over the face of the sea. Yet not a single man got so much as a glimpse of the three dories from the *Moween.* It may seem a bit farfetched to imagine that the ocean literally opened up and swallowed them, yet, their sudden and complete disappearance together with their crews does present an aura of mystery. They were by no means the first nor the last dories and dorymen to vanish without a trace, but in most all the cases of that nature which I have followed one dory, only was involved.

Whereas it was densely foggy at the time the men went astray, the fog cleared up the following day. The win, though fairly strong, did not develop enough power to swamp dories. For these reliable craft even when loaded and are manned by inexperienced men can take a tremendous amount of buffeting, which incidently, was one of the prime reasons why boats of that type were selected to equip fishing vessels, by the men of all nations who frequented the great offshore Banks during the days of dory trawling.

If one of the men in each of the three dories was inexperienced, then their dorymates certainly were not, for these would be the dory skippers and dory skippers, hardly without exception, were experienced dory handlers. I am aware that a solitary dory would be a mere chip on the broad bosom of the North Atlantic Ocean, but three dories, surely must have presented a far bigger picture, that is, of course if all of them stayed together, this we must assume that they did, when they became aware that they had gone astray.

There is an area of the Atlantic Ocean which goes out from Cape May, New Jersey to the edge of the Continental Shelf. Following the Shelf around Florida into the Gulf of Mexico, it continues through Cuba, Jamaica, Haiti, the Dominican Republic, Puerto Rico and other islands of the West Indies and comes up through the Bahamas, twenty inhabited islands, plus hundreds of smaller islands, then up once more to Bermuda.

This area has been saddled with many sinister sounding titles. Writer Adi-Kent Jeffrey called it the Bermuda Triangle; writer John Goodwin, The Hoodoo Sea. It is also known as the Triangle of Death, Triangle of Tragedy, Pentagon of Death, Port of the Missing, the Devil's Triangle. Author John Wallace Spencer in his book, first published during 1969 and which went into its eleventh printing in February, 1974, has titled the area, Limbo of the Lost. That particular stretch of water has well and truly earned the foregoing names. For more than a thousand people and over a hundred ships and planes have mysteriously disappeared within its boundaries; in the greater majority of cases, leaving no grace. Awesome, ghostly appearing, deserted ships have been discovered reeling about without a soul onboard and without a visible reason as to why their crews and passengers had abandoned them.

The brigantine, *Marie Celeste*, may not have been the first vessel to be found sailing aimlessly about, crewless, but I feel safe in asserting that the mystery surrounding that vessel was the most written about, talked of case in the world. I first read the strange story of the *Marie Celeste* sixty years ago when it appeared in a book published in England. I have read it in various publications, approximately twenty times since. In addition, down through the years, I have heard a great number of persons discussing that episode of sea mystery.

The *Marie Celeste* was classed as a brigantine, because she was a two-masted ship which was square rigged on the foremast and fore and aft rigged on the mainmast. That type of vessel was also often erroneously called an hermaphrodite brig.

According to the story which I read in the English book, on the afternoon of December 4, 1972, the *Dei Gratia* (by the grace of God), another brigantine, commanded by Captain David Morehouse was sailing between the Azores and Portugal, bound for Gibraltar, when the captain's attention was suddenly attracted by the actions of another vessel which to his trained seaman's eye meant that all was not well onboard. This vessel had every sail set and her rig appeared to be in perfect condition, but every few minutes she would shoot or luff up into the teeth of the wind, then fall off to leeward again, run along for a while then come into the wind once more, a process which she kept repeating. The vessel's peculiar actions informed Captain Morehouse more eloquently than words that the craft was not under the control of a helmsman. He decided to investigate, putting over a boat with three men, he ordered them to intercept and board the strangely acting craft; which they did. However, they returned a short while later to acquaint Captain Morehouse with the fact that the vessel was the *Marie Celeste* and that they had found no one onboard her, either living or dead. Partly consumed meals were discovered both in the captain's cabin and in the crews' quarters. The ship's boats, they stated, were found resting in their chocks and evidently had not been disturbed. A state of perfect order was observed both on deck and below. There was no evidence to indicate that the crew had mutinied or that the vessel had been boarded by pirates.

The sailors from the *Dei Gratia* did observe one thing that later was the cause for much speculation, whenever the fate of the *Marie Celeste* was being discussed; a deep, freshly made axe cut on her taffrail (top rail surrounding the stern of the ship). The writer of sixty years ago would up his story by offering his own interesting theory as to what had happened to Captain Benjamin Brigs of the *Marie Celeste*, his wife and eight seamen who made up his crew. His theory is set forth as follows.

'It was meal time, the captain and his wife were busily engaged eating their repast in his cabin. The other men were in the forecastle occupied likewise, one man, only was on deck and he was at the wheel. The day was fine and clear, so the officers did not deem it necessary to post a sailor on lookout duty, in the bows of the ship (an unlikely as well as an unlawful piece of hindsight). Then,' opined the writer, 'a giant squid or an octopus surfaced astern of the *Marie Celeste*, snaking a tentacle in over the vessel's taffrail, he seized the man at the wheel and proceeded to drag him overboard. The sailor's agonized cries for help caused the captain, his wife and the other crewmen to scurry up on deck and rush aft to assist him. But such a monster possesses many tentacles which are generously equipped with oversized suction discs. So, making good use of these, he whipped all hands overboard to their doom, while they were valiantly attempting to rescue their shipmate.' In the writer's opinion, one man managed to get hold of an axe before he was dragged to his death, delivering at least one hefty chop at the creature, which apparently failed to kill or disable it. 'That is why,' continued the author, 'the freshly made axe cut was found on the vessel's taffrail.'

The *Marie Celeste* story as it was written by John Wallace Spencer and which appears in his book, Limbo of the Lost, differs in some respects from that of the earlier account just related. The old time narrative states that the ship's boats were found in their chocks. Spencer tells us the *Dei Gratia's* men had discovered the boats to be missing. Story number one declares that the *Marie Celeste's* sails were set and in good condition. Spencer describes them as being torn and out of kilter. The dining room tables, according to Spencer, were clean, indicating, he says, that the crew were not about to eat. However, in the story written more than half a century ago, the boarding party found partly eaten meals both in the captain's cabin and in the crews' quarters. Spencer's account makes no mention of an axe cut on the vessel's taffrail.

It is quite understandable how old stories become changed and very often embellished with the passing of time, but in the case of the *Marie Celeste* at least, the basic quality of both narratives remain concrete, for regardless of whichever version is exactly correct, there is one fact that stands out very clearly, which is, Captain Benjamin Briggs, his wife and eight crewmen either took a hasty departure from the vessel for some urgent reason, or else they were taken off her by some unknown agency.

The question as to why the ship was abandoned when she was, apparently not in danger of sinking and under reasonably good weather conditions, has never been answered. Captain Briggs and the other people who were onboard the *Marie Celeste* could not shed any light on the mystery, for they were never seen or heard from again. Captain Morehouse put his mate and two seamen onboard the derelict with a view to salvaging her. Six days later the *Dei Gratia* arrived at Gibraltar and the *Marie Celeste* turned up there the following day, December 13, 1872.

By making that seven-day journey manned by only three men who were required to handle work which normally took eight men to perform, the *Marie Celeste* had proven beyond a doubt that her seaworthy qualities were excellent.

A salvage hearing began on December 18, 1872, which did not conclude until March 14, 1873. Captain Morehouse of the *Dei Gratia* and his crew were accused of foul play, conspiracy and murder. They were eventually cleared of those charges and divided the $8000.00 in salvage money.

The *Marie Celeste* had always been considered a jinxed ship, for she experienced a series of mishaps both before and after the abandonment, that is if she was indeed voluntarily abandoned by Captain Briggs. In any case she was the first known vessel to provide a puzzling mystery whilst voyaging across the area, what is now commonly called the 'Bermuda Triangle'. Or as John Wallace Spencer more aptly names or renames it, 'The Limbo of the Lost'.

The account concerning the *Marie Celeste* may be considered as only incidental to this book. I inserted it simply because I desired to draw attention to mysterious disappearances which have occurred at sea, as well as to offer the opinion that not only within the confines of the Limbo of the Lost have such incidents taken place. For off the coast of Newfoundland, Nova Scotia and New England, schooners and dories have vanished without leaving a solitary clue as to what manner of finality overtook them. The disappearance of the three dories and six men from the American banker, *Moween* is a case in point. When ships were caught out in severe storms, then vanished into the port of missing ships, reasonable explanations for the disappearances became readily apparent. Men wise to the ways of the sea would say, "She sprang a leak," "She got hove down," etc., or such and such a shoal or rock broke as she passed over it. In the case of a vessel which had sprung a leak when beset by a roaring tempest and the men at the pumps were unable to gain on the water gushing into her and it was too rough to escape in dories, the schooner foundered and her crew perished.

If a vessel became hove down (which means that after being struck on the broadside by a giant comber, she was thrown over on her beam ends or was turned completely bottom up) the craft could, and no doubt many of them did, descend to the bottom like a stone.

If a mountainous wave broke on a schooner as she was passing over an underwater rock or shoal, then unless she was extremely fortunate she too, would be added to the list of the missing.

It has been pretty well recognized also, that many vessels were cut down by steamers, particularly during periods of dense fog or in snowstorms with none of their crewmembers surviving.

But what of those vessels which mysteriously disappeared when there was no wind storm raging, no gigantic seas rolling and during the total absence of fog or snow? In that connection I will deal with one case only, that of the Newfoundland Banks fishing schooner, *Partanna*, which was lost with all hands in April, 1936.

Although a considerable number of Newfoundland's fishing ships over the years have disappeared with their entire crews, those tragedies have not, nor apparently cannot be explained. They have been forgotten. The loss of the *Partanna*, however, after a lapse of forty-two years, still remains fresh in the minds of a large number of people who reside on the south and southwest coasts.

The interest in the ill-fate which overtook the *Partanna* may be kept alive by the fact that ever since the vessel sank beneath the waves, supposedly, between Cape Pine and Cape St. Mary's, an aura of mystery seems to have hovered around her disappearance.

Whereas the schooner's loss did not provide food for world-wide discussion and argument as did the mystery overshadowing the crewless *Marie Celeste*, yet, locally, whenever aging skippers and dorymen get together in settlements along the south and southwest coasts the conversation very often veers around to questions and answers related to the *Partanna* and her crew. The same questions and answers which have been going the rounds for four decades. Countless opinions which have been offered by some as a possible solution, have been rejected by others. The pros and cons have been carefully weighed time out of mention by those experienced Banks fishermen, but up to the present time nobody has been able to come up with a satisfactory answer.

Many of the men who lived on the southern shore of the Avalon Peninsula at the time of the loss of the *Partanna* might have been able to enlighten present day researchers respecting certain items of wreckage, including dories, which were reported to have been washed ashore near St. Shotts, but unfortunately those men are no longer with us.

The *Partanna* was built in the shipyard of S.B. Ernst Company in Mahone Bay, Nova Scotia, during the winter and spring of 1924. She was first registered in Lunenburg in the summer of 1924. Her first owner was Acadian Supplies, Ltd. R.S. Corkum was listed as owner-manager. The vessel was re-registered in St. John's, Newfoundland in 1934. Her new owners being Samuel Harris Export Company, Grand Bank, Newfoundland.

When the Samuel Harris Export Company was declared bankrupt, the *Partanna* was taken over by the firm of Grand Bank Fisheries, Ltd.

In March, 1936, the schooner set sail from the harbour of Grand Bank on her first spring trip. Onboard were the following crewmembers:

Charles Ansty	Garnish	Captain
Morgan Hickman	Grand Bank	Mate
Edwin Walters	Garnish	Cook
Joseph Brown	Garnish	Doryman
Aaron White	Garnish	Doryman
Earl Marsh	Garnish	Doryman
Ernest Grandy	Garnish	Doryman
Thomas R. Grandy	Garnish	Doryman
William M. Grandy	Garnish	Doryman
Victor Day	Garnish	Doryman
Thomas Cluett	Garnish	Doryman
Joseph Cluett	Garnish	Doryman
Wilson Hickman	Grand Bank	Doryman
Stanley Burt	Grand Bank	Doryman
Clyde Briggs	Grand Bank	Doryman
Clayton Walsh	Grand Bank	Doryman
William Dunford	Grand Bank	Doryman
Norman Burt	Grand Bank	Doryman
Philip Baker	Grand Bank	Doryman
Robert Rose	Grand Bank	Doryman
Willoughby Mullins	Grand Bank	Doryman
Kenneth Pike	Bay L'Argent	Doryman

The *Partanna* was typical of the big, handsome fishing vessels which had been built in Nova Scotian shipyards during the 1920s-40s. Her gross tonnage was 172, net tonnage 109. Her length, overall was 144 feet. Her beam was 26 feet and her depth was 10 feet, 8 inches. The schooner was considered to be the largest and one of the most able in the Newfoundland Banks fishing fleet. At the time of her loss the *Partanna* was twelve years old. So one could safely say that as far as the life span of those vessels went she was only in her infancy.

When Captain Ansty left the town of Grand Bank, he sailed into Fortune Bay and picked up a baiting of herring; then took his departure for the Grand Banks.

Captain Charles Ansty at the wheel of his schooner Flash'. Ansty and his entire crew died when his banker 'Partanna' vanished somewhere between the Grand Banks and Cape St. Marys in 1936 —(Courtesy Caleb Marsh).

The *Partanna* was carrying ten dories. Arriving on the fishing grounds, in a location just east of Whale Deep, Captain Ansty anchored, put over his dories and commenced fishing. A berth away from the *Partanna* was the Newfoundland banker, *L.A. Dunton* in command of Captain Clarence Williams, also anchored and fishing. One afternoon, Captain Williams observed Captain Ansty weighing anchor and setting sail towards land. Knowing that the *Partanna* did not have any more than seven or eight hundred quintals of fish onboard (she could carry twenty-five hundred quintals), the *Dunton's* skipper concluded that Ansty was heading for either Placentia Bay or St. Mary's Bay to pick up another herring baiting. The date would be on or about April 25, when the *Partanna* had disappeared from Captain Williams range of vision. It was, apparently the very last time she was ever seen.

On April 29, word was received in Grand Bank to the effect that the

Partanna had been lost with all hands in the vicinity of St. Shotts on the southern shore. It was reported that half of the vessel's mainboom with the sail still furled on it and tied up had been discovered floating off that settlement by some fishermen. Two of the *Partanna's* dories were reported to have been found in a lonely cove on the west side of Trepassey Bay.

Down through the years two stories have been circulating respecting those dories. One version had it that the dories, when found, were completely wrecked where the seas had driven in on the sharp rocks, and they were supposed to have been identified only by the fact that sections of their top side boards still carried the *Partanna's* name.

The second story which surfaced at the time the vessel disappeared is being retold down to the present day. For example, while I was in Labrador City in 1974, I met a man who told me the second story. Then in May, 1976, a man from Fortune Bay again told me the story which carried the same details. The second story has been related as follows:

'Two dories marked *Partanna* were discovered in a lonely cove on the southern shore (Trepassey Bay is not mentioned specifically). When located the boats were undamaged and had been hauled up on a beach well above the highwater mark. On the for'ard thwart in one of the dories lay a pair of white woolen mitts of a kind used by Banks fishermen. On the wristbands of those mitts were the initials: J.C. Now, it was the practice for Banks dorymen to have their mitts marked in that manner, with the initials of the owners being worked in with wool of a darker colour to make identification of one's property easy. It could also prevent a shipmate from taking and using a pair of mitts without bothering to seek the owner's permission.

'The only man on the *Partanna* with the initials J.C. was doryman, Joseph Cluett.

'Then those same initials were found carved on the trunk of a fir tree a few yards inland from where the dories had been discovered.'

Today, some old fishermen living on the southern shore have told me that the *Partanna's* dories were not found on the southern shore, but on the Cape Shore, in the vicinity of Point Lance. Other southern shore fishermen state that although they never saw any wrecked dories, they have always understood that splintered sections of the boats were found on the west side of Trepassey Bay, the same as was reported in the first story.

Meanwhile, elderly residents of the Cape Shore, who were grown men at the time of the tragedy occurred and who remember the incident very well, claim that no dories from the *Partanna* were ever located in the vicinity of Point Lance or near any other settlement along the Cape Shore.

Then an ex-fisherman from Placentia Bay told me that at the time the *Partanna* vanished, he was a doryman on another banker and he can recall vividly that groups of men from southern shore settlements were searching the woods and marshes and scanning the ponds for several days, inland from the area where the dories from the vessel were reported to have been found. The searchers being under the impression that some crewmembers might have escaped the fate which overtook their vessel, then had wandered away into the woods to become lost or perhaps they may have fallen through the ice in one of the ponds and drowned. Oldtimers remember that the winter of 1936 was very severe, with heavy frosts and many snowstorms. So, even in April the ponds were still frozen over, but the ice on them had become very weak owing to the advance of spring. If any men did manage to get ashore from the *Partanna* there was the possibility of them dying from exposure as April nights can be very cold, even frosty at times. Then, if the men had suffered injuries when escaping from the doomed banker, they could have succumbed as a result of those injuries after they had gotten safely ashore.

According to legend, Mutton Bay and Cape Mutton in Trepassey Bay were so named because of a certain species of livestock a ship was carrying when she was wrecked in that locality during a terrific storm a long, long time ago. Apparently, after the vessel struck she was quickly battered to pieces by gigantic waves. Some time after the storm which destroyed the ship had abated, a couple of fishermen from one of the settlements, when passing along by that section of coast noticed that the shoreline was strewn with wreckage which was mute evidence that some ship had been lost there during the big storm. The men landed to investigate. While they were walking along the littered beach, one of them suddenly observed a small flock of sheep grazing amongst the nearby trees. As the animals were of a breed totally unfamiliar to them they realized that the ship must have had them onboard and that they had, somehow, managed to swim ashore.

The fishermen concluded that all the ship's company had perished. So they decided to round up the sheep and take them home seeing that the animals were without an owner. It was while the fishermen were rushing about attempting to corner the sheep that they literally stumbled over the decomposing bodies of two men lying in the grass growing between the trees. By the outlandish clothing on the remains and knowing in any case that no man had been reported missing from any settlements, they now had stark proof that at least two crewmembers, or passengers, had contrived to get ashore from the stricken vessel. Drenched to the skin roughed up by the seas, as they must have been, the voyagers had evidently died from exposure and possible injuries.

Because of the human bodies having been found in the area one would imagine that the indentation and the point of land would have been named Deadman's Bay-Cape. But somebody must have decided on Mutton Bay and

Cape Mutton which after all are not so gruesome nor so frightening. Very appropriate too, because of the flock of sheep that was discovered there.

Cross Island is situated in Placentia Bay, two miles southeast of Baine Harbour. This island which is two miles long by a half mile wide was never permanently inhabited, as it is a bleak place that contains no harbour to shelter boats, during severe winter storms. As the island was nearer to good fishing grounds than was their home ports, some fishermen had erected shacks there which they occupied during the summer fishing season only.

A couple of months after the *Partanna* had been lost, a deaf and dumb fisherman named Richard Synyard of Parker's Cove, Placentia Bay landed on the island. While walking along the beach he picked up a piece of one of the bow name plates which had belonged to the *Partanna*. The section contained the first four letters of the vessel's name, i.e. PART. The fisherman brought it to Baine Harbour and gave it to a businessman named John Rodway, who nailed it up on the inside of his fish store, where it remained for several years. Eventually, one of Mr. Rodway's sons presented the nameplate section to Caleb Marsh, well-known taxi-driver of Garnish, whose brother Earl had gone down with the *Partanna*. Mr. Marsh in turn donated the relic to the Fishermen's Museum in Grand Bank, where it is now on display.

Around the time that Mr. Synyard discovered the nameplate section on Cross Island, a piece of the *Partanna* second nameplate was picked up by a fisherman from Isle Valen, Placentia Bay, when he discovered it floating off that settlement. Presumably the finder's name was Lockyer. I have interviewed quite a number of Lockyers, former residents of Isle Valen (the settlement was abandoned during the resettlement program several years ago) but none of them could tell me who actually picked up the nameplate section. But the fact that it was picked up is confirmed by Mr. Wilfred Rodway, formerly of Baine Harbour and Mr. Ernest Lockyer, formerly of Isle Valen. Both these gentlemen assure me that they viewed it many times while it was nailed up to the side of a stage in Isle Valen.

The section picked up off Isle Valen contained one more letter than did the piece that was found on Cross Island, i.e. PARTA. Today, nobody knows what became of that section.

After it had been firmly established that there was no hope for the *Partanna* and her crew, the late Eli Ansty of Garnish, brother of Captain Charles Ansty, came to St. John's, then visited settlements on the southern shore in an attempt to ascertain what had caused the tragedy. Whatever information Mr. Ansty may have gleaned in that locale was never disclosed. It appears that after Mr. Ansty returned to St. John's he was informed that shortly after the *Partanna* was reported missing, a steamer had entered the harbour of the Capital with a damaged bow and was then on drydock having repairs effected.

According to my informants of today (close relatives of the Anstys) Eli made several attempts to get certain Government officials to accompany him to the drydock to have an inspection made of the damaged steamer and to question members of her crew as to the manner in which she had sustained the damages. But it seems that the officials offering one excuse or another, would not accompany Mr. Ansty to the dock nor clear the way for him so as he could survey the damaged steamer himself and interview her crewmembers.

When Mr. Ansty returned to his home in Garnish the people whose relatives had disappeared with the schooner and who had eagerly and anxiously awaited his return hoping that he had unearthed some pertinent facts concerning the ill-fated vessel, were told very firmly that he was not discussing the tragedy at all, and that he wanted to hear nothing further concerning it.

Some fishing skippers and dorymen are of the opinion that the *Partanna* was running over Lamb's Rock at the time a huge sea broke which completely engulfed her. Lamb's Rock is situated twenty miles off the land and it rises above the seabed that extends between Cape Pine and Cape St. Mary's. The rock bears the name of the fisherman who discovered it approximately one hundred years ago, Patrick Lamb of Red Island, Placentia Bay. There is a depth of five fathoms of water over the rock, however, the soundings will vary somewhat with the rise and fall of tides.

Several ex-fishermen tell me that they have witnessed Lamb's Rock breaking when high seas were running. But according to men who were at sea in the general vicinity of the rock at the time the *Partanna* was lost, if the vessel did run over that submarine elevation she, in their opinion, would have been in no danger as they claim the waves were not big enough to break in that depth of water. Other fishermen offer the opinion that the *Partanna* met her end on St. Mary's Quays, reefs that lie seven miles off the bill of Cape St. Mary's. For a greater part of the time St. Mary's Quays are under water, but at extremely low tides, sections of them become exposed.

Another belief regarding the loss of the *Partanna* one which is shared by many old time fishermen, is that the vessel was cut down by a steamer. That opinion may very well have been spawned after the story regarding the steamer on the St. John's drydock with the stove-in bow commenced to be spread around.

Following the loss of the *Partanna* it was reported that Captain John Dodge, master of the banker, *Mary Ruth*, had informed Captain Ansty that the *Partanna's* compass was out of kilter and that if he, Ansty, steered the usual course by that faulty compass, he would end up on St. Mary's Quays.

This warning was supposed to have been delivered to Ansty by Dodge as the *Partanna* was leaving the Banks. Then, according to a former crewmember of the banker, *Beatrice and Vivian*, her master, Captain James Gosling, boarded the *Partanna* three or four days prior to the time Captain Ansty sailed from the Banks on his final trip. Captain Gosling's purpose for going onboard the *Partanna* was to check positions with Captain Ansty.

On Gosling's return to the *Beatrice and Vivian*, he remarked to his cook, "From the soundings I took before going onboard the *Partanna* I would say that Ansty's compass is away off from being true. If he steers by that compass on a hundred mile run he will end up at least twenty-five miles off course."

My informant does not know if Captain Gosling had advised Captain Ansty that the latter's compass was defective But it is quite reasonable to assume that he did.

If Captain Ansty's compass was faulty at the time he was visited by Dodge and Gosling, it must have been faulty before they boarded his vessel. That being the case, one has to wonder why Ansty did not have the compass adjusted or replaced, as the soundings which he would take from time to time must have told him that he was not arriving at the locations on the fishing grounds for which he had been headed. Yet when Ansty had taken on his first baiting, he sailed for the Grand Bank and arrived at the location already mentioned. It is possible that he made the location by dead reckoning or without the guidance of his compass. As many veteran skippers arrived exactly where they desired to go by using their good judgement or dead reckoning.

Many fishermen on learning of the warning given to Captain Ansty by Captain Dodge and presumably by Captain Gosling, respecting his compass, uttered such statements as: "Charl Ansty was a stubborn, hard-headed man, he wouldn't accept advice nor heed warnings from any man."

At the beginning of the *Partanna* story, I mentioned that an aura of mystery surrounded the vessel's disappearance. Well, no less than a half dozen old Banks fishermen have remarked to me, quite recently that the loss of the *Partanna* is one mystery which will never be solved. These oldtimers refer to the incident as a mystery. Why? As a matter of fact there are a number of if's and how's which may be related to the loss of the vessel.

Fishermen who were at sea while the *Partanna* was sailing to keep a blind date wtih grim destiny and who were only scant miles from her route of advancement claim that there was no wind storm, just a brisk breeze. There was no fog and no snow squalls. The weather was absolutely clear, conditions were ideal, they say, for any ship to have, what they term, was a fine time along.

If such ideal conditions existed why did the captain have his big mainsail furled on the boom and tied up? There is hardly any doubt but that he was in a hurry to make land, pick up a fresh baiting then return to the fishing grounds as speedily as possible. All fishing skippers that I ever knew or heard of were always in a hurry on such occasions. Some of them drove both their schooners and their men harder than did others. Those captains were called hustlers. They were the ones who were mainly concerned with securing a full load of fish in the shortest possible time and by all accounts Captain Ansty was a hustler.

The main sail of a schooner was exactly what its name typifies it to be. For it was the tallest, widest, sheet of canvas, to dominate a deck. It was the real pusher, especially during a brisk breeze which would constitute a fine time along. Only the for'ard half of the *Partanna's* mainboom was ever located. It had been snapped off almost dead center. The mainboom of that vessel measured seventy-five feet in length and it had a diameter of twelve inches at the sheet sling (near the stern). 'It was fashioned from American hard pine, commonly called pitch pine. That wood carries both a semi-soft and hard grain, similar to Douglas Fir. But the pitch pine is a tougher fibred stick. It has a greater degree of resiliency than does the Douglas Fir and will not snap off so easily when under severe strain.

Time and again many vessels whose mainbooms were just as stout and tough-fibred as the one that was on the *Partanna* had been snapped off at points of stress, when the big sail had been hoisted and the vessels were running under heavy wind pressure. The fact that the mainboom on the *Partanna* had been broken in two with the sail furled on it and tied up, when by all reports the kind of weather which had existed at the time did not warrant such a precaution, has to be regarded as mysterious, whichever way one may desire to consider it.

On a two-masted schooner the mainmast is stepped about half-way between the stempost and the stern. The jaws of a mainboom rest on a narrow ledge of wood which completely encircles the mainmast. That circular ledge is called 'the saddle'. As the *Partanna's* seventy-five foot mainboom had been broken off at almost dead center it means that the breakage occurred at from thirty-six to thirty-eight feet aft of the mainmast, which places it well towards stern. The fact that both of the *Partanna's* bow nameplates were broken in two means that whatever force connected with the vessel must have shorn her bow section off as completely as if she had received a karate chop from a gargantuan hand.

The question is, what agency snapped off the ship's mainboom at, apparently, the same time that her bow section was severed? Whereas the broken nameplates from both the port and the starboard bows tend to point to a collision with an ironclad ship, yet it would have been impossible for that same ship to sheer off the vessel's bow and crash through the after section of her hull to break off the mainboom simultaneously. It was not impossible, but highly improbable for two ships to have ploughed into the *Partanna* with both of them striking her at the same moment. If that did occur then another angle to the mystery is apparent.

To return to the two dories which were supposed to have been located in a lonely cove hauled up well above the highwater mark. If the story is true then the dories must have been placed in that position by human power. As above the highwater mark means, of course, beyond the highest point which tides rise. In that story I find that part where a pair of woolen mitts, bearing the initials of doryman Joseph Cluett, which were found in one of the dories and those same initials being discovered also, carved on the trunk of a nearby tree, particularly fascinating. I am of the opinion that these details alone lend a great deal of truth to the story. For fishermen as a general rule did not permit their imaginations to run riot to the extent that would enable them to concoct such a story.

Fishermen worked hard, lived hard and all too often died hard, and as one of them once remarked to me, "I'll probably go to hell after all, which is damn hard."

Those were the days when it was extremely unhealthy to say to a fisherman that he was a liar, even if you were smiling when you said it. With very few exceptions our fishermen were devoutly religious. When they went ashore they attended church services regularly. They would never utter curses or mouth obscenities in the presence of women or children. They regarded Almighty God very seriously because they firmly believed in His existance. They scorned and despised a known liar. He was shunned by them for they knew that his word could not be trusted. Consequently,if it became known that one of their number had deliberately fabricated a falsehood respecting the finding of the *Partanna's* dories it would have gone ill with him. For as far as those fishermen were concerned an incident which involved the loss of so many lives was certainly not the subject to tell lies about.

Then there was the statement of the Placentia Bay fisherman who vividly recalls how men were searching an area a considerable distance inland from the southern shore coastline. Those men must have believed some of the crewmen had escaped from whatever fate overtook the *Partanna.* The fact that such a search was made again proclaims that there must have been considerably more than a mere segment of truth to the hauled up dories story. For without some evidence to show that men had indeed landed from the vessel, the southern shore residents would not have even considered making an inland search.

If there be certain individuals who class stories of that kind as stagehead tales, or more harshly, plain lies, then I am afraid that I would have to disagree with them, for I honestly believe that such narrations cannot be born, grow up, then live throughout two score years without having a solid basis in fact.

Before Captain Ansty took his departure from the Banks there is no doubt but that he had his ten dories taken aboard, nested and lashed or gripped down to their cradles, as that was the usual precaution taken in case a schooner should encounter heavy weather. It is probable also, that some members of the ship's crew, particularly those who happened to be on deck when the vessel ran into difficulties, might have managed to sever the gripes, get a couple of dories down in the water and board them before the *Partanna* plunged to the bottom, then have rowed ashore, as had happened in the Cape Mutton incident.

On July 11, 1918, the American fishing schooner, *Georgia* was rammed by the steam collier, *Bristol*. The vessel was struck between the fore and main rigging and was nearly severed in half. She sank in four minutes. Fortunately her crew of seventeen men were on deck at the time, more fortunately still, the *Georgia's* seine boat was trailing alongside. All seventeen men jumped into the boat and were saved. The schooner's griped down dories went to the bottom with her.

On June 28, 1925, the American banker, *Rex*, was cut down on Quero Bank by the seventeen thousand ton Cunard liner, *Tuscania*. The sharp bow of the big steamer sliced into the *Rex* on the port bow near the cathead (davit-like iron arm on which the anchor is secured) and cut right through the vessel with her prow coming out through the starboard side just for'ard of the main rigging. The *Tuscania* had been going so fast that it was some time before she could be brought to a stop to put over lifeboats. All the schooner's dories had been smashed to splinters in the collision. Fifteen members of her crew died. Nine were saved, they having been picked up by the liner's lifeboats. The completely severed vessel went down to the bottom in seconds.

It may be interesting to note here that despite their very violent collisions with those schooners, neither the collier, *Bristol*, nor the liner, *Tuscania* received so much as a scratch. Still the two vessels were just as sturdily con- structed as was the *Partanna*.

Here was a coal collier and a passenger liner which were built in separate yards, of vastly different tonnages and whose bow reinforcements must have been affixed by different methods, not suffering even minor damage in those collisions, then why would the bow of another steamer be so badly battered in a collision with a wooden-hulled schooner that the captain was forced to have her drydocked for repairs.

Of course there is no real evidence in mere speculation, but in view of the fact that neither steamer even had their paint scratched when they collided with the schooners *Georgia* and *Rex,* I feel compelled to conclude that the *Partanna* was not destroyed by a steamer. That a steamer with a stove-in bow appeared in St. John's drydock shortly after the *Partanna* disappeared could have been a coincidence. As at that time of the year there were probably many icebergs drifting around in the Atlantic and it is quite possible that the damaged steamer might have collided head-on with one of them.

The nameplates, also called nameboards, of schooners built in Nova Scotia were fashioned from white pine, a sturdy member of the soft wood family. Those plates were invariably painted black regardless of the colour of the vessel they adorned. The letters forming the names were handcarved deeply into the wood, then were painted golden yellow, orange or buff. The brightly coloured letters showed the names up in sharp contrast to the black and green painted hulls making them easily readable from quite a distance.

The nameplates were fastened with screws to the upper sections of the for'ard bulwarks of a vessel. The nameplates of submerged schooners have been found many times washed upon beaches or were picked up at sea. Always they have been found intact or in one piece. Some of them when discovered have had the paint, both dark and light colours, completely scrubbed off with the edges of the boards considerably rounded from the continuous action by water and churning sand. Those nameplates are so light in weight that they may be wave-tossed up against boulders, cliffs and the gravel of beaches countless times without breaking into sections. They are similar to numerous other pieces of light weight wood which have been found on beaches and wedged tightly into the crevices of rocks where they have been driven by the force of the waves without sustaining breakage.

In the Atlantic also, but far removed from the route the banker *Partanna* had pursued, the broken bow nameboard of another vessel was recovered after the craft had disappeared with her entire crew. The location, Limbo of the Lost or the Bermuda Triangle if you prefer that title.

On the night of October 29, 1966, the eighty-five gross ton, sixty-seven foot tugboat, *M/V Southern Cities* left Freeport, Texas, bound for Tuxpan, Mexico. This was her fifth voyage since July 25. She was honouring a verbal contract which called for the towing of the one thousand and thirty-one gross tons, sea-going bulk cargo barge between Freeport and Tuxpan.

Three days after setting out on what was to be her last voyage, the *Southern Cities* owner received report from the tug's master to the effect that she was ninety-five miles south of Port Isabel, Texas. She was forty-three miles offshore with another two hundred and thirty miles to go. The captain, G.A. Reynolds, reported also that the tug was making six knots, the weather was fine, no problems were being experienced and it was estimated that she would arrive at Tuxpan on the morning of Thursday, November 3.

It was further acknowledged that another report would be made on the following morning, November 2. It was to be relayed through the *M/V Texan*, another tug located approximately eighteen miles southeast of Tuxpan.

On the morning of November 2, the *Southern Cities* owner was advised that no report had been received. The following morning still brought no report from the vessel. At the request of the *Southern Cities* owner an intensive search was made by air and surface craft. On November 5, the barge was located one hundred and five miles north of Tuxpan. The barge was totally undamaged. Her cargo was intact. The six hundred foot long, eight inch, polypropylene tow-line was still fast to the barge and the chafing chain and hawser which had been secured to the towing bitt of the *Southern Cities* were also intact.

At 2:05 p.m. on the same day that the barge was located two broken sections of the tug's nameboard were recovered. When the pieces were fitted together it was observed that two letters were missing. The shortened name read: 'Uthern Cities'.

Respecting the *Partanna* case as you read in this chapter, a number of little mysteries combine to add up to one big mystery, with the broken name boards not being the least of them. For the broken name boards from both the *Partanna* and the *Southern Cities*, apart from everything else, do present a mind-boggling mystery. To once again echo the words of old-time Banks fishermen, "The *Partanna* mystery is one that will never be solved."

Apparently, the mystery surrounding the disappearance of the tug *Southern Cities* and her crew will not be solved either. For twelve years have passed since the vessel became separated from the barge she was towing and simply vanished. Yet up to the present day no person has been able to come up with a solitary clue to what caused her to disappear so rapidly that her crew did not have time to transmit a radio distress message.

On November 28, 1966, the Department of Transportation, United States Coast Guard, Marine Board of Investigation released a report which stated in part: 'In the absence of survivors or physical remains of the ship, the loss of the *M/V Southern Cities* cannot be determined. Although there is no evidence indicating a failure of the vessel's radio equipment, the failure of the vessel to transmit a distress message appears to justify the conclusion that the loss of the vessel may have occurred so rapidly as to preclude the transmission of such a message.'

Today in the town of Grand Bank, from whence the *Partanna* sailed on her final, fatal voyage in the spring of 1936, there stands a modern school, which was constructed on Main Street six years ago. Following its completion, the John Burke High School pupils were requested to suggest a suitable name for the edifice. One pupil, Lloyd Hillier, submitted the name, 'Partanna Academy' which was accepted. That fine building now serves as a fitting memorial to a hardy, capable fishing captain, an efficient cook, a crew of brave dorymen and a handsome, able schooner.

All that remains of the ill-fated banker 'Partanna' is this section of one of her bow nameplates, picked up on Cross Island, P.B. by a fisherman. It is now in the museum in Grand Bank. A piece of her other bow nameplate was picked up by another fisherman floating off Isle Valen, P.B. This section has disappeared. — (Courtesy of Nfld. Museum).

A Grandy type, Nfld. dory awaiting shipment to her new owner. —(Photo by Jerry Kelland).

Her battles with Atlantic storms over, this old fishing dory rests peacefully in the back yard of a motel in Gloucester, Mass. —(Courtesy of Gordon W. Thomas, Ipswich, Mass.)

Bibliography

Andrew Merkel, 'Schooner Bluenose', Ryerson Press, 1949

Samuel T. Williamson, 'The Lowells of Amesbury', Yankee, November 1961

'The Chronicle-Herald The Mail-Star', August 23, 1960

Michael Harrington, 'Off Beat History', St. John's Evening Telegram

Mrs. Bobbi Robertson, 'Daily Colonist', 1875 to 1886 editions

S.J. Favazza, Chairman Gloucester Fisheries Committee, Brochure on 350th. Anniversary Celebration of Gloucester

Gordon W. Thomas, 'Fast and Able', Life stories of great Gloucester fishing vessels, 1973

Feenie Ziner, 'Bluenose, Queen of the Grand Banks', Chilton Book Co., Philadelphia and Thomas Nelson & Sons, Ontario

'Daily News', St. John's, Newfoundland, August 1935

'Evening Mercury', St. John's, Newfoundland, September 1886

John Wallace Spencer, 'Limbo of the Lost', Phillips edition, June 1969-73, Bantam edition, 1973-75

John Wallace Spencer, 'Limbo of the Lost Today', Phillips Publishing Co. and Bantam Books, 1975

Murray Bernard, 'The Indomitable Dory', Imperial Oil Review, June 1966

Harry Carter, owner-editor, 'Newfoundland Stories and Ballads', St. John's, Newfoundland